THE COMPLETE

Grand Illinois Trail

GUIDEBOOK

THE COMPLETE

Grand Illinois Trail

GUIDEBOOK

The Midwest's Biggest
Outdoor Adventure

By Todd Volker

FirstServePress

PEORIA, ILLINOIS 61651

Published by FirstServePress, Peoria, Illinois

Maps by Matt Kania
Book Design and Production by Todd Sanders

ISBN: 0-9726176-1-2

This book is dedicated to the memory of
Mr. Vern Gielow,
an eloquent advocate for the Great River Trail
and the Grand Illinois Trail

Contents

Acknowledgments

A book like this requires many friends along the way to see it completed. I would like to note the great help and kind support of these fine people. It has been a pleasure to meet and work with each of them:

Dick Westfall, Illinois Department of Natural Resources
George Bellovics, Illinois Department of Natural Resources
Vern Gielow, Great River Trail
Ders Anderson, Openlands Project
Ed Barsotti, League of Illinois Bicyclists
Steve Moser, Hennepin Canal State Parkway
Judi Jacksohn, Hennepin Canal State Parkway
Jean and Paul Mooring, Illinois Prairie Path Association
Don Kirchenberg, Illinois Prairie Path Association
Richard Stark, Oshkosh, Wisconsin
Amy Madigan, Illinois Department of Natural Resources
Al Sturges, League of Illinois Bicyclists
Amy Easton, Illinois Historic Preservation Agency
Mary Michaels, Illinois Historic Preservation Agency
Ralph Schultz, Will County Forest Preserve District
Don Fisher, City of Joliet
Rick Strader, Rockford Park District
Judy Roby, Rockford Park District
Doug DeLille, Bi-State Regional Planning Commission
Jim Hochgesang, Lake Forest, Illinois
Ray Hoven, American Bike Trails
Bev Moore, Illinois Trails Conservancy
Joe Taylor, Quad Cities Convention and Visitors Bureau
Bob Lukens, Chicago Southland Convention and Visitors Bureau
Beverly VanDerZyl, Galena/Jo Daviess County Convention and Visitors Bureau
Richard Campbell, East Peoria, Illinois
Monica Knapp, Peoria, Illinois
Randy Neufeld, Chicago Bicycle Federation

The author wishes to thank his kind and generous wife, Linda Volker, conscious of the many impositions placed upon her by this work. I wish to thank my associates of FirstServePress: design and production supervisor Todd Sanders, Marylou Sanders and Matt Kania. I count any errors here as my own.

There are many ways to experience the Grand Illinois Trail and northern Illinois. Let me know if you run across any other items to add in future editions!

TODD VOLKER

Using this Book

The Complete Grand Illinois Trail Guidebook is a one-stop reference resource for the Grand Illinois Trail system. The Guidebook is a great overview of the trail system and its parts. The Grand Illinois Trail is broken into four large sections: North, South, East and West. Each section contains all the information pertinent to the Grand Illinois Trail: notes on local trails (named subsections), road routes, side features, maps, photos and useful resources.

The Grand Illinois Trail is a loop trail, so you can pick it up or leave it at any point. Subsection descriptions of trails may be found going in either direction. Simply reverse the description details if you are taking the Grand Illinois Trail in the opposite direction.

Use the special map in back to plot your trip and record your progress toward Trail Blazer recognition. You can also use the trail diary to record your impressions along the way.

Enjoy!

Getting Started

Introduction

Take to the Trail

There is a joy to being on the trail. You can see it in people's eyes. It is a combination of fresh air and friends, a mix of exercise and relaxation.

It makes you happy.

You can bike on trails. You can walk on trails. You can run on trails. You find neighbors out there. And there are trail events and trail rides that give you a chance to talk and meet new people.

People love trails and the whole trailbuilding movement is a Big Tent jamboree of bikers, nature-lovers, scouts, farmers, walkers, runners, mountain bikers, outdoorsmen and conservationists. They are a good thing if you live in the city and they are a good thing if you live in the country.

Trails offer something for just about every outdoor interest and trails bring the outdoors close to home. Trails offer something for every age. Young children ride with their parents. They use trails as the setting for imaginative adventures and for practical transportation around the neighborhood. Older children take off and exercise and explore by themselves. Adults exercise or wander, as hard or as easy as they choose.

The Grand Illinois Trail claims a special place in the Midwest. The Grand Illinois Trail is huge, running a massive loop around the suburbs and across northern Illinois. It is over 500 miles long, making it one of the longest loop trails in the United States.

Not only is it a trail-system that is built up of several already-popular trails, but the Grand Illinois Trail offers a wide variety of trail experiences.

On the Grand Illinois Trail you can trek from one corner of the state to the next. You can pedal along the blue shores of Lake Michigan, and take the trail on to the great Mississippi River. You can hike along scenic, rugged river bluffs. This lake-to-river connection is a magical connection.

And on the Grand Illinois Trail you can explore old stagecoach routes, follow along railroad corridors and river bottoms, and experience Illinois and Illinois nature in much of the way the original settlers experienced it.

And of course, the trail runs between towns and between neighborhoods, making a route that can be used for enjoyable errands and trips.

The Grand Illinois Trail offers the very best that Illinois has to offer: the trail system includes stops at such noteworthy destination gems as Starved Rock State Park, the Chicago Lakefront, Mississippi Palisades State Park and historic Galena.

The trail route also provides access to the unique natural environments of Apple River Canyon State Park, Lake Le-Aqua-Na State Park and Rock Cut State Park. It also opens a host of smaller natural areas for exploration.

And the Grand Illinois Trail also manages to be routed along some of the most valuable rivers in the state. Here you find the Illinois River and the Mississippi River. These are two rivers that define the heartland. Here along the trail is the Fox River and the Chicago River. And here, too, you find the Rock River, a beautiful stream.

The Grand Illinois Trail is more than a place for recreation. The trail is also a route to exploration and discovery. It is a unique way to learn more about the history of Illinois. The trail goes through major cities and alongside important industries. It runs through natural areas and farmland, as well as newer suburbs and established suburbs. These all have their own sensibilities and the Grand Illinois Trail lets you experience these diverse places.

It is a place where lazy breezes toss big bluestem grasses, and where soybeans grow green and then yellow under the sun. Here you find ancient trees. Buffalo roamed here. French explorers and traders set up camp. And here are the remains of great, watery canals—the first transportation technology that served countless farmers and merchants. The Fox River, with its countless mills, and the Illinois River, with her steamboat and packet points.

The Grand Illinois Trail also follows its way through precious natural resources. Being the prairie state, you will find many kinds of prairie along the Grand Illinois Trail. There are "garden prairies" tended meticulously as showplaces for all types of prairie plants and grasses. There are sand prairies complete with cactuses. There are wet prairies and there are dry dolomite prairies.

You may pause to watch a pair of mallards, male and female, bobbing their way as they search for breakfast. You might find soaring hawks cartwheeling in the sky as they scan the ground for mice. You may scare a slumbering carp that has been silently sunning in a canal.

Out and about on the Grand Illinois Trail you can see the impacts of the great Ice Age upon the land. The trail route follows the course of melting glacier waters and traverses glacier outwash regions filled with gravelly moraines. Part of the Grand Illinois Trail—its northwest corner—treks into unglaciated Jo Daviess County, known as the "driftless area," a region unbothered by the glacier's heavy crunch. It is a look into an earlier Illinois geology.

It is incredibly easy to get on the Grand Illinois Trail. Chances are, it's right outside your door. It ranges in a broad circle, running from Chicago and the western suburbs, follows the Fox River valley toward Wisconsin, then turns west toward Rockford. A combination of trails and country roads heads toward Galena, and the route follows the Mississippi River to the Quad Cities.

From the Quad Cities, the trail follows the two major Illinois canals—the Hennepin Canal and the I & M Canal—into Rockdale next to Joliet. From Joliet, there are off-road trails and city streets that bring you back to Chicago and the great blue horizon of Lake Michigan.

Major cities—Rockford, Elgin, Joliet, the Quad Cities, Chicago—are touched along the Grand Illinois Trail route.

All in all, the Grand Illinois Trail connects the resources of 12 existing trails, 12 major parks and at least 45 cities and villages. It is an integral part of trail development in northern Illinois. Some trails, such as the Jane Addams Trail and the Burnham Greenway, were specifically built or further developed in order to help create the Grand Illinois Trail. Other trail developments are planned, or underway, that are expressly designed to connect to the Grand Illinois Trail.

Building the Vision

Doing the Grand Illinois Trail route adds spice to being on a trail. It is an adventure—a very doable adventure—and you can set your own pace for completion. It is the perfect way to escape the stress of a busy week since trails take you away from the grind of traffic and the electronic buzz. A day on the trail is a mini-vacation. The Grand Illinois Trail surrounds you with a moving and changing panorama of sights and sounds and attractions.

The Grand Illinois Trail idea was born in the early 1990s by community leaders in La Salle-Peru. There was interest in joining the two canal trail systems, and the endpoints of the canals are in the Illinois Valley area. These leaders liked the idea of linking the canals and finding a way for hikers and bikers to cross the state. Their declared goal was to build the link that would let bikers dip their tires in the water of Lake Michigan and ride the trails all the way west to the Mississippi River, there to dip tires in the great Father of Waters.

This took place at the same time that the federal government had established federal funding for transportation "enhancements." Called ISTEA, the transportation funding authorization generated a new and historic approach to transportation. It provided for transportation enhancements to improve all aspects of travel and transportation, and not just automobile travel. The enhancements also help to smooth out some of the harsh effects of old-style highway projects. The concept was enormously successful with the general public. . . less so with the powerful Highway Lobby.

The canal trail link was a good idea. As the Grand Illinois Trail became better known, new possibilities developed and other communities wanted to join. More pieces were added to the plan. The Illinois Department of Natural Resources committed more staff time, and finally a staff member, to the GIT project. George Bellovics was named Grand Illinois Trail Coordinator in 1993.

In May 1994, the Illinois Rails-to-Trails Conservancy ran their Grand Adventure, sending executive director Mike Ulm and board member Kandee Haertel around an early version of the GIT circuit. They became the very first official Trail Blazers, a unique club of people with intimate experience of the complete GIT route. By stopping and chatting with local reporters, Ulm and Haertel generated critical media publicity for the idea.

A large forum to review and discuss the GIT concept took place in August 1993 at Starved Rock. More than 150 people attended representing park district, tourism groups, preservation interests, transportation planners, and trail user groups. The directors of the Illinois Department of Transportation and the Illinois Department of Natural Resources joined in support of the Grand Illinois Trail concept.

The IDNR developed a state trails plan in 1995 that pointed out the Grand Illinois Trail route and urged its completion. The Grand Illinois Trail was seen as a way to build upon existing interest in trailbuilding with an overall organizing principle: the Grand Illinois Trail's loop across northern Illinois.

"'Let's think big,' that started it. When we first came up with the idea in the state trails plan in 1995 we were cautious and careful about the concept," says Dick Westfall. Westfall, greenways and trails supervisor at the Illinois Department of Natural Resources, was an early advocate of the trail. "Everyone thought it was a great idea and embraced the concept. Everyone wanted to link up to it."

"Since then it has become, regionally, the way to create a network of trails. The Grand Illinois Trail is a spine with local connections coming off of it." Says Westfall, "We see it as an idea of networking. The Grand Illinois Trail now connects to the ADT (American Discovery Trail) and the Mississippi River Trail. Now we are seeing linkages from the local to the state to the national level."

The fact that the trails all connect is important. Public approval of the Grand Illinois Trail route became louder after 1995. The past several Conservation Congresses, forums for state and local outdoors groups, have overwhelmingly supported the Grand Illinois Trail. It was even supported in the position papers of gubernatorial candidate

George Ryan in 1996. The most recent Conservation Congress made the formal recommendation to the IDNR that:

The IDNR and Illinois Department of Transportation should give funding priority to construction of the Grand Illinois Trail and priority connecting spurs.

These recommendations were based on the observation that the Grand Illinois Trail enhances state tourism revenues, improves the quality of life in trail communities and also helps to add acreage to habitat valuable for wildlife. This matches the general feeling that the Grand Illinois Trail is a highly accessible recreation trail that can be used by a wide range of age groups and a wide range of recreational users.

The IDNR has been optimistic about the Grand Illinois Trail. According to Dick Westfall:

"This project is a case where what *is* and how it *goes* is a joint decision. It's not DNR going in, saying we want this trail. It's gone in directions we haven't anticipated, and because of this, it's something that takes advantage of what's out there. But the Grand Illinois Trail makes trail development better by linking together what's out there into a bigger experience. A big part of its appeal is because it's a loop—you get there and get back—and that really sets it apart from other trails."

A great deal of work has already been done on the Grand Illinois Trail. More remains to be done. Some of the major projects that have helped build the Grand Illinois Trail include:

- Funding for the Jane Addams Trail

- Funding extensions of the Great River Trail

- Funding elements of the Burnham Greenway

- Assistance with extending the I & M Canal trail from Channahon into Rockdale, just outside of Joliet.

- Funding the $12 million resurfacing and bank reconstruction of the Hennepin Canal.

The development of the trail has involved many working partnerships among as many as 90 different governmental entities and nonprofit organizations. Local suggestions and local management and direction have been important to the success of this joint effort. Local spurs and ancillary trails to the Grand Illinois Trail exist everywhere along the route. And more are projected and being discussed.

The most recent big development is the GITAP ride. In June 2003, Chuck Oestreich with the League of Illinois Bicyclists put together the first-ever Grand Illinois Trail and Parks (GITAP) ride. They sold out immediately. The week-long GITAP ride uses most of the GIT route, with stops at state parks and campgrounds.

The future of the Grand Illinois Trail is clear. It is one of America's most unique trailways, a combination of rural and suburban and urban trail along famous rivers and historic canals, ranging across broad prairies for some 550 miles. It will generate national attention. Furthermore, the Grand Illinois Trail is the backbone for trail development in northern Illinois and it will be made increasingly stronger and important as more trail spurs are opened.

Take to the Trail

From a car window speeding on the interstate, Illinois is nothing but a one-dimensional cornfield as flat as a pizza box. But the Grand Illinois Trail changes this relationship between you and the state.

The amazing thing is that the speed and tempo that you get on a good walk, or on a good bike ride, is fun. It is true that sometimes getting there is half the fun, and biking and hiking are, simply and totally, fun. Using the car a lot can make you feel stressed. But the Grand Illinois Trail gives the exact opposite feeling. Some of the most peaceful weekends possible are found out on the trail. One full day on the trail—parsing your way along an old rail corridor, for instance— actually gives the kind of mental refreshment you might get from a full week of vacation!

One of the most amazing and most elemental kinds of pleasure is how great plain water tastes after you have been riding a bike for a few miles.

Good exercise just feels good. You might be tired at the end of the day, but it is a *good* tired. In a way, this is the kind of tiredness that also brings a sense of personal accomplishment.

And the neat thing about the Grand Illinois Trail is that it is all so convenient and so accessible.

Lightweight bikes are easy to ride and after a while it is easy to forget that you are pedaling. In a way this is a true technological marvel: bike technology is personally liberating and lets you get out and around and explore. There is no glass between you and the world around you.

I will never forget the fun of finding a very small, very cold little garter snake that found a place in the sun for itself on the trail. These little surprises are among life's most enjoyable pleasures.

The Grand Illinois Trail wraps around northern Illinois in a way that brings out some of the state's really finest highlights. And the trail system gives you different kinds of trail experiences: there are sections that are quiet and you can feel nature around you. There are portions that are busy with people and activity, and you can find yourself in the middle of a town festival, a nice surprise.

Remember that the Grand Illinois Trail is a new trail system. The dedicated professionals from the IDNR continue to work on upgrading The Grand Illinois Trail partners to make The Grand Illinois Trail a growing and vital resource.

Quick Tips for the Trail

- Dogs sometimes chase riders on country roads. So look to see a doghouse when you approach a farmhouse. This may just give you a head start!

- Stop, stretch and rest every so often.

- Be sure to eat something on a long ride, even if you don't feel hungry.

- The route through the South Section is easily camped and it makes a good, short vacation if you do the entire stretch.

- Eat spaghetti the night before a long ride. This gives you a good carb base.

- For more control use low gears on patches of very loose gravel.

- Plan your trip to take into consideration eating at a local restaurant.

- Follow the rules of the road when you are on-road.

- Take along a camera: you'll be surprised at how many cool things there are to take pictures of.

- Stop by a historical society museum along the way: they always have something interesting!

- Try the cheese-and-crackers packets along with granola and energy bars for a nice change of pace.

- Avoid fried foods and fast foods before you begin a long hike or bike ride.

- Most roads in Illinois run North-South and East-West. The northwest corner, Jo Daviess County, is not so predictable.

20 Questions

MOST OFTEN ASKED
ABOUT THE GRAND ILLINOIS TRAIL

George Bellovics, Grand Illinois Trail Coordinator,
Illinois Department of Natural Resources

1. *Just what is the Grand Illinois Trail?*

The Grand Illinois Trail is a unique assemblage of local trail systems in partnership with the DNR including various city and township roads which creates an interconnected trail system in Northern Illinois.

The Grand Illinois Trail links Lake Michigan to the Mississippi River; it connects cities to countryside, links people to places. It is configured in a loop, so every point of beginning is also an end. Each city equally along the way is the beginning and end of the Grand Illinois Trail.

We very much envision the Grand Illinois Trail to be a catalyst for other trails to link into. It is a corridor, not a linear park. What is important is not the trail itself but the region where the trail lies. The more integrated the trail is to the community and region, the more the trail becomes a destination. It becomes a linear community in its own right. Trails increase the quality of life. It becomes a community project. It brings in more interests than hiking and biking—it brings in the bird watchers, sports clubs, scouts, there are health benefits, garden clubs. They all realize a part of their mission in the trail. It creates concentric circles from the community at large; this is an alternate transportation *movement*.

2. *Who runs it?*

The beauty of the Grand Illinois Trail is the diversity of experiences along the way. Each local experience is dependent on local administration of the trail. This is part of the ambience, rather than standardize it.

Each local jurisdiction maintains its trail, and the DNR maintains its trails. Buffer treatments and trail integration depends on our various partners. But the engineering is standardized. This extends to the programming function. All programming is done locally.

3. *Is the Grand Illinois Trail hilly?*

Yes, in parts it is hilly—within reason. Of course the hillier parts are in Jo Daviess County, where the hills make up an important component of the trail experience. But there are a few hills throughout the route. But it's mostly flat!

4. *How safe is the Grand Illinois Trail?*

The majority of the Grand Illinois Trail involves organized trail systems. The lessons we have learned from trails across the country is that trails are inherently safe because the community is involved. Like everything else in life, take precautions and be prepared.

5. *When is the best time of year to ride the Grand Illinois Trail?*

We would anticipate the majority use of the trail between April and November 15. This could be sooner, could be later depending on weather, but the majority of use will be during that time frame.

6. *Which is the best section for starting the Grand Illinois Trail?*

Since it's a loop trail you can pick it up anywhere and end it anywhere. A lot of users may not ride the whole trail but will ride sections. Some major themes of the Grand Illinois Trail include culture and history, geography and geology, urban-rural. There are slices of history all over the place that you're riding through.

7. *What kind of bike or bike gear will I need?*

If you have a road bike, we recommend a touring tire that can take varying surfaces. The Grand Illinois Trail has a variety of surfaces—oil and chip, limestone screenings, asphalt. You can do the whole thing on a mountain bike but you might want to use a road-based tire rather than knobby tires. A hybrid bike is the best of both worlds.

8. *What is the trail surface like?*

There is a variety of surfaces: oil and chip, asphalt, limestone screenings. In one area we're using an experimental surface which uses an organic epoxy compound as a stabilizer added to aggregate base material. Cactus plants from New Mexico and Arizona are used to make the epoxy. The trail rides like limestone screenings but is as durable as concrete.

9. Can I camp anywhere along the route?

Yes, there is camping both at DNR sites and at local private campgrounds.

10. Where's the bathroom?

There are ample facilities along the way. These are provided by the local trail supervisor in most parts.

11. How many miles will I average per hour?

In general a good clip is from eight to ten miles per hour. In some cases the ambience and place you're riding through will capture you and extend your stay.

12. Can I rent a horse along the trail?

Yes, at some locations there are stables. In fact there are equestrian campgrounds along the way. In limited areas there are riding stables. Keeping in mind, uses of the trail depend on the locale—which includes horseback riding, snowmobiling, cross-country skiing, rollerblading, canoeing.

13. Are kids allowed?

Are kids allowed? Of course they are! We always encourage children to ride in groups that are supervised. Especially kids under age ten.

14. What are the best things to see along the Grand Illinois Trail?

We encourage all users to explore the Grand Illinois Trail and to seek out their own piece of happiness, for as William Shakespeare once said, "oh how bitter it is to see happiness through the eyes of another man!"

15. Can I ride my motorcycle/off-road vehicle on the Grand Illinois Trail?

Absolutely not.

16. Are there any organized Grand Illinois Trail rides during the year?

We have a Trailblazer program where the department encourages users to explore the whole trail through one year. Locally on our partner trails there are organized rides.

The League of Illinois Bicyclists have developed a tour of the Grand Illinois Trail route that covers much of the route. The Grand Illinois Trail and Park Ride (GITAP) is a new event that has received a lot of attention and interest, and we expect to see this become a standard fixture of the Grand Illinois Trail.

17. *What's the next project the IDNR is doing after they build the Grand Illinois Trail?*

We provide technical assistance to many communities to connect a functional alternative transportation system connecting people to places.

18. *Who do I talk to after I've completed the entire route?*

Contact the League of Illinois Bicyclists. If you've done the entire route in one year you become a member of the Trail Blazer Society, and you get the Trail Blazer shirt.

19. *Where do I start? When do I start?*

You can start today just by getting familiar with the route! Realistically, you might want to start in the spring and take it in stages, or make plans to do the whole route.

20. *What parts of the Grand Illinois Trail are best for paddling?*

It depends on your level of experience and the type of canoe you have. The Hennepin Canal is akin to pond canoeing, versus stream canoeing. You can canoe the Rock River, the Des Plaines River, the Du Page River, Fox River, Pecatonica River, Richland Creek and Bureau Creek. There are many various paddling opportunities along the Grand Illinois Trail at various points.

Trail Access Points

It is fun to take the Grand Illinois Trail in stages. This lets you bike or hike just the right amount for your ability or interest. The nice thing is that this approach can also allow you to work your way around the Grand Illinois Trail at your own pace. The Grand Illinois Trail is easy to reach and all sections have trailhead access points convenient to major roads. Most have restroom and water facilities.

South Section TRAIL ACCESS

Trail	Access Point	Location	Directions
I & M Canal	Lock 14	La Salle, IL	Trail access is just off Illinois Route 351 immediately south of downtown La Salle. Reach Route 351 at Interstate 80, Exit 77.
I & M Canal	Gebhard Woods State Park	Morris, IL	From Illinois Route 47, pick up Illinois Route 6 west, then follow park signage to park location.
I & M Canal	Channahon State Park	Channahon, IL	Take Interstate 55 to Exit 248 and follow Illinois Route 6. Follow park signage.
Hennepin Canal	Lock 3	Bureau Junction, IL	Take Illinois Route 29 directly to trailhead.
Hennepin Canal	Lock 21 Day Use Area	West of Wyanet, IL	Take U.S. Route 6 directly to trailhead.
Hennepin Canal	Sheffield Visitors Center	Northeast of Sheffield, IL	Visitors Center is off Interstate 80 at Exit 45.
Hennepin Canal	Lock 24 Day Use Area	North of Geneseo, IL	Take Interstate 80 to Geneseo Exit 19. To park, take Chicago Street north. It becomes 1500E/ Grange Road.
Hennepin Canal	Timbrook Field	Colona, IL	Take Colona Exit 6 off Interstate 80, take Cleveland Road west and then follow local signage.
Great River Trail	Empire Park	Hampton, IL	Access park from Illinois Route 84.

14

Trail	Access Point	Location	Directions
Great River Trail	Thomson Causeway Recreation Area	Thomson, IL	Access trailhead from Illinois Route 84, follow Main Street to trailhead at the Causeway.
Great River Trail	Hiawatha RR Coach Visitors Center	Savanna, IL	Take Illinois Route 84 to downtown Savanna.

West Section TRAIL ACCESS

Trail	Access Point	Location	Directions
Great River Trail	Empire Park	Hampton, IL	Access park from Illinois Route 84.
Great River Trail	Thomson Causeway	Thomson, IL	Access trailhead from Illinois Route 84, follow Main Street to trailhead at causeway.
Great River Trail	Hiawatha RR Coach Visitors Center	Savanna, IL	At downtown Savanna.

North Section TRAIL ACCESS

Trail	Access Point	Location	Directions
Jo Daviess GIT route	Apple River Canyon State Park	Outside of Apple River, IL	Take U.S. Route 20 to Illinois Route 78.
Jo Daviess GIT road route	Lake Le-Aqua-Na State Park	Outside of Lena, IL	Take U.S. Route 20 to Illinois Route 73.
Jane Addams Trail	Freeport trailhead	Freeport, IL	Take U.S. Route 20 around Freeport to trailhead access.
Rockford Rec Path	Sinnissippi Park	Rockford, IL	Downtown Rockford at riverfront.
Rockford Rec Path	Rock Cut State Park	Rockford, IL	Take Illinois Route 173 to north park entrance.

Trail	Access Point	Location	Directions
Prairie Trail	Downtown Richmond	Richmond, IL	Take Illinois Route 31 or Illinois Route 173.
Prairie Trail	Prairie Trail Bike Shop	Algonquin, IL	Take Illinois Route 31 to trail access.
Fox River Trail	Grand Victoria Casino	Elgin, IL	Downtown Elgin
Illinois Prairie Path Volunteers Park	Downtown Wheaton	Wheaton, IL	Take Roosevelt Road/Rt. 38, then north on Main Street to park access.
Illinois Prairie Path	First Avenue access	Maywood, IL	First Avenue just north of Congress Expressway
Chicago Lakefront Path	Navy Pier	Chicago, IL	Take Lake Shore Drive to downtown, follow signs to Navy Pier
Burnham Greenway	Calumet Park	Chicago, IL	Indianapolis Boulevard and Avenue E intersection
Thorn Creek Forest Preserve	186th Street Access at Lansing Woods	Lansing, IL	From Interstates 80/94 take Torrence Avenue south to 186th Street.
Old Plank Road Trail	Ingalls Park	Joliet, IL	Take U.S. Route 30 to Hillcrest Road, then take Park Road to access point in park.

Making the Most of the Trip

Know the local history; this will help you see things you have never seen before.

A lot of the Grand Illinois Trail experience is about transportation: rails, highways, stagecoach lines, canals, interurbans. A lot of Grand Illinois Trail country was settled right after the Black Hawk War died down.

Don't expect to use racing tires on your bike. Try to find some wider tires, preferably with some kevlar to them. You probably should try heavy-duty, puncture-resistant inner tubes and have a spare tube and air pump.

The best time to view nature is during the early morning or in the evening. You might be surprised at what you find: muskrats, bald eagles, bats, raccoons, beavers, deer, and coyotes.

The best time to view prairie plants is probably late June. Prairie has a great diversity, so you can find interesting things throughout the year, but June sparkles up most prairies.

The best time to spot wildflowers is in April or early May.

Some days turn out good, some turn out bad. The more sections you do, the more prepared you end up being and the more enjoyable it becomes.

You miss out on some things if you don't talk with the people you meet on the trail or during a rest stop.

Doing the Grand Illinois Trail is actually a tone-up and weight-loss program in disguise. You may not realize it, but the Grand Illinois Trail sections make you stronger.

Take along a camera. There are lots and lots of good photo opportunities. And if you do the whole Grand Illinois Trail route, you will have a fine scrapbook, and a fun way to remember and relive the experience.

Interesting how the Grand Illinois Trail changes perceptions about Illinois. It's not perfectly flat. It's not entirely planted over in row crops. There is a lot of nature out there.

Surprising how great water can taste! Be sure to drink frequently since it is easy to get dehydrated on a warm summer day.

There really is nothing like the broad blue sky over the flat Illinois landscape. It's a great thing. Whenever someone talks about beautiful seasides and mountains, remember the big skies over Illinois.

If you mainly bicycle, consider hiking at least one portion of the Grand Illinois Trail. This gives you an even closer look at nature and geography. Some of the best sections for hiking include the Pecatonica Path, the Hennepin Canal from Geneseo to Colona, the I & M Canal from Channahon to Morris and the Prairie Trail from Glacier Park to Richmond.

Trail Jaunts

The Grand Illinois Trail offers a number of excellent trail segments. You can add them up to do the whole trail—use the master map in back to chart your progress.

These are some of the better one-day trips that can be found on the Grand Illinois Trail.

Shorter Day Trips

Trail Section	Route	Distance
I & M Canal Trail	Lock 14 in La Salle to Utica and back.	9 miles
Illinois Prairie Path	From Wheaton to Elmhurst and back.	20 miles
Fox River Trail	From Elgin to Algonquin and back.	21 miles
Jane Addams Trail	Up and back on the Jane Addams.	15 miles
Hennepin Canal	Lock 3 in Bureau Junction to Wyanet Lock 17 Day Use Park.	15.5 miles
Pecatonica Path (hiking and mountain biking)	From Dakota Road outside Freeport to Meridian Road outside Rockford.	21 miles

Mid-Sized Day Trips

Trail Section	Route	Distance
I & M Canal Trail	Gebhard Woods to Channahon State Park and back.	30.2 miles
I & M Canal Trail	Lock 14 in La Salle to Fox River Aqueduct in Ottawa.	29.5 miles
Hennepin Canal Trail	Lock 24 in Geneseo to Timbrook Field in Colona and back.	34.2 miles
Long Prairie Trail	From Roscoe to Capron, Illinois and back.	23 miles
Chicago Lakefront Path	From Navy Pier to Calumet Park and back.	28 miles

Mid-Sized Day Trips

Trail Section	Route	Distance
Old Plank Road Trail	Loop from Joliet to Chicago Heights and back.	46 miles
I & M Canal Trail	Channahon State Park to Gebhard Woods State Park and back.	30.2 miles
I & M Canal Trail	From Gebhard Woods State Park to Lock 14 La Salle and back.	73.2 miles
Prairie Trail	From Algonquin to Richmond and back.	44 miles
Illinois Prairie Path	From Wheaton to South Elgin and back.	32 miles
Great River Trail	Empire Park, Hampton to Thomson Causeway.	42.2 miles

Overnighters

Recommended overnight trips include taking the I & M Canal Trail from Channahon State Park to Starved Rock State Park and back, staying overnight in the Starved Rock area; taking the Hennepin Canal from Lock 3 in Bureau Junction to Geneseo, staying overnight in Geneseo, and back; and the Great River Trail, from Empire Park in Hampton to Mississippi Palisades State Park in Savanna and back, staying overnight in Savanna.

Trail Riding Tips

1. Hydrate and power up. Be sure to pack a water bottle or two. You'll be surprised at the extra power you can get from water. This is especially the case if you add a little fruit juice to your water. Mix in some Welch's Grape Juice. Remember to drink before you get dry!

2. If you are doing longer distances, be sure to carry along a supply of snacks to keep your energy up. Granola bars work great.

3. Bring along an extra tire tube (or a tire patch kit), bike tools and an air pump.

4. Sunglasses are handy for keeping bugs out of your eyes. They also reduce eyestrain.

5. Take along a light portable camera to record what you find along the trail.

6. Leave the trail better than you found it. Don't litter.

7. Use bicycle gloves. These substantially reduce road shock.

8. Buy a bell for your bike. It's fun, low-tech and useful. And you can ring at kids—they absolutely love it!

9. Bring along a friend.

10. Don't expect to use road tires on your bike on unpaved portions of the Grand Illinois Trail. Try to find some wider tires for your bike. Kevlar and puncture-resistant tires are a good idea and work well across many trail surfaces. Consider puncture-resistant inner tubes as well.

11. Cell phones are useful in emergencies.

12. Consider wearing long-sleeved t-shirts for added protection.

13. Use sunscreen and consider tying a bandana around your neck to ward off sunburn.

14. Consider your fit with your bike. When seated on the saddle, your leg should be only slightly bent at the knee at full extension. Can you reach the handlebars without making a full stretch?

15. Consider upgrading your factory bike seat with a better saddle. This one change can result in a big difference over long distances.

16. Review your route before you ride it, especially when taking road routes involving a number of turns.

Bike Safety Tips

1. Always wear a bicycle helmet. Use a Snell, ASTM or ANSI-approved model.

2. Make sure your bike is in good working condition. Give it a good look-over before setting out on a long ride. Check your tire inflation regularly.

3. Ride predictably and use hand signals, especially in heavy city traffic.

    - For a left turn, just point your left arm out and point the direction

    - For a right turn, bend your arm at a 90-degree angle at the elbow, with your hand pointing upward

    - For a stop, bend your arm at a 90-degree angle, with your hand pointing downward.

4. Keep to the right and pass on the left. When passing someone on foot or on bike, use a bell warning or say aloud, "passing on your right (or left)."

5. Stop at night. The IDNR allows trail use only from sunup to sundown.

6. Slow down easy on loose gravel and go slow around tight corners where visibility is low.

7. Be careful of any loose clothing or gear that can get caught in the bike!

8. Keep an eye out for loose gravel, for holes in the ground, and for trash or debris on the ground.

9. When you are on a road, obey the traffic signs. Scan behind yourself for traffic and check before you make lane changes or turns.

10. In tough situations, keep both hands on your brakes and stay alert. Move off the trail if you make a stop.

The Grand Illinois Trail

South

Joliet City System
★
Illinois & Michigan Canal Trail
★
Kaskaskia Alliance Trail
★
Hennepin Canal Trail
★
Road link to Empire Park/
Great River Trail

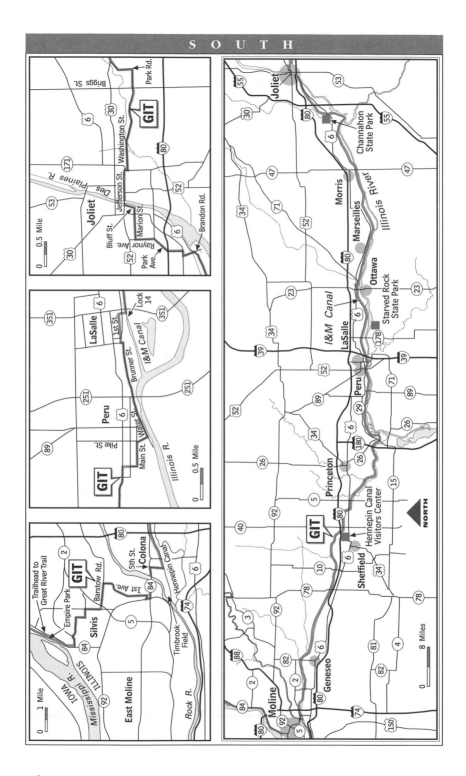

Overview _____

The South Section of the Grand Illinois Trail should be called Canal Country. The South Section is the great connecting route between Lake Michigan and the Missippi River.

The South Section begins with the Joliet City System, a set of designated local streets that are safe road routes for touring through Joliet from the Old Plank Road Trail to the Illinois & Michigan Canal Trail.

Scenic and following closely along the Illinois River waterway, the Illinois & Michigan Canal is rich in natural heritage and historical and cultural interest. It ends near the State Park Region of Illinois that is crowned by the great natural heritage and lore of Starved Rock.

The Hennepin Canal goes through tall corn country in Bureau, Henry and Rock Island counties. It is a level trail and the Hennepin Canal is fully watered along its course from the Illinois River at Bureau Junction to the Rock River in Colona. Running between the two state canal trails is the Kaskaskia Alliance Trail. This is a road route that closely follows along the Big Bend of the Illinois River—the point that the Illinois River slows down its stream and turns south through the middle of the state. The South Section ends at Empire Park in Hampton, Illinois where it connects to the Great River Trail.

A lock near Geneseo along the picturesque Hennepin Canal portion of the Grand Illinois Trail

27

SOUTH SECTION POINTS OF INTEREST

Union Station, JOLIET
Joliet downtown murals
Will County Civil War Monument, JOLIET
Silver Cross Field, JOLIET
Billie Limacher Bicentennial Park, JOLIET
Rialto Square Theater, JOLIET
Channahon State Park
DuPage River spillway, CHANNAHON
Dresden Lock and Dam
McKinley Woods
Aux Sable Aqueduct
Canalport Plaza, MORRIS
Nettle Creek Aqueduct, MORRIS
Gebhard Woods State Park, MORRIS
M. J. Hogan Grain Elevator & Visitor Center,
    SENECA
Pearl Street Bridge, MARSEILLES
Illini State Park, MARSEILLES
Fox River Aqueduct, OTTAWA
Reddick Mansion, OTTAWA
Washington Park, OTTAWA
Lincoln and Douglas Debate Statues,
    OTTAWA

Ottawa Scouting Museum
W. D. Boyce Memorial, OTTAWA
Buffalo Rock State Park
Illinois Waterway Visitors Center, UTICA
Starved Rock
La Salle County Historical Museum, UTICA
Split Rock
Little Vermilion Aqueduct
Lock 14 on the I & M Canal
La Salle City Hall, LA SALLE
Hegeler-Carus Mansion, LA SALLE
Westclox Building, PERU
Maud Powell statue, PERU
Lock 3 on the Hennepin Canal,
    BUREAU JUNCTION
Hennepin Canal Lock 17 Lift Bridge,
    WYANET
Hennepin Canal Visitor Center, SHEFFIELD
Summit Basin on the Hennepin Canal
Geneseo Historical Society Museum
Green River Aqueduct
Rock River at COLONA

GRAND ILLINOIS TRAIL THROUGH JOLIET

FROM BRANDON ROAD / I & M CANAL TRAIL TO OLD PLANK ROAD TRAIL

Brandon Road north to Meadow Avenue
Meadow Avenue east to Wheeler Avenue
Wheeler Avenue north to Park Avenue
Park Avenue northeast to Raynor Avenue
Raynor Avenue north to Marion Street
Marion Street east to Bluff Street
Bluff Street north to Jefferson Street
Jefferson Street (cross river) east to Eastern
    Avenue
Eastern Avenue south to Washington Street
Washington Street east to Park Road
Park Road north to Ingalls Park/Old Plank
    Road Trail Joliet Access

FROM OLD PLANK ROAD TRAIL TO BRANDON ROAD / I & M CANAL TRAIL

Park Road south to Washington Street
Washington Street west to Eastern Avenue
Eastern Avenue north to Cass Street/
    U.S. Route 30
Cass Street/U.S. Route 30 west to Bluff Street
Bluff Street south to Marion Street
Marion Street west to Raynor Avenue
Raynor Avenue south to Park Avenue
Park Avenue southwest to Wheeler Avenue
Wheeler Avenue south to Meadow Avenue
Meadow Avenue west to Brandon Road/I & M
    Canal Trail Access

Joliet City System

Channahon I & M Park Access to Old Plank Road Trail

Joliet is perhaps the easiest city for pedestrian, hiker or bicyclist along the Grand Illinois Trail. It is an effortless route. There are no disturbing jogs or jots to the roads. Intensive city planning efforts, along with ample, casino-provided revenue, have transformed civic dreams to bricks-and-mortar reality. It has paid off for Joliet's downtown.

Chicago Street offers a lot to tourists and travelers. The Rubens Rialto Theater in downtown Joliet, a fabulous and restored theater—the kind of thing that made the glory days glorious—offers a consistently good program of performances and events. The vaudeville greats all bounced the stage boards at the Rubens Rialto.

Joliet, Illinois, county seat of Will County, population 106,221, was first incorporated 1845, and was first settled in 1831 by Charles Reed. In 1833, Joliet was "Juliet," and had its first post office. The name was changed in 1845. The year 1848 turned Joliet into a boomtown, as the Illinois & Michigan Canal was opened to commercial navigation. The town had earlier prospered supplying limestone and other supplies to canal workers and contractors. The canal legacy surrounds Joliet. There are Irish names and Catholic churches. Limestone can be found everywhere.

Stone was the city's first great industry. Tons upon tons of limestone deposits were blasted up and delivered forth. Thousands were employed in the quarrying business, and thousands of structures across Illinois—churches, houses, and commercial buildings—still stand today, made of Joliet stone.

There is an interesting rivalry here. Some call the rock "Joliet Limestone" or "Joliet Marble," while others call it "Lemont Limestone" or "Athens Limestone." Actually the stuff is not limestone (calcium carbonate) but dolomite (magnesium carbonate). Dolomite just looks the same as limestone, and it is hard to tell apart from limestone. The rock in Joliet is from the same great, buried wall of 420 million year-old Sugar Run dolomite that you find cropping up along the banks of the Rock River in Rockford.

Joliet is a city of bridges and water, today and yesterday. The I & M Canal's north portion runs from the Bridgeport neighborhood of Chicago down to Joliet. Canal boats would then enter the Des Plaines River at Joliet and make their way to reenter the I & M Canal at Rockdale. Now the Sanitary and Ship Canal runs through the city carrying barges through the Illinois Waterway, bringing barges from the Illinois River to the Cal-Sag Channel and Calumet Harbor.

From the start, Joliet early on was well suited to heavy industry. Coal and limestone and water meant iron and steel. Joliet factories led the nation in steel production, making spikes, bolts, rails and rods. Andrew Carnegie, when he was just starting out, was awed by the size of Joliet's Illinois Steel Company. Joliet has also been home to plants of General Electric, United States Rubber and Caterpillar.

The bustling Elgin, Joliet and Eastern railroad, a belt line shunting freight cars around the outskirts of Chicago, made Joliet home. Union Station downtown has always been busy with trains, coming and going. Engines of the Rock Island line, the Atchison, Topeka & Santa Fe, the Illinois Central and Penn Central all came through Joliet.

And the city has been the location of other unusual companies. The Gerlach-Barlow poster calendar company was here, producing hundreds of thousands of sometimes kitschy, sometimes romantic, sometimes artistic advertising calendars. A half-dozen wall paper factories were once operating in Joliet, making enough each day to wallpaper the distance from Joliet to New York and back, an impressive imaginary road if there ever was one.

For years Joliet was keeper of the state's main penitentiary, brought up to this city from Alton. This castellated concoction, this stone box of a prison, sent terror into the hearts of children and petty criminals. For decades, the word "Joliet" resounded in the ears of cornhuskers and city slickers as the place of hard rock and hard time.

With riverboat revenues, Joliet has been reborn. It has a friendly downtown and it is remarkably easy to get around without a car. The city center has much to see, and it should be impossible to visit Joliet

Up she goes! Here a downtown bridge in Joliet swings up to let by the tugboat Karla.

without seeing Billie Limacher Bicentennial Park. The riverside park offers beautiful views of downtown Joliet. The west edge of the park is ringed with a hard jaw of exposed limestone bluff. Joliet limestone is a beautiful thing—creamy yellow with an almost expressive texture.

The Grand Illinois Trail route runs on Joliet city streets from the I & M Canal trailhead at Brandon Road in Rockdale, at Joliet's south side, to the Old Plank Road Trail at the east side of town. It is about 20 miles through Joliet city streets.

It is hilly on the west side of the river but once you cross the Des Plaines River, the route is fairly well flat.

Following the Joliet City System Trail

Useful trailheads are at Brandon Road and at Channahon State Park just south of Illinois Route 6 in Channahon. Channahon State Park is just off Interstate 55 at Exit 248.

Another fine access point is at Lower Rock Run Preserve at the intersection of U.S. Route 6 and Empress Road. This is an area run by the Will County Forest Preserve District and it can be easily reached from Interstate 80.

Channahon State Park has an information center, Class D camping at $6 per night and picnic grounds. There are ample parking, drinking water and restroom facilities. A good place to go fishing. The DuPage River has a spillway here. It is a short distance down the trail to McKinley Woods and the Dresden Lock and Dam.

Lock 6 on the I & M Canal is at Channahon State Park, and you can get a good photo of the lock with the locktender's house in the background here.

Get on the I & M Canal Trail and head east. Very soon, less than half a mile out, you pass under the U.S. Route 6 bridge. After this, the trail crosses a busy local street at grade. About three miles from the park are a half dozen huge sycamores, ancient and reaching into the skies. It makes sense to see them here. Sycamores, willows and cottonwoods like moist bottomland soil. The trail here, of course, is classic eight-foot crushed limestone.

The I & M Canal Trail takes a concrete ramp under a local road and Interstate 55 just over four miles from the park. At this point you will find a new, ten-foot wide path. This is the new I & M trail extension into Rockdale outside of Joliet. Just ahead is a short trail spur, built by the Channahon Park District. This is a "wetland trail" and it makes sense—you can spot turtles here.

There is a railroad crossing the trail at about five and a half miles out. Egrets can be found among the cottonwoods and ash trees.

The Lower Rock Run Preserve is at 6.5 miles out. The park has a short trail leading to an observation deck, looking over a pond and Rock River Creek. Rock Run has water, parking for 72 cars and a picnic shelter. Just past this is the Rock Run Corridor trail spur.

At 8.3 miles, there is another railroad spur crossing the I & M trail, heading into the Johns Manville Roofing Rockdale plant. South of this is the Caterpillar facility at Joliet. A bridge ahead takes you under Mound Road.

About 10 miles out from Channahon State Park is Brandon Road in Rockdale, just outside Joliet. The main I & M Canal State Trail ends here. There is a short, seven mile trail called the Heritage Trail that runs along the I & M Canal from the north side of Joliet into Lockport and a bit beyond.

The Brandon Road trailhead is nothing special. There is parking for your car. A burned and abandoned Brockway Plastics plant is next to this, in its own way an attractive ruin. Further south along Brandon Road is the Brandon Road Lock and Dam on the Illinois River.

Turning left, take Brandon Road north to Meadow Avenue.

Meadow Avenue is a busy road. Go east for about two blocks to Wheeler Avenue. Wheeler is steep. There is a quiet neighborhood park, West Park, at the hilltop. At this point you are not quite 11 miles from the Channahon State park trail access.

Wheeler Avenue bridges over Interstate 80. Immediately after the bridge take a 45-degree angle right, turning onto Park Street. Follow Park Street and you will run into Raynor Street after about five blocks. Take Raynor Street north.

Raynor is an active city street and it is in good shape. Just three blocks ahead is Marion Street. This will take you down to downtown Joliet. On the way, at Marion and Center Street intersection is the Patrick C. Haley Mansion, a hefty stone Romanesque Revival house.

Marion Street turns onto Bluff Street as it approaches the River. The Billie Limacher Bicentennial Park is on the west side of the Des Plaines River in downtown Joliet. Here are great walkways, performance areas, "interpretive ruins" of some of Joliet's earliest shops and industries, along with water fountains and portable toilets. Here, in the 1850s, merchant John Paige bottled flavored pressurized water—early soda pop!

Wheel about the park. You will get better acquainted with Joliet and there are beautiful murals portraying local history here and throughout the downtown city center. You can get a fine walking-tour of these murals at the Chicago Avenue visitors center. It is an interesting way to view history.

It is three blocks along Bluff Street to the Jefferson Street Bridge. Right after the bridge is the Joliet Municipal Building and two blocks past this is the Will County Courthouse.

The Joliet Municipal Building is unassuming and merely functional. It is a newer building draped in ivy. But take a look at the Will County Courthouse! It would be just right in a Star Trek movie, the kind of New Frontier, Mod-Utopian architecture that bespeaks 1968 with a bang! Oddly enough, when it was built county leaders moved an 1884 Civil War monument right in front of the courthouse. This makes for a real juxtaposition. The monument notes major battles of the war: Gettysburg, Appomattox, Chickamauga and others. Designed by J. C. Cochrane, placed by local masons in high rites, it is a time capsule on display. You can imagine the personal memories of triumph and pain this must have evoked on the day of its dedication.

Just beyond the Will County Courthouse is Chicago Avenue. The street is pro-pedestrian, with inviting shops and restaurants. The Heritage Corridor Convention and Visitors Bureau office is at 81 N. Chicago (they have plenty of Joliet information). Rubens Rialto Theater is just down the street at 102 N. Chicago Avenue.

Also downtown is Silver Cross Field, a new minor league baseball field that is home to the Joliet Jackhammers. Silver Cross Field is located just beyond the Will County Courthouse on Jefferson Street. Continuing on Jefferson Street you can find Union Station, a handsome historic railroad station at 50 E. Jefferson. Union Station is on the National Register of Historic Places.

Joliet Township High School is perhaps the most solidly built high school in the nation. It is an immense, monolithic stone construction that will remain for a long time at 201 E. Jefferson. The school is also on the National Register. Just south of here is Joliet's East Side Historic District.

Stay on Jefferson Street until you reach Eastern Avenue, then take Eastern Avenue south one block to Washington Street. Washington Street is a long stretch and it runs east to Park Road. Turning left (north) on Park Road, travel up to Ingalls Park and the Old Plank Road Trail access point.

Pilcher Park is only a half-mile north of Ingalls Park. This was originally a park and arboretum, given to the city by Robert Pilcher, a sturdy pioneer, a loyal citizen, a "lover of nature and his fellow men—a dreamer whose dream held," according to park statuary. The park is a treasure along winding Hickory Creek and it contains a nature center and opportunities for fishing, bird-watching and picnicking.

The route west through Joliet is a bit different than the route that takes you east through the city. The routes are adjusted to take one-way streets and bridges into account. Heading west from Ingalls Park, take Park Road south to Washington Street. Then take Washington Street west to Eastern Avenue. Turning right (north) head up Eastern Avenue toward downtown Joliet and Clinton Street. (Clinton is two blocks north of Jefferson Street). Turn left on Clinton and head toward the river. You will pass the city library, and here there is a good map kiosk with a display of downtown routes. Two blocks west of the library, take a right turn and go north one block to Cass Street.

Cass Street is a busy road. It is U.S. Route 30 through town. Cross the Cass Street bridge. Once over the river, get on Bluff Street to join the regular west side Grand Illinois Trail routing.

Joliet Additional Trails

The Heritage Trail:
Joliet-to-Lockport on the I & M Canal Trail

The 61.5-mile long I & M Canal Trail ends at Brandon Road in Rockdale. But a short section of the old canal towpath, called the Heritage Trail, has been made into an 11-mile long trail that begins at the city's north side and runs up to Isle a la Cache Park in Romeoville.

Along the way, the Heritage Trail runs past the Gaylord Building Historic Site in Lockport, the headquarters for the I & M Canal Visitor Center, and it also hosts a branch of the Illinois State Museum. The Gaylord Building is on the National Register of Historic Places and it is actually operated by the National Trust for Historic Preservation.

Access to the Heritage Trail is about the very north end of Chicago Street in Joliet, at the intersection of Chicago and Columbia Streets. This access point is also a self-guided interpretive center for the nearby Joliet Iron Works Historic Site. This is near the newly abandoned Joliet Penitentiary.

Wauponsee Glacial Trail

This 26-mile long route runs from the Old Plank Road Trail to the Kankakee River. It will take an asphalt path to Sugar Creek Preserve, and then a limestone path through to Midewin National Tallgrass Prairie and on to the Kankakee River. The south access point will be at Custer Park next to the Kankakee River. Another access point will be built at Sugar Creek Preserve, off of Laraway Road.

Joliet Junction Trail

The 4.4 mile Joliet Junction Trail will run from the I & M Canal Trail to Joyce Street, and then is routed on an abandoned railbed to Alessio Prairie in Crest Hill. It provides access to Theodore Marsh.

Rock Run Greenway Trail

This proposed route will run from the I & M Canal Trail north to Houbolt Road, through and around Joliet Junior College and Joliet Regional Airport (at this point, a city street route will connect over to the Joliet Junction Trail). The routing connects with the Rock Run corridor up to Ingalls Avenue and Theodore Marsh access.

DuPage River Trail

This proposed trail route will run from Channahon, on River Road, to Seil Road, then east to Shorewood Park. The route then will parallel the DuPage River up to Naperville and DuPage County.

Joliet POINTS OF INTEREST

Bird Haven Greenhouse and Conservatory
225 N. Gougar Road
Tropical house, cacti room and show house.

Jacob Henry Mansion
20 S. Eastern Avenue
A fabulous creation, a Second Empire mansion of the first order, on the National Register.

Joliet Iron Works Historic Site
Collins Street, east of Joliet City Center
Tour ruins of early blast furnace technology, a fine way to learn local history. Here, from the 1870s to the 1930s, Joliet made a reputation for its steel. Self-guided interpretive exhibits.

Rialto Square Theatre
102 N. Chicago Street
A landmark in every sense of the word, the Rialto offers regular public tours. On the National Register of Historic Places.

Slovenian Women's Union of America
Heritage Museum
431 N. Chicago Street
A smaller museum focused on local history and Slovenian heritage.

Hiram B. Scutt Mansion
206 N. Broadway
An historic mansion with strong architectural interest.

Joliet Area Historical Museum
Cass and Ottawa Streets
Compendium collection of local history and historical artifacts that tell the story of Joliet.

Pilcher Park Nature Center
Gougar Road near U.S. Route 30
Large established park with hiking, biking and cross-country skiing possibilities. Scenic and located along Hickory Creek.

A Healing Place:
Midewin National Tallgrass Prairie

They made TNT at the Joliet Army Ammunition Plant south of Joliet, near Wilmington. Storage bunkers and rail lines crisscrossed the site. Built in 1939 to make munitions for European allies and then for World War II, the arsenal was also kept busy for the Korean Conflict and for Vietnam.

At its peak during World War II, the arsenal employed 14,000 people. It even had passenger train service to Chicago.

But today the place is different. The former army plant is the site of the Midewin National Tallgrass Prairie. Midewin is Potawatomi for "healing." There is a lot of healing to be done here before the 19,000-acre park turns into waving prairie.

Tallgrass Prairie is the rarest major biome, or ecosystem, on the North American continent. Tallgrass prairie requires more annual rainfall than the drier lands of the Great Plains. In Illinois and other midwestern states, prairies became farm fields.

The task for the USDA Forest Service administering the site is to gradually rebuild a tallgrass prairie ecosystem from the ground up. Midewin is currently about 2% prairie, and about half of the site is put to agricultural purposes—row crops, cattle grazing and hayfields. A 20-year phase-in period for development will allow local farmers to adjust to the loss of leasable farmland in the area. It also allows Midewin staff a chance to create a substantial nursery for prairie plants.

It is the largest prairie redevelopment in the world.

Eight million people live within a short drive (down Illinois Route 53) from Midewin National Tallgrass Prairie. It will be connected to the Joliet area by the Wauponsee Glacial Trail. Already the site is home to the Upland Sandpiper and the Loggerhead Shrike, and other grassland bird species. With a new visitors center, an interpreter and volunteer guides, Midewin currently fields a schedule of bike tours, wildflower walks, habitat studies, birding events and butterfly expeditions.

Illinois and Michigan Canal

From Joliet to La Salle

[T]ime, as it flows through communities over decades and centuries, is not always an enemy and a thief, undermining worth, gnawing through value. Just as often, time is a ripener and a repairer, a force that can heal, scour, comfort, burnish, and recombine, sometimes restoring value, sometimes generating it.

—Tony Hiss

When you bike or hike the I & M Canal section of the Grand Illinois Trail, you travel back in time to a more understandable world. The trail is on the actual canal towpath, built once in the 1830s and built up a second time during the 1930s by the Civilian Conservation Corps. The locks are made of hand-dressed stone, with timbers of white oak. The locktender houses and buildings are straightforward. The canal was the major transportation route through this part of Illinois in the 1840s, and so it attracted town sites to it: Morris, Seneca, Marseilles, Ottawa, Utica and La Salle. It was the interstate highway of its day.

The Illinois & Michigan Canal is the Commercial Godfather of Chicago. It gave Chicago reach into the rest of the country. It let Chicago become a commodity trader, dealing in wheat and corn brought up through the canal from downstate.

Everyone saw it from the start. By plowing a canal between the Chicago River and the Illinois River, a magic connection could be made—the Great Lakes could reach the Gulf of Mexico, opening up the American interior. The great French explorers who marshaled through Illinois commented on this. President James Madison even talked about the great connection in his formal State of the Union Address of 1814. It was about the very first thing everyone wanted to do once Illinois became a state. Said Madison:

How stupendous the idea! How dwindles the importance of the artificial canals of Europe compared to this water connection. If it should ever take place—and it is said the opening may be easily made—the (Illinois) territory will become the seat of an immense commerce, and a market for the commodities of all regions.

Madison's vision took another 22 years to realize. But the idea was just too good to put aside: this was the "canal boom" era in a young America eager for "internal improvements" that would generate wealth.

Fort Dearborn on the Chicago River in 1833. Fifteen years later, the Illinois & Michigan Canal would route commercial and passenger traffic from the Illinois River up to Lake Michigan.
(Photo courtesy of the Illinois State Historical Library)

The famous Erie Canal (completed in 1825) had met with unheard-of, unexpected success. It spilled New Yorkers, Yankees and other immigrants into northern Illinois all eager for farmland. A young Abe Lincoln jumped on the internal improvements bandwagon in his first political campaign. The proposed Illinois route set off a huge chain of real estate speculation that led to the skyrocketing growth of Chicago. And this made many a local fortune.

Construction began in 1836 at Bridgeport. Canal headquarters and Lock 1 were established at Lockport, Illinois. A series of 15 locks form "water steps" descending from the high Lake Michigan pool down to the lower Illinois River water level. There are canal aqueducts over the Aux Sable Creek, Nettle Creek in Morris, the Fox River in Ottawa and the Little Vermilion River in La Salle.

The I & M Canal was originally built to end at Ottawa, but practical requirements pushed the last locks further west to La Salle. This was as far as steamboats could navigate up the Illinois River without scraping boat bottoms against the rocky river bed.

The I & M Canal was designed to be 97 miles long, with a width of 60 feet, a depth of six feet and a water width of 30 feet. The water depth in the canal "prism" was to be six feet deep. Native limestone hauled from Joliet quarries formed the locks. Watergates were made of incredibly durable white oak. Mortar came from naturally occurring hydraulic cement mined in Utica at the Blackball Mine. All told, the price tag for this massive landscape transformation was $6.4 million dollars in 1848. In today's terms the price tag would be $144,923,726.32.

Canal boats were 100 feet long stern to bow and about 17 feet wide. They were made of wood, with deep storage berths. The 150-ton boats were actually pretty well designed, and they were specially balanced to move easily through the canal system. The

Expert stonecutting craftsmanship on Lock 12 on the I & M Canal outside of Ottawa.

boats had no motors, no sails, and no oars. Instead, local boys walked the towpath—masters of the mules that steadily pulled the canal boats.

Canal packet boats averaged a speed of about five or six miles per hour, and made the La Salle to Chicago trip in 22 to 26 hours. Heavier cargo boats traveled at a rate of about three miles per hour. One fast trip on the "Queen of the Prairies" made the trip in just 20 hours. Compare that to the 44 hours a stagecoach trip would take to cover the same distance!

The I & M Canal drew a foreign-born labor force into a young Illinois. These workers were mainly Irishmen drawn by good pay in America and hard times in the Old Sod. Along the route the Irish influence is clear and certain: the Bridgeport neighborhood with St. James of the Sag Church, St. Patrick's Church in La Salle, constructed of cut stone and St. Columba's (Patron Saint of Ireland) Church in Ottawa. Irish backs built the canal; English speculators bought the canal bonds. And Illinois legislators would mire the State of Illinois in debt until 1871, since the General Assembly grievously overextended itself with its costly taste for internal improvements.

Fifty-Dollar State Bank of Illinois Bond for the Illinois & Michigan Canal Fund. Workers and suppliers were issued thousands of dollars of this stuff.

(Illustration courtesy of the Canal Corridor Association).

The canal opened in 1848. Payback came quickly. Chicago boomed and reached into her downstate neighbors for trade. Another boom took off back in Buffalo, New York, the point at which the Great Lakes waterway system met the Erie Canal. Buffalo was at the other end of the Great Lakes equation.

The commercial implications were so obvious that the directors of the Rock Island railroad voted to extend their project to Chicago (the railroad was originally supposed to run only from Rock Island to La Salle). The Chicago, Rock Island and Pacific Railway opened its full route in 1854—offering year-round service and a much faster trip. The railroad parallels the I & M Canal from La Salle to Morris.

The railroad took the passenger trade and some commercial business from the canal. But the railroad was always more expensive than the canal for shipping bulk commodities like corn and wheat. Tonnage on the I & M Canal peaked in 1882, when over one million tons were shipped that year on this stupendous water route. Competing rail lines cut prices and eventually took away much of the bulk commodities business from the canal.

The opening of the first Sanitary and Ship Canal in 1900 effectively ended the canal's commercial life. The I & M was then mainly used for pleasure boating. Barge traffic could take the Calumet River to the Des Plaines River, and then reach the Illinois River. The construction of the Chicago Sanitary and Ship Canal in 1922, and the massive rejiggering of the Illinois and Des Plaines Rivers created the Illinois Waterway system in 1933.

The same year that the canal was formally closed to navigation, 1933, was also the year it began life as a recreational parkway. Five units of the Civilian Conservation Corps worked on the canal in the 1930s, building parks and shelters, creating trails, planting trees, doing erosion control projects and repairing canal damage. These infrastructure improvements can be seen and are still used today, along the entire length of the canal. Gebhard Woods in Morris and the McKinley Woods in Channahon show outstanding examples of the CCC work.

In 1984 the Illinois & Michigan Canal became our country's first National Heritage Corridor. This designation reinvigorated interest in the canal and a number of organizations now work toward recreational improvements and events. Once more the I & M Canal is recognized for its vital role in building the state. Recent large-scale projects have been underway in La Salle (the Lock 14 park), Ottawa (downtown Riverwalk), Morris (downtown Canalport Plaza and at Gebhard Woods), and Seneca (the M. J. Hogan Grain Elevator and Visitor's Center). The I & M Canal trail was extended east from Channahon to Brandon Road in Joliet (it scoots under both Illinois

The Grand Illinois Trail route travels back in time through an older era of construction.

Route 6 and Interstate 55), and new trail was built from Joliet north to Lockport.

Planners call for extending the I & M Trail from Lockport into the western Chicago suburbs, possibly connecting with the Fox River Trail. This part of the I & M Canal trail from Joliet to Lockport is called the Heritage Trail. A 3.3-mile section of I & M trail already runs through Cook Country Forest Preserves in Willow Springs.

There is an increasing number of heritage celebrations and events all along the Illinois & Michigan Canal Corridor. These range from scholarly talks to children's festivals to van tours for the handicapped to farm tractor parades. The Starved Rock Runners take to the canal limestone. The Hogan Grain Elevator site in Seneca offers a full program, and there are other cultural, entertainment and recreational activities offered through the Gaylord Building in Lockport.

The I & M Canal route takes you through the state park region of the Illinois River. Noted state parks in the area include the venerable Starved Rock State Park and Buffalo Rock State Park, Matthiessen State Park, Illini State Park, Gebhard Woods State Park, William Stratton State Park, Channahon State Park and McKinley Woods State Park.

The Grand Illinois Trail relies on the canal route from Joliet to La Salle. The natural idea of linking the 61.5-mile Illinois & Michigan Canal trail with the 70-mile long Hennepin Canal was the impetus for the concept of the Grand Illinois Trail.

The I & M Canal originally ran further, from Joliet to Bridgeport, where the canal connected to the South Branch of the Chicago River. At Lockport, site of Lock 1 and canal commissioner headquarters, the area has been revitalized. The Gaylord Building at 200 W. Eight Street downtown was built in 1838 as a massive stone granary. It is now home to parkway administration and a north outpost of the Illinois State Museum. This museum gallery often hosts cultural and historical programs.

A view of the Nettle Creek Aqueduct on the I & M Canal in Morris.
(Photo courtesy of Edward Ranney).

The I & M Canal and its towpath, heading through Gebhard Woods State Park.
(Photo courtesy of Edward Ranney).

Following the I & M Trail

The I & M Canal State Trail runs 61.5 miles. It can be biked in one day by a strong biker, but it is also possible to break this into several smaller trips, such as La Salle to Morris, or Channahon to Ottawa. Main trailheads are at Channahon State Park, Gebhard Woods State Park, Ottawa and Lock 14 in La Salle. The I & M Canal State Trail is routed almost entirely on the old canal towpath. For some short stretches, and a length between Seneca and Marseilles, the route runs on low-volume roads. This Seneca-to-Marseilles portion was originally a section of an old stagecoach route through the Illinois Valley.

The trail follows the original canal towpath on a crushed limestone trailbed. It is perfect. The route is gentle and level, and for much of the route the canal is watered and especially scenic. The canal structures add to its interest. This is great territory for hikers and bikers. Snowmobiling is permitted in the winter if there is at least four inches of snow. Portions of the canal retain water, making these sections especially scenic. And canoeable—you can wet your paddle between La Salle and Utica, and between Channahon and Morris.

The terrain is part of the Grand Prairie section of Illinois, a broad glacier plain extending across 18 counties in Illinois, including La Salle, Kendall, Will and Grundy counties. This was the largest range of tallgrass prairie in the state, and the Grand Prairie section was known for its flatness and its marshes. Buffalo roamed wild here until 1814. The Grand Prairie was the easternmost edge of a vast prairie system that extends west to the Rocky Mountains.

In the 1840s, just before the advent of railroads, there were many stage lines that ran through the I & M canal country. A portion of the current trail route between Marseilles and Seneca actually runs right on the old stagecoach road. Kind of cool, actually.

Start the I & M Canal at Channahon, Illinois. The best place to begin is at <u>Channahon State Park</u>. The park is just off of Illinois Route 6 east of Channahon, and west of Interstate 55. There is plenty of good parking, restrooms and drinking water. Channahon State Park is a good base camp for exploring both the I & M Canal trail, the Des Plaines Conservation Area and <u>Midewin National Tallgrass Prairie</u>.

This is a watery part of the state. Channahon is near the confluence of the DuPage and Des Plaines rivers, and the confluence of the Des Plaines and Kankakee rivers. This is the birthplace of the Illinois River.

Channahon, Illinois, population 7,344, incorporated 1961, is a popular I & M spot and it is here that the I&M Canal crosses the DuPage River. A long planked bridge crosses above the river spillway, carrying the trail route on its back. The distance from Channahon State Park to Morris is about 13 miles. For about half of this distance, the canal closely follows the Illinois River. The Commonwealth Edison nuclear power plant at Dresden can easily be seen through the trees from the canal towpath. Just across the river is Goose Lake Prairie State Park, a 2,537-acre prairie, and Heidecke Lake.

Heidecke Lake is a 1,300-acre lake up to 12 feet in parts, and a place to fish for muskie, bass and catfish. Goose Lake Prairie is 2,537 acres of pure Illinois prairie. It is the kind of place where you can see prairie flowers and grasses throughout the summertime, and it is the largest stand of prairie in the Prairie State. There are seven miles of interior trails, and you can reach the park by taking Route 47 south to Pine Bluff-Lorenzo Road to Jugtown Road.

Aux Sable Creek meets the I & M Canal at eight miles from the Channahon State Park access. This stretch is a great introduction to canal technology. The I & M Canal needs an aqueduct to carry it over the lower Aux Sable Creek. The Aux Sable site deserves a medal—it is an effective use of historic preservation to bring us in touch with the past. Here you can find a restored canal locktender's house near Lock 8.

Between Channahon and Morris, you can find evidence of riverbank erosion. The slapping of boat wakes has caved in, or nearly so, several of the attractive old CCC retaining walls on the Illinois River.

Almost part of the tree! An old hickory has fungi feet.

An artistic wood and steel bridge crosses over the I & M Canal Trail.

Morris, Illinois, population 11,928, first incorporated 1853, is a classic canal town and it is the county seat of Grundy County. The city came into existence due to commerce on the I & M Canal. This is still seen today. The Coleman hardware company operated next to the canal, as did the local brewery. The city contains the Evergreen Cemetery gravesite of Chief Shabbona, a Potawatomi Indian, who was what they used to call a "good Indian," meaning that he helped white settlers as they arrived in northern Illinois. Chief Shabbona had fought with the British during the War of 1812, fighting the Americans. But by the 1830s, Shabbona was a voice of accommodation and assistance to white settlers.

Canal Port Plaza is a great entryway into downtown Morris. Downtown Morris offers many shops and restaurants. You can spin off to Gebhard Woods State Park which rambles across 33 acres just to the north of the canal. It is a finely wooded park that was given to the State of Illinois by a local sportsmen's club in the 1930s and then built up by the Civilian Conservation Corps. It is a nice stop and nicely shaded, with restrooms and running water and an information center. The picnic areas and pond are attractive. Just east of Gebhard Woods State Park is the restored Nettle Creek Aqueduct, a fine stone project built by the CCC boys.

Seneca, Illinois, population 2,053, incorporated 1865, is quiet town now, but in the 1940's, Seneca was bustling. Under the direction of the Chicago Bridge & Iron Company, a massive shipbuilding operation was established. This brought over 11,000 workers to Seneca, building Navy landing craft, and building the

The M.J. Hogan Grain Elevator in Seneca is now a canal museum.

town in the process. These LSTs landed tanks and men on battlefront shores in Normandy, Okinawa, North Africa and points around the globe.

The restored M.J. Hogan Grain Elevator and Visitor Center is a good rest stop. You can get water, and there are restrooms. The Center provides a good orientation to the area, a bit of history about Illinois agriculture, and it is a towering remembrance of the time when all commercial activities in town revolved around corn and canal traffic.

The grain elevator once served as many as 400 wagonloads of corn a day, using steam-powered engines to haul bushels of corn up to storage bins. These bins could direct grain straight into canal boats or railroad grain cars below. The Seneca elevator had a 70,000-bushel capacity and stands 65 feet tall. It is the last remaining grain elevator along the canal and it dates to 1860.

Marseilles, Illinois, population 4,655, incorporated 1861, is a smaller canal town. In 1911, a hydroelectric facility was built in order to power the Chicago, Ottawa and Peoria interurban. This was an extensive light-rail commuter line that operated in the Illinois Valley, from Joliet to Princeton. You could easily connect in Joliet with Chicago-bound trains. It never did send an extension down to Peoria, although there were spurs to Streator and Ladd. The hydroelectric plant is on the National Register of Historic Sites for a number of reasons, including being partly designed by Daniel Burnham, the famous architect. A cheap and popular form of transportation, the interurban system went defunct because of the new-fangled Automobile.

By the way, Marseilles is home to a major training base for the Illinois Army National Guard, located on the south side of the Illinois River. And also on the south side of the Illinois River is Illini State Park, a good place for camping. Operations on the Marseilles Lock and Dam on the Illinois River can be viewed up-close from Illini State Park.

Ottawa, Illinois, population 18,307, was first settled in 1823 and incorporated in 1837, and is the county seat of La Salle County. The town was laid out by the I & M Canal Commissioners in 1829 and was designed to be Chicago's twin on the opposite end of the canal. It has a lovely location at the junction of the Fox and Illinois Rivers just below the river bluff.

The I & M trail runs straight through town, crossing the Fox River in the recently-restored, highly scenic, Fox River Aqueduct. This structure was built in the 1840s by David Sanger & Sons Construction Company of Ottawa. The aqueduct runs for 464 feet over seven limestone piers that were set directly on bedrock. The state recently spent close to $2 million to restore the Joliet limestone piers to an original condition, so this is a good place to be impressed by stonework.

There will be additional public parking at the west end of the aqueduct, making this a decent trailhead for the canal, and also for the city's riverwalk along the Fox River. Early conceptual planning here calls for re-watering the canal through the length of the city, restoring this as a recreational amenity.

Ahead, at the Columbus Street crossing, is a very small house on the south side of the trail. This is the last standing canal tollhouse, currently disguised as a barbershop, although plans are being made for its restoration.

Ottawa is a good place to take a quick jog off the trail. Two blocks from the trail is one of Ottawa's earliest public parks, Washington Park. This is the site of the first Lincoln-Douglas debate, held in August 1858. Here the two political giants matched wits (and gnashed teeth) over the issue of slavery expansion into the western territories—and by implication whether there should be slavery at all in a free country.

They Set the Prairie On Fire: *Artist's models from the Ottawa statue grouping. Lincoln and Douglas spoke at Ottawa and Freeport and both cities recall their great debates.*
(Photo courtesy of the City of Ottawa).

The large <u>Lincoln and Douglas statues</u> are new additions to the park, dedicated in 2002. They are original representations, done by Rebecca Childers Caleel after exhaustive research. The Lincoln statue has been described as among the best artistic representations of the Railsplitter by Lincoln scholars Harold Holzer and Wayne Temple.

Washington Park includes a fine old <u>Civil War monument</u> inscribed with the names of numerous La Salle County volunteers who paid the ultimate price for freedom and union. During summer months the park contains an 1890s-style popcorn wagon—a local tradition kept popping away. Try the popcorn. The overall design of Washington Park recalls a time when parks were specifically designed to create quiet, peaceful settings.

Just north of, and across the street from, Washington Park is <u>Reddick Mansion</u>, at 100 W. Lafayette Street. This is a grand Italianate structure built in 1856. Its interior plaster ceilings are worth a look, and two main rooms are kept in period fashion. It was for many years the town library. The mansion grounds have been given a nice historic landscaping treatment, and the building serves as offices for several organizations, including the Ottawa Area Chamber of Commerce. The <u>Ottawa Visitor's Center</u> is at the ground floor, and can provide valuable tips for additional sightseeing.

William Reddick was an Irishman who did very well for himself in La Salle County, arriving in Illinois to work on the I & M Canal, and finally getting real wealth through real estate sales. His mansion provided hospitality to U.S. Senator Stephen Douglas just before the Lincoln-Douglas debate in Ottawa, Reddick himself would later serve as county sheriff and state senator.

Just to the east of Reddick's mansion, across the street, is the Third District Illinois Appellate Courthouse at 1004 Columbus Street. The Greek Revival courthouse was built from 1857 to 1860 and wings were added in 1871. Lincoln saw it being built but never practiced in it.

Ottawa was given a choice in 1848. The town could either be home to the new state land-grant college (the one that eventually grew to become the University of Illinois) or the city could be the northern home to the Illinois State Supreme Court. Ottawa politicos chose the court. For many years the Illinois State Supreme Court was a court that operated on a seasonal circuit across the state. This traveling circus of paper ended in 1877. Since then, the Ottawa courthouse has been subsequently used as one of the state's five appellate courts. The courthouse hears cases from across 21 central Illinois counties.

Ottawa has been a summer get-away for various Chicago personages, including Marshall Field. One such Chicago millionaire was William D. Boyce, owner and president of Boyce Publishing Company. Boyce made a fortune producing millions of newspaper inserts and mass-market monthlies. But a curious twist of fate happened to him. In London on a business trip in 1909, on a dark and foggy night, he became lost. But a helpful Boy Scout gave him directions. Boyce was struck at the great possibilities of the scouting movement. And he brought scouting to America, becoming the esteemed Founder of the Boy Scouts of America.

Since then, Boy Scouts have educated generations of youth in woodcraft, mechanics, citizenship, sports and virtue. The Boyce Mansion in Ottawa got knocked down years ago, but the city memorializes the scouting movement in the Ottawa Scouting Museum at 1100 Canal Street. The Museum contains memorabilia from all types of scouting, not just the Boy Scouts, and it has an active events schedule. And the grand man himself has a grand gravesite on a bluff above the Illinois River in the Ottawa Avenue

Cemetery. Here, overlooking the river is a fine bronze statue of the "Lone Scout." Scouts are able to follow a hiking route, the W.D. Boyce Trail, which runs along both sides of the Illinois River from Ottawa to Starved Rock State Park and back.

For many years Ottawa was at the center of an extensive glassmaking industry, which used local silica. It retains a reputation for Peltier marbles. And U.S. Silica, formerly Ottawa Silica Company, still works its quarry on the west edge of town. The I & M Canal trail goes right past U.S. Silica, and one of the great advocates of the I & M Canal, Edmund Thornton, was for many years the president of U.S. Silica.

Utica, Illinois, population 977, incorporated 1867, was first settled in 1852. The village has an interesting bit of history: it's been moved twice. First developed as the village of Science, Illinois, Utica was sited on the south side of the Illinois River. But rivers flood, and Science was definitely in the floodplain. The town uprooted its stakes and took to the north side of the great river. But alas! this townsite flooded as well. The current village of Utica is officially "North Utica" because of this.

The La Salle County Historical Society Museum is located in the heart of downtown Utica at the intersection of Mill and Canal Streets. The Museum occupies the Clark Warehouse, a stone warehouse along the canal. The warehouse is so solid it could withstand World War III. The historical society collections are extensive, and are a caliber above the ordinary local museums. See the holdings in canal and railroad history, local industrial history, ethnic history, Native American history and scouting and military history. The Museum is a good place to pick up books, guides and pamphlets on the Starved Rock area.

Across the street on an uneven diagonal lies Duffy's Tavern on Mill Street. Duffy's, built in a triangular shaped building wedged toward Canal Street, is a Local Institution. This is the place to get a cold beverage.

Father Marquette, a Jesuit priest who accompanied the great French explorers La Salle and Jolliet, built the Immaculate Conception mission here on April 14, 1675. He offered the first Christian services here among the Illini tribes in 1675, and an impressive bas-relief monument recalls the event. It is at St. Mary's Catholic Church at 303 Division Street.

The Illinois Waterway Visitor's Center is worth a stop. Located south of Utica and south of the I & M Canal Trail on Dee Bennett Road, the Illinois Valley Waterway Visitor's Center gives a close-up look at river navigation and the history of the Illinois River. Operated by the U.S. Army Corps of Engineers, the Illinois Waterway Visitor's Center is open from 9 A.M. to 5 P.M., seven days a week. This is a great place for viewing river traffic activities, and for getting a great view of Starved Rock, which is right across the way.

Stretching for two and a half miles along the north side of the Illinois River, the Grand Village of the Kaskaskias was located here in the 1600's. It was here that the earliest French explorers found the major encampment of Native Americans in the Illinois Country. The village was occupied by members of the Illiniwek Confederacy—the Kaskaskias, the Tamaroas, the Illini, the Peoria, the Moingwena, the Cahokia and the Michigamea. The Grand Village had about 6,000 residents. Here Father Marquette first met the Illiniwek Indians, and it was here that the legendary explorers Henri Tonti and Cavalier seigneur de La Salle established the French fur trade in the Illinois Country.

Scientific excavation of the site shows that the Illiniwek lived in houses made of mats lashed to bent saplings. They wore animal skins along with decorative feathers and tattoos, and wore jingling ornaments. Their diet was nicely varied—ground corn, squash, beans, turkey, deer and bison. The Illini were semi-nomadic, moving according to hunting and harvesting schedules.

The French built an alliance with the Illiniwek. Together, they were to control the fur trade in the Illinois Valley. But in 1680, British-allied Iroquois moved in from the Great Lakes and fought to gain control of the industry. They were tough and experienced fighters. They routed the Illini, and in 1683 Henri Tonti returned to build Fort St. Louis atop Starved Rock. The Illiniwek remained at Starved Rock until 1691 when operations shifted south to Peoria. Later attacks by the Sioux, Fox, Sauk and other tribes pressed the Kaskaskias and other Illini tribes into southern Illinois.

Starved Rock State Park, established in 1911, is the second oldest state park in Illinois and one of the most loved and one of the best visited. Starved Rock State Park contains 18 fantastic stone canyons, many lookout points, and an enviable place in midwestern Indian lore. A fine, Adirondack-style rustic lodge is on the river bluff, built in the 1930s by the Civilian Conservation Corps. Its Great Hall is an Illinois landmark, and the Lodge is on the National Register of Historic Places.

It is a little-known, but amazing, fact that architect Joseph F. Booten designed Starved Rock Lodge in a ten-day burst of architectural creativity. Booten also designed the smaller CCC lodge at Black Hawk State Park in Rock Island.

The Legend of Starved Rock needs to be recounted. It is a long-lived bit of Illinois lore. According to legend, the great chief Pontiac was stabbed to death at a peace meeting by a member of the Illini. United in vengeance, the Potawatomi, Kickapoo and Miami tribes chased the Illini to Starved Rock. The desperate Illini took shelter atop Starved Rock, and remained there under siege, until they died of starvation. Hence the name Starved Rock. If this happened, if part of this happened, it would have most likely taken place around 1769.

The Starved Rock Visitor Center, opened in 2002, gives a good introduction to the human and natural history of the park area. It has a fine model of Fort St. Louis on Starved Rock, built by students of the Illinois Math and Science Academy.

Also in the Starved Rock region are Buffalo Rock and Matthiessen State Parks. Buffalo Rock has good picnic facilities, a pair of bemused buffalo and the Effigy Tumuli earthenwork art. There is a fine I & M Canal trailhead just across the road from Buffalo Rock State Park.

Buffalo Rock has gone through many changes over the years. It was briefly the site of another Fort St. Louis, built after the first one at Starved Rock. It became Fort Ottawa in 1760, held by French soldiers and French sympathizers during the great French and Indian War. During the canal era, there was talk of building a settlement at Buffalo Rock. By 1903 it was owned by religious "Holy Rollers" and they held large revival meetings on the site. After that, it was a summer camp for tuberculosis patients. For a time, the Crane elevator company owned Buffalo Rock and used it as a company summer resort. Employees could take the trolley down. It was sold to the state in 1922.

Matthiessen State Park, southwest of Starved Rock, has prairie lands, fine woods and scenic dells along the Vermilion River. It offers great cross-country skiing in the wintertime. Matthiessen State Park was originally the country estate of Frederick Matthiessen, co-founder of the M & H Zinc Company of La Salle. He was a golfer, and Deer Park Golf Course next to the park was built from his pioneering links. The name "deer park" comes from Native American use of the Vermilion River dells to pen deer during winters. These dells have an interesting assortment of ferns, mosses and liverworts.

The I & M Canal Trail pushes into Utica from the east. Cross over the first pedestrian bridge, and continue on Canal Street, past the historical society museum. Cross Clark Street. Ahead is a trailhead for the canal, with parking for 30 cars and a portable toilet. Another pedestrian bridge takes you over the canal and back to the south towpath trail. Be alert to the low railroad bridge as you start off.

The route between Utica and La Salle is short, but it is packed with many features.

Pecumsaugen Creek cuts across the canal. Just up this canyon are the Blackball Mines, source of hydraulic cement for the canal.

It is at Split Rock that you can see a minor wonder of the world. Here, some 510 million years ago, the underlying Ordovician rock was thrust skyward, tilting and exposing the upper layers of rock. (It is because of this tilt that early French explorers noted that coal, *carbonne d'terre*, could be found along the river here). Take a look at the lines, or striations, on Split Rock. This is the approximate angle of the La Salle Anticline, a great buckling of

The I & M Canal and its towpath near Split Rock east of La Salle.

The view from atop Split Rock. This looks out across the Illinois River and bottomland fields near La Salle.

rock layers. This geological upthrust is responsible for the many mining activities in La Salle County, since it brings to the surface silica-rich St. Peter Sandstone, gravel and coal layers. Knowing about the La Salle Anticline is a key to knowing something about the area.

But it took dynamite to make Split Rock, a stony finger cut to allow the canal its path westward. At one time the local interurban line ran directly over the canal to the north side, where there was a summer dance pavilion. You can clamber to the top of Split Rock, but it takes some time and energy and concentration. Small toeholds have been scraped into the rock.

Ahead, as you enter La Salle, you can see the operations of the Illinois Cement Company next to the canal aqueduct over the Little Vermilion River. The old steel truss bridge above you at this point was used by the Illinois Central railroad as it struck its way through the middle of the state.

Lock 14 in La Salle is ahead. The Abraham Lincoln Bridge carrying Interstate 39/51 over the Illinois River has "authentic" looking stone facings to match with the canal aesthetics.

The Lock 14 trailhead is a work in progress. There is parking and a portable toilet. The actual lock was rebuilt, to original specifications, in 1982. Just beyond the lock is the Steamboat

Basin, a wide area for docking and unloading passengers and freight. The very last lock on the I & M Canal, Lock 15, is submerged. A short local trail takes you almost a mile west to the joinder of canal passage and the Illinois River.

La Salle, Illinois, population 9,796, first incorporated 1852, was first settled in 1830 by Simon Crosiar, an itinerant trader. The town grew because of its location at the end of the canal, and canal workers built their cabins along the river bluff line above the canal. Almost immediately after this, large-scale coal mining operations, along with zinc production, became important. Her sister city, Peru, was known for her steamboats.

This part of Illinois became quite a manufacturing center. Coal mines operated throughout the Illinois River valley (one company even ran a work tunnel under the Illinois River). Several zinc smelters operated, taking advantage of the local coal and access to lead mine tailings from the Galena/Mineral Point mining district. Western Clock Company, Westclox, made thousands of buzzing Big Bens here. The area was also home to a number of breweries, including the maker of the regionally popular Star Model beer. Maze Nails has long manufactured its line of special zinc-coated roofing nails in the area.

La Salle has been called a city of churches, and the many different ethnic groups each seemed to have claimed a church of its own. St. Patrick's for the Irish, St. Hyacinth's for the Poles and St. Joseph's for the Germans.

The I & M Canal Trail ends at the Lock 14 park in downtown La Salle. The Kaskaskia Alliance Trail is the next section on the Grand Illinois Trail. The Kaskaskia Alliance follows county roads and state blacktops over to the Hennepin Canal trailhead at Lock 3 in Bureau Junction, Illinois.

I & M Canal Additional Trails

The Heritage Trail

The <u>Heritage Trail</u> runs along the north part of the I & M Canal for 11 miles from Joliet to Romeoville. Pick it up on the north side of downtown Joliet, at the <u>Joliet Iron Works Historic Site</u> (at Columbia and Chicago Streets). The trail passes along Locks 1 to 4, and Dellwood Park, up to the <u>I & M Canal Visitor Center/Gaylord Building Historic Site</u> in downtown Lockport and beyond to Isle a la Cache in Romeoville.

The Ottawa Riverwalk

The <u>Ottawa Riverwalk</u> extends a short spur along the lower Fox River, from the <u>Fox River Aqueduct</u> to the local YMCA and downtown.

La Salle Short Loop

In La Salle, a short loop trail spins through <u>Lock 14 Park</u>. On it you can see the juncture of the canal with the Illinois River. A local plan calls for using a former railbed to access the <u>Hegeler-Carus Mansion</u> and the east side of the city.

Hopalong Cassidy Trail

Streator makes an interesting connection to the canal route, with its <u>Hopalong Cassidy Trail</u>. This is a combination biking-canoeing trail. From Ottawa take Illinois Route 23 south to Streator. In downtown Streator, canoe down the <u>Vermilion River</u> toward the Oglesby/Starved Rock takeout point on Ed Hand Road.

I & M Canal MILEPOSTS ————————————————

I & M Canal Trail/Channahon Access to Brandon Road/Rockdale	10 miles
I & M Canal Trail/Channahon Access to McKinley Woods	3 miles
I & M Canal Trail/Channahon Access to Morris	13 miles
Morris to Seneca	11 miles
Seneca to Marseilles	5.5 miles
Marseilles to Ottawa	7.5 miles
Ottawa to Buffalo Rock State Park Access	5 miles
Ottawa to Utica	9.5 miles
Utica to Lock 14 Access/La Salle	4.5 miles

I & M Canal LANDMARKS

Little Vermilion River Aqueduct, east of LA SALLE
Split Rock, east of LA SALLE
Stone canal warehouse/La Salle County Historical Society building in UTICA
Last remaining canal tollhouse, downtown OTTAWA
Fox River Aqueduct, OTTAWA
M. J. Hogan Grain Elevator, downtown SENECA
Gebhard Woods State Park, MORRIS
Nettle Creek Aqueduct, MORRIS
Canalport Visitors Center, MORRIS
William G. Stratton State Park, MORRIS
Aux Sable Aqueduct between MORRIS and CHANNAHON
Dresden Island Lock and Dam on the Illinois River
McKinley Woods, west of CHANNAHON
DuPage River Spillway at Channahon State Park/I & M Canal Trail Access

Trails for America!

by Reese Lukei, Jr., *National ADT Coordinator*

The creation of the American Discovery Trail was a Herculean accomplishment of linking thousands of miles of hiking, biking, and horseback riding trails from the Atlantic to Pacific. With one terminus at Point Reyes National Seashore, California, and another at Cape Honlopen State Park, Delaware, the ADT is a route heavy with superlatives: it runs through 15 states and the District of Columbia, passes within 20 miles of 32 million Americans and touches more than 10,000 sites of historic, cultural, or natural significance.

The ADT is a collection of more than 200 local, regional, and national trails, each with its own constituency and caretakers. The ADT will allow trail users to see beyond their local links to the expanse of America from coast to coast. It is the only east-west path traveling cross-country.

From the beginning, the ADT was to be as accessible as possible. It passes through metropolitan areas and incorporates many urban and rural hiking trails as well as paths for bicycles, horses, and for those with disabilities. Today the ADT is formally recognized in each state it traverses and has been incorporated into the trail system and outdoors and transportation plans of those states. In Illinois, the ADT northern branch consists of the Old Plank Road, the I & M Canal, the Kaskaskia-Alliance and the Hennepin Canal trails.

The ADT parallels the southern portion of the Grand Illinois Trail.

The Illinois River

The Illinois River is the outstanding natural feature of Illinois. The river is home to Illinois' industry and to much of Illinois' wildlife, and the river defined the Illinois Country for the state's very first settlers.

There really are two Illinois Rivers. Or perhaps there are three Illinois Rivers, if you count the Illinois Waterway system from Lake Michigan to the Des Plaines River. The Illinois River has its formal origin at the confluence of the Des Plaines River and the Kankakee River, near Channahon, Illinois at the outskirts of Joliet. It runs for 270 miles, a broad water swinging through the state, and the Illinois River enters the Mississippi River at Grafton, Illinois, roughly 40 miles north of St. Louis. You can tack on an extra 57 miles if you include the Illinois Waterway.

The Illinois River has a 200,000 acre floodplain, and its 26,000 square mile watershed contains 44% of Illinois. About 95% of Illinois' urban areas are within the river's great watershed. As a channel of commerce, boats on the Illinois River haul 60 million tons each year. The river handles 60% of the state's commodities, including more than half the state's corn crop, and an incredible 23% of all U.S. grain crosses on the river's watery shoulders.

It is two rivers pressed into one river. Its watery dividing point is near Hennepin, Illinois at the Great Bend. It is here that the Illinois River enters the ancient riverbed of the Mississippi River as it courses southward. And from this point, heading north, the Illinois River is a relatively young creature. It was the geography-smashing Illinoisan glaciers that pressed the Mississippi River hard to the west, pushing it into its present channel. And it was a much later glacial epoch that created the upper portion of the Illinois River.

Geographers believe that a huge, cold lake of glacier water was formed 13,000 years ago, located at around present-day Lake Michigan. This became a huge reservoir known by geographers as Lake Chicago—a lake that finally shattered its glacier walls, its waters bursting forth through the valley, carving the channel of the upper Illinois River.

This prehistoric event is called the Kankakee Torrent, the great flood that gouged the riverbed. Signs of the torrent are all around us. The river valley is much narrower above the Great Bend. The river elevation is a sharp descent in the newer river course. At Starved Rock, it is the work of years of water draining from the prairies that created the dells.

Illinois was settled along its rivers and streams by white settlers who could not imagine that prairie dirt was anything more than desert, that prairie grass was a sign of its worthlessness.

And before the farms and the settlers, the native Americans and the French traders and trappers stayed close to the waters as well. The river provided fish, and its forested valley held game. It was the easiest way to travel.

Travellers' accounts spell out the beauty of the river and the lushness of its woods. French explorer Henri de Tonty's journal notes that one spectacular catfish caught in the Illinois River was food for 22 of his men!

"We have seen nothing like this river. . . as regards to its fertility of soil, its prairies and woods; its cattle, elk, deer, wildcats, bustards, swans, ducks, parroquets, and even beaver. There are many small lakes and rivers," recorded French explorer, Father Marquette, in 1673.

Early settlement in Illinois proceeded through the Illinois River, with Peoria a major city in the territory. French explorers developed strategic holds on the region by establishing forts at Starved Rock and at the broad central part of the river known as Lake Peoria.

Illinois Agriculture

Illinois is the world's biggest producer of soybeans and one of the tops in growing corn. Almost all of downstate Illinois is planted in these two row crops. But farmers in Illinois also plant sorghum, oats, wheat and hay.

Soybeans are fabulous plants. An acre of Illinois farmland typically will produce from 40 to 60 bushels of soybeans. They are one of the best sources of edible oil, livestock feed and biodiesel fuel. Soybeans also are the source of soymilk and meat substitutes like tofu. The word "ubiquitous" comes to mind.

Illinois soybeans are the world's best, bar none, and they're shipped to points and places around the globe. When a farmer says "beans" he's not talking Jolly Green Giant green beans. He's talking about a highly-respected food commodity.

And the same is true for corn. Maize has been planted in Illinois for centuries. But most of the corn you see today is "field corn". Field corn is used to make ethanol. It is also raw food material, and it's typically used for such things as high fructose corn syrup, key ingredient in soda pop and gummi bears. But for the most part, field corn goes to feed beef cattle. Only a small percentage of Illinois corn is "sweet corn," the kind of stuff you'd want at a picnic. Average yields per acre for corn is around 115 to 200 bushels depending on seed and soil types.

Growing these crops takes soil, seed and fertilizer. And plenty of summer sun and rain. A year on the farm usually begins in the spring, with tilling the ground. Farmers use a field cultivator to turn over the soil so that field stubble will decay. Sometimes farmers go no-till and simply plant seed without turning over the soil. They do this to save on tilling costs and to reduce the amount of topsoil lost to erosion.

Farmers use a drill or planter to plant seed in the spring, usually in late April. The land may also receive a dose of intense fertilizer, often nitrogen in the form of anhydrous ammonia, before planting. Planting, cultivating, fertilizing and then spraying herbicides and insecticides as the plants begin to grow are the things you do in the spring. Sometimes stump-winged cropdusters spray the crops for bugs in the early summer, flying tight, swallow-like turns at the row ends before making another run down the rows.

Weeds are also kept in check by using row cultivators, which turn up the soil between the row crops.

And certain genetically-modified bean hybrids are lab-built to match specific commercially-available herbicides (hence, "Roundup-Ready" soybeans). Other genetically-manipulated beans offer higher oil content or higher yields per acre. Illinois farmers seem consigned to use genetically-manipulated seeds simply to compete on the world market.

Summertime comes and the fields soak up the moisture. There really is a growing period of around three and a half months for corn and soybeans in northern Illinois. Farm activity during the summer includes harrowing and weed-cutting. This reduces plant competitors for soil nutrients and moisture. Things pretty much slow down in the summertime.

But in the fall, just as in the spring, farm managers and farm workers take to the field and work long, furious hours at bringing in their crops. They know from experience that the weather isn't dependable in September and October, that moisture conditions rapidly can change, and that they need to harvest as quickly as possible. Often the weather doesn't cooperate. And tractors don't work well in mud! Harvesting requires the use of large combines to bring in the crops.

This is all a great change from just a generation ago. Back then, farmers actually lived on the land that they worked, and they often diversified their crops and raised livestock on the side. But agriculture is a big industry now, and the main business advice for some time has been for farmers to "get big or get out."

P R A I R I E !

Most of the open prairie was covered with high beard grass, usually interspersed with tall-growing flowers, such as prairie arch, cup plant and compass plant, a number of gaudy sunflowers, several species of osage, and large purple patches of ironweed, often mixed with various thorohwoks, asters and ragweed. Indian plantain, leafcup, horseweed and lujssop were abundant while dragonhead, prairie clover, blazing star milkweed, orange lilies and wild roses added to the gorgeous black-eyed Susans, purple coneflowers and bright fur marigolds. . . . In the Spring, strawberries bearing abundant scarlet fruits, were scattered far and wide; wild phlox added gay splash of blue and pink, the blue phlox, the Greek valerian and the bluebell were usually found in the more moist areas. Wild garlic was abundant. The blue Iris made a rich spot of color and the unicorn plant and the bendtongue occasionally grew in great patches. For acres at a stretch the Summer fields glowed with vivid goldenrod.

—CLARENCE ALVORD

Kaskaskia-Alliance Trail

La Salle to Bureau Junction

The Kaskaskia Alliance Trail takes its name from the Kaskaskia Indians. This area of the Illinois Valley was home to the famous Grand Village of the Kaskaskia, a city of four to six thousand residents on the flats right across from Starved Rock. Archaeological studies date the village to 500 A.D. Pressure from American colonists in the eastern states pushed Iroquois and Algonquin tribes into the Illinois territory. These Indian tribes, fierce and more experienced in warfare than the Illini, decimated the native Illinois tribes, such as the Peoria, the Kaskaskia, the Tamaroa, the Cahokia, the Michigamea and the Moingwena.

And the "Alliance" part comes from its practical work in tying together the two major canal trails, the Illinois & Michigan Canal Trail and the Hennepin Canal Parkway State Trail.

The Kaskaskia-Alliance Trail is utilitarian. It does its job and that is all there is to it. The trail closely follows U.S. Route 6 and local roads in bridging the 15-mile gap between the two canal trails.

The Kaskaskia Alliance goes through the Illinois Valley communities of La Salle, Peru, Spring Valley, DePue and Bureau Junction. This region rests along two important geographical and geological regions: the northernmost edge of the vast and luxurious bituminous coal field and along the great river route that the Illinois River makes coursing through the state. Because of these factors the Illinois Valley was actually one of the earliest industrial areas in Illinois.

Following the Kaskaskia-Alliance Trail

If you are taking the Grand Illinois Trail in stages, this area is a good place to begin exploring the trail. Day parking at <u>Illinois & Michigan Canal Lock 14</u> in La Salle is a fine location at the eastern end of the Kaskaskia-Alliance route. A large parking area at <u>Hennepin Canal Lock 3</u> is the trailhead at the western end.

From the canal parking lot, ride one block north to First Street. This is downtown La Salle.

<u>La Salle</u>, Illinois has a population 9,796 and it was incorporated 1877. The <u>La Salle City Hall</u> (1906) at 745 Second Street is a rare bit of Dutch Revival architecture, the kind of eye treat that's rare

The I & M Canal water gate at Lock 14 in La Salle was made of heavy-duty white oak and built to last.

to find. It was designed by local architect Victor Matteson. The nearby Eureka Savings Bank (1993) at 250 Marquette Street is a recent building that shows a vigorous modern use of traditional Illinois limestone: it is rare to see contemporary buildings built with such an architectural concern. The bank was designed by John Richards of the local firm Richards/Johnson & Associates.

Downtown La Salle includes the Hotel Kaskaskia at the corner of Second and Marquette Streets, a large hotel that once was favored by traveling salesmen and is on the National Register of Historic Places. The Hotel Kaskaskia is a classic high-style hotel, with rooftop "gardens." A good restaurant here is the Uptown on First Street.

Other interesting features include the former company headquarters of the La Salle Coal Company (at the very east end of First Street), now a private residence, and St. Patrick's Church (1853) at 725 Fourth Street, a fine stone church constructed by the Irish canal stonecutters. Ministers of the parish, formed back in 1838, provided mission services to much of northern Illinois. What would it be like to hear the confession of a canal digger?

The Illinois Cement Company on the east side of La Salle was formerly the German-American Cement Company (changing its name due to wartime sentiment in 1917). It has been grinding away at the countryside for over 90 years now and shows no sign of slowing down.

The Hegeler-Carus Mansion in La Salle was an historic meeting place for East and West.

One of the area's grandest historic houses, the Hegeler-Carus Mansion at 1307 Seventh Street is open to public tour. Built in 1874, the Second Empire house was home to a local industrialist, Edward Hegeler, and later to Dr. Paul Carus, editor of the Open Court Publishing Company. The Hegeler-Carus Mansion is known for its strong architectural detail as well as its importance in the history of scholarly publishing. D. T. Suzuki, the noted Zen scholar, worked at a young age with Dr. Carus on Open Court publications.

Of this mansion, Gustave Koerner, an Illinois Lieutenant Governor of the 19th century, wrote:

> Socially, we could not enjoy ourselves better. Owing to the large zinc works, rolling-mill, sulphuric acid manufactory and extensive coal mines, owned by two highly-intelligent Germans, Messrs. Matthiessen and Hegeler, quite a number of highly educated gentlemen are employed by this firm as superintendents, geologists and metallurgists. The principals live in handsome houses, filled with large and elegant libraries, paintings, engravings and bronzes. Their residences are surrounded by fine lawns and parks. Gymnasiums, billiard rooms, ten-pin alleys, and in fact everything that is now called "modern improvements" are to be found in these almost palatial residences.

Continue along First Street heading west. The street descends to the river elevation and passes railroad tracks near Monari's 101 Club. This street is now called Water Street.

A particularly impressive view of the abandoned <u>Western Clock Company</u> factory (*aka* <u>Westclox</u>, makers of the famous "Big Ben" and "Baby Ben" alarm clocks) is seen from Water Street. This view shows the building as a kind of glittering palisade on the side of a river bluff. Western Clock Company was originally founded in 1885 by Charles Stahlberg as United Clock Company. The company went bankrupt and was reorganized in 1888 by local industrialist Frederick Matthiessen. The company at one time employed 100 people just to polish watch casings. At its height in the 1930s Westclox employed 5,000 people and had a daily production of 30,000 clocks.

The Grand Illinois Trail route passes by <u>Maze Lumber</u> ("Since 1848") under the Illinois River U.S. Route 251 bridge. Continue west. This is the former site of downtown Peru, once noted for its amazing iron storefronts, and a scene of riverboat commerce. (Outwash bars from the Vermilion and Little Vermilion river mouths made the Illinois River navigable only to La Salle and Peru). Peru's Water Street district includes the <u>Red Door Inn</u>, a fine local restaurant. And it offers some great Illinois River views.

Peru, Illinois, with a population of 9,835, was incorporated in 1890. A notable site in Peru is the grand bronze <u>statue of Maud Powell</u>, the first world-caliber female violinist, who grew up in Peru. The statue, on Fourth Street in downtown Peru, was created by Brother Joseph Heyd of nearby St. Bede Academy and was dedicated in 1993.

From Water Street, pick up Pike Street to head back up the river bluff. (This is just before Mertel's, and Olson's Metal is at the Pike Street-Water Street intersection). Since this is a river bluff, the next three blocks are a workout for your legs, but the road is not much used. Take Pike Street north to Main Street. Curiously, Main Street in Peru is residential.

Take Main Street for four blocks, then turn onto Henry Street, which takes you past <u>Sunset Park</u>. Henry Street runs north to Fourth Street, which is U.S. Route 6 through town.

The Kaskaskia-Alliance Trail follows U.S. Route 6 west, passing St. Bede Academy and entering Spring Valley. <u>St. Bede Academy and Abbey</u> is managed by brothers of the Order of St. Benedict, and was for many years a kind of junior college. It now enrolls high school students from across the area, and it is known for its excellence. A neat little on-campus print shop houses a working linotype machine!

The Grand Illinois Trail takes the U.S. Route 6 shoulder to Spring Valley. The routing includes the famous "S curves" on Route 6 into Spring Valley. These "S curves" require skilled cycling, and they consist of a rapid descent, turn and ascent. Go slow. Brake with caution. Be sure your helmet is on.

You whiz into Spring Valley. Spring Valley, Illinois has a population 5,398, and was incorporated in 1886. The city began its existence as a coal town shipping out Carbondale #2 coal. The city currently operates a coalmine park at 100 E. St. Paul Street, and this park property has provisions for overnight camping.

Spring Valley hosts a phenomenal walleye fishing tournament every year, attracting top fishermen from across the nation. The city has a great public boat launch facility, located off Illinois Route 89 just south of town.

If you wish to go downtown, take Cornelia Street south to St. Paul Street. But the main Grand Illinois Trail routing through Spring Valley follows Dakota Street through town. Continue on Dakota west. As it curves out of town, Illinois Route 6/Dakota Street is renamed "Richard Mautino Drive."

But don't stay on this road: Dakota Street takes a weird split from U.S. Route 6/Richard Mautino Drive just at the local McDonald's. Watch the traffic, cross Illinois Route 6 to Dakota Street.

You should be on the road that goes past Hall Township High School. This is Dakota. Continue along Dakota Street to the very end of the street and here take Marquette Street. Turn left, and head south toward the Illinois River.

Perhaps they named the street after the great French explorer, perhaps not. But at one time there was a Marquette, Illinois, a tiny town buried somewhere on the river bluff between Spring Valley and DePue. It might be that the street got its name from being the road to Marquette. You can search for the town of Marquette, Illinois but it is impossible to find the old townsite.

Marquette Road heads south and then turns west at the bottom of the riverbluff. Here it becomes a "scenic byway," a gravel road infrequently traveled. This river bottom area happens to be a kind of "nature preserve-by-default." Since it is difficult to build anything in the area there is plenty of significant old trees and undergrowth. Plans are in the works to put in a hard road here in the near future.

The road runs to DePue, Illinois. Continue along Marquette Road bottom road for about 3.5 miles to reach DePue. This is one of the curious sections of the Grand Illinois Trail where you can be surrounded by nature in a matter of minutes, and find quiet and calm despite being in a pretty settled area.

This bottom road is gravel and straight and it follows the Rock Island rail lines. It is scenic country, with views and glimpses of the Illinois River and Illinois River backwaters. This is the kind of place where you can view a huge flock of white herons, hundreds of herons, scuttling across the sky in sweeping waves, flying straight and then turning back upon themselves.

On Marquette Road there is not much traffic. As you near DePue, you will pass an outdoor exhibit of antique agricultural equipment.

DePue, Illinois, population 1,842, was incorporated in 1901. DePue is known for its boat races at Lake DePue. These races date back to the very founding years of the sport. The DePue races attract national-level competition every July.

De Pue is home to Lake De Pue Fish and Wildlife Area along the Illinois River. The Area consists of wetlands and Spring Lake and Lake DePue. The Donnelly Fish and Wildlife Center is across the Illinois River from the village of DePue. This area is primarily a nature preserve. Gaylord Donnelly, the Chicago printer and publisher, enjoyed duck hunting and he liked the area so much that it became a favorite place to hunt on weekends.

This is a mecca for migratory waterfowl. The birding expert Frank C. Bellrose has noted that the Big Bend area of the Illinois River is an entry point to the lower Illinois River valley, and that this area is an important American migration corridor. If you have ever bought a duck stamp you have helped out the Donnelly complex, which gets a portion of the fee. The fishing on the river is good, with walleye, sauger, large and smallmouth bass.

The bottom road from Spring Valley enters DePue by crossing over a steel truss bridge. In town the road is named Marquette Street. Follow this to the end of the street, where it intercepts Depot Street. At this point, veer left. This road goes past the site of the former New Jersey Zinc Works. The site was toxic but years of reclamation have moderated its dangers.

Follow Depot Road down to the depot—now the Selby Township Library—a wonderful reuse of an older structure. Cross the rail tracks here and one block later pick up Fourth Street.

Take Fourth Street west to East Street, and then take East Street north to Willow Street. (In DePue, East Street runs north and south).

Using the existing railbed of the old Chicago, Ottawa & Peoria Traction Railway was discussed early on as the routing for the Grand Illinois Trail through this part of the state. Talks are still in the works here, and a road route connects DePue and Bureau Junction. The Chicago, Ottawa & Peoria was an interurban commuter rail line that ran through much of the Illinois Valley, running from Chicago to Princeton, but it was discontinued in the 1930s due to competitive pressures from the automobile.

In DePue, take Willow Street west. This is a straight city street until the very end of the street. At this point Willow Street takes a right turn. The road changes to gravel. And now comes one of the few real physical challenges of the Grand Illinois Trail, a half-mile long hill that will require some real leg stretching. Stand when you pedal. This short stretch demands caution as well as a good amount of physical exertion: the road has twists and turns. This will take you to the top of the bluff line just above the Big Bend of the Illinois River.

The road gets better at the top. It becomes just another farm road and it joins Illinois Route 29 just ahead. Get on Illinois Route 29.

Illinois Route 29 does not get a lot of traffic, but most cars will travel at around 65 mph. Not a great deal of road shoulder here, but the drivers are reasonable and will move around you a bit. The best thing about this stretch is that it is basic road cycling. Nothing too arduous after that hill up the bluff.

Just outside of DePue is <u>Paul Miskowiec, Sr. Park</u>, which is a wonderful country park, the kind that you do not see often enough. The park is used for summer picnics and gatherings, and it contains some wonderful old oaks. The park has restrooms and drinking water. At about this point the Illinois River takes its great sweep southward through the middle of the state.

There is a huge sand and gravel operation here, taking advantage of sand left by the Wisconsonian glacier eons ago. Believe it or not, the Mighty Mississippi River roiled and churned its course through here about 10,000 years ago, and it was at this point that the Mississippi connected to the original Illinois River. But glacial action literally pushed the Mississippi west to its present course.

Follow U.S. Route 29 west past the park toward Bureau Junction, Illinois. The town takes its name from being a rail junction—here the railroad connects with its spur heading along the river south to Peoria. But the town was also a junction point for the Hennepin Canal and the Illinois River. And it remains the junction point for two state roads, Illinois state routes 26 and 29.

At the Illinois Route 29 and Route 26 intersection just outside of the town of Bureau, continue south on Route 26.

Bureau Junction, Illinois, is often called Bureau, and it has a population of 368. The town was incorporated in 1901.

Bureau at one time was a classic juncture point between a number of transportation routes: the Rock Island line ran through here, the Hennepin Canal ended here and the rail route to Peoria struck off from this point. Nowadays, hunting and fishing are big things and there are a number of local hunting clubs along the river that not only are good for hunters, but also have a positive conservation impact. This part of the state is well known to fishermen, duck hunters and deer hunters.

This entire transportation route along the Illinois River is sometimes called the "Illini Trail" due to the fact that it is an ancient, prehistorical route and for thousands of years native Indians used the river road. And so did the early white settlers, tracing a line of new communities along the Illinois River up from St. Louis to

Chicago. The Grand Illinois Trail is the latest manifestation of human transportation moving through this area.

The endpoint of the Kaskaskia Alliance Trail is at Lock 3 at the east end of the Hennepin Canal. A new trailhead has been constructed here, and the Lock 3 access point is directly off Illinois Route 26. It is easy to find. (Note that Lock 2 on the Hennepin Canal is in the center of Bureau, and Lock 1 has been long submerged under the Illinois River).

KASAKASKIA-ALLIANCE TRAIL SUMMARY

EAST TO WEST	WEST TO EAST
I & M Canal Lock 14 north to First Street (La Salle)	Hennepin Canal Lock 3 east in Bureau Junction to Illinois Route 26
First Street west to Water Street (Peru)	Illinois Route 26 east to Illinois Route 29
Water Street west to Pike Street	Illinois Route 29 east to Willow Street
Pike Street north to Main Street	Willow Street east to East Street
Main Street west to Henry Street	East Street south to Fourth Street
Henry Street north to Fourth Street/ U.S. Route 6	Fourth Street east to Depot Street
(U.S. Route 6 to Spring Valley)	Depot Street north to Marquette Street/Marquette Road
U.S. Route 6/Dakota Street west to Dakota Street Turnoff	(Marquette Road to Spring Valley)
Dakota Street west to Marquette Street	Marquette Road east to Marquette Street
Marquette Street south to Marquette Road	Marquette Street north to Dakota Street
(Marquette Road to DePue)	Dakota Street east to Dakota Street/U.S. Route 6 Turnoff
Marquette Road/Marquette Street west to Depot Street	(Dakota Street/U.S. Route 6 to Peru)
Depot Street south to Fourth Street	U.S. Route 6/Fourth Street east to Henry Street
Fourth Street west to East Street	Henry Street south to Main Street
East Street north to Willow Street	Main Street east to Pike Street
Willow Street west to Illinois Route 29	Pike Street south to Water Street
Illinois Route 29 west to Illinois Route 26	Water Street (Peru) east to First Street (La Salle)
Illinois Route 26 west to Hennepin Canal Lock 3 in Bureau Junction	First Street (La Salle) east to I & M Canal Lock 14 in La Salle

Marquette on the Illinois

From Father Jacques Marquette's account of meeting the Illini in 1673.

When one speaks the word "Illinois" it is as if one said in their language, "the men,"—As if the other Savages were looked upon by them merely as animals. It must be admitted that they have an air of humanity which we have not observed in the other nations that we have seen upon our route.

They are of a gentle and tractable disposition; have several wives, of whom they are Extremely jealous; they watch them very closely and Cut of Their noses or ears when they misbehave. I saw several women who bore the marks of their misconduct.

Their bodies are shapely; they are active and very skillful with bow and arrows. They also use guns, which they buy from our savage allies who Trade with our French. They use them especially to inspire, through their noise and smoke, terror in their Enemies; the latter do not use guns, and have never seen any, since they live too Far toward the West.

They are warlike, and make themselves dreaded by the Distant tribes. . . the Captains are distinguished from the warriors by wearing red Scarfs. These are made with considerable Skill from the Hair of bears and wild cattle. They paint their faces with red ocher. . . They live by hunting, game being plentiful in that country, and on indian corn, of which they always have a good crop. Consequently, they have never suffered from a famine. They also sow beans and melons, which are

Excellent. . . Their Cabins are very large, and are Roofed and floored with mats made of Rushes. They make all Their utensils of wood and Their Ladles out of the heads of cattle, whose Skulls they know so well how to prepare. . .

There remains no more, except to speak of the Calumet (peace pipe). There is nothing more mysterious or more respected among them. Less honor is paid to the Crowns and scepters of Kings than the Savages bestow upon this. It seems to be the God of peace and war, the Arbiter of life and of death. It has but to be carried upon one's person and displayed, to enable one to walk safely through the midst of Enemies—who, in the hottest of the Fight, lay down Their arms when it is shown. For that reason, the Illinois gave me one, to serve as a safeguard among all the Nations through whom I had to pass during my voyage. . . .

It is fashioned from a red stone, polished like marble, and bored in such a manner that one end serves as a receptacle for the tobacco, while the other fits into the stem; this is a stick two feet long, as thick as an ordinary cane, and bored through the middle. It is ornamented with the heads and necks of various birds. . . The Calumet dance, which is very famous among these peoples, is performed solely for important reasons; sometimes to strengthen peace, or to unite themselves for some great war; at other times, for public rejoicing. . . .

Hennepin Canal Trail

Bureau Junction to Colona

Here the water went down, the icebergs slid with the gravel, the gaps and the valleys hissed, and the black loam came, and the yellow sandy loam.

—CARL SANDBURG, *Prairie*

The Hennepin Canal was a boondoggle. Just an outright flop. It was a grand engineering triumph and a dismal economic failure. In no way did things turn out the way they were planned.

Skip back to 1870. Railroads are already in place all over Illinois. The great span across the wide Illinois prairies had long been made; the Quad Cities to Chicago connection was complete by 1854 with the opening of the Chicago-Rock Island line. Not only did the Rock Island railroad mean the beginning of the end for the Hennepin Canal's older sister, the I & M Canal, but it also meant that there would be minimal need for canals in the future. Canal boats were slow, they had limited freight space, and canals froze over during the winter.

So why didn't this project get killed? Why was the Hennepin Canal built? Politics.

The construction of the Hennepin Canal was a triumph of persistence and politics over economic good sense. Officially christened the "Illinois-Mississippi Canal," that name never stuck—although you can still find it on some road maps. The canal never really became a working canal and was never much connected to the economies of its nearby towns.

Joseph Galer, an early Illinois pioneer who had been an engineer on the Erie Canal, first explored the region with thoughts of canals in 1834. He figured the area between two rivers, the Rock and the Illinois, might make a good canal passage. So, as he put it, he "took his blanket and gun and surveyed the route." Galer presented his idea to Dr. Augustus Langworthy of Tiskilwa who owned a good portion of land along the route. The two of them managed to get the Hennepin Canal idea introduced into the same big, sloshing bucket of internal improvements legislation that initiated the I & M Canal.

Indeed, the Hennepin Canal was viewed as an important part of a broad internal waterway system that would connect the Upper Mississippi River Valley to the Great Lakes and beyond, to the eastern seaboard. This was the dream: one of a long line of swaying and shimmering internal improvement projects that went dancing before the Illinois General Assembly in 1836.

A rare photo of the bottom of a canal! Here is a look at the Hennepin Canal as it was being constructed, probably near the canal's east end at Bureau.
(Photo courtesy of the Illinois State Historical Library).

But politics canned the canal. Established communities on the lower Illinois River and along the Mississippi River were successful in blocking the potential competitor, fearing diversion of some of the Great Lakes commercial traffic.

But the dream endured. It took shape. In the 1860s the Granger movement renewed public interest in canals and a formal Army Corps of Engineers survey was completed in 1870. The survey noted that the practical use of the canal would require it to be part of bigger, better water links to Lake Michigan. The I & M Canal was already too small, and use of the upper Illinois River would require large-scale civil engineering. The study called for the construction of the Hennepin Canal at a size twice that of the canal that was eventually built.

Canal conventions were held regularly in the 1870s and 1880s in Rock Island and in Henry and Bureau counties. Canal promoters even got the Buffalo, New York chamber of commerce to endorse the idea, trying to make the point that the idea was of national transportation importance. The New York state legislature joined this endorsement.

Another engineering survey was made. But no action was taken. (This sounds familiar). But by the 1890s, organized farm pressure in the form of populist politics made Washington take notice and act— the 1890 River and Harbor Act authorized the construction of the Hennepin Canal.

But the same act that created the Hennepin Canal also doomed the canal. The federal authorization called for a much smaller canal—due to St. Louis and New Orleans political opposition and due to local concerns about the water that would be diverted from the Rock River. And due to the very real concern in 1890 about the usefulness of a canal that was designed to be hooked up to the already obsolete I & M Canal and the unnavigable upper Illinois River.

Politics created the canal. Politics condemned it.

Major W. L. Marshall of the U.S. Army Corps of Engineers supervised canal construction. Construction on the canal began in 1893 and ended in 1907. Commercial traffic first entered its waters in 1908. The Hennepin Canal is noteworthy for being the first large-scale application of poured concrete technology for entire canal locks. This technique was later used with great success in the building of the Panama Canal.

Ghostly remnants of old concrete structures still appear in thickets along the route, and poured concrete was used to build various buildings, sheds and ramps. You get the impression that they basically liked working with the concrete—the concrete telephone posts weigh 750 pounds apiece.

Major Marshall devised the "Marshall gate" for the canal—a horizontally opening canal gate with a pipe mechanism that allows the gate to open and close by water pressure. You can see the only remaining example at Lock 16 between Tiskilwa and Wyanet. The final price tag on the canal was $7,319,563 million dollars.

The men who built the canal were locals drawn from neighboring farming communities. But recent immigrants to America found employment on the project as well. Almost a quarter of the workers were Irish. Germans, Swedes, Belgians, English and Danes made up the rest.

The canal was designed to lift boats from the Illinois River to a highpoint at the canal's summit pool and then lower boats back down to the Mississippi River. Gravity working on water did the trick. The canal was built with 33 locks. Most of these are along the main body of the canal from Bureau to Colona. But the last three locks were placed on the Milan Section, a short five mile canal section that parallels the Rock River and provided good navigation through to the Mississippi.

A 29-mile long feeder canal was built expressly to bring water to the Hennepin Canal and it runs from Rock Falls to the summit pool between Locks 21 and 22. On a map, the Hennepin Canal looks like an upside-down "T".

The canal prism was built to a size of fifty-two feet wide at the bottom and eighty feet wide at water line, with a working depth of seven feet. It has a 300 foot-wide right-of-way across the Illinois prairie. There are turnouts, passing lanes for boats, about every five miles. There are 89.8 miles of canal prism in good shape. There were originally nine aqueducts on the canal; six of these water bridges remain. The IDNR currently works to keep the canal depth at five feet. The Hennepin Canal is watered throughout its course.

The first boat to travel the Hennepin Canal, running 75 quiet and watery miles from Bureau to Rock Island, was the *U.S. Marion*, carrying its load of government officials, engineers, and local dignitaries.

The Hennepin Canal was designed to compete with railroads on freight charges, thus reducing the costs of shipping coal and agricultural commodities. It would drain the wet lowlands in Bureau and Henry counties. And it would cut 419 miles off the existing water route from Chicago through St. Louis up to the Quad Cities.

But from its very opening, the Hennepin Canal could never do all these things. It was built to an obsolete scale much too small for modern shipping. By the time the river connections were improved, the 19th century dimensions of the canal doomed it to obsolescence. And the railroads, by 1907, were firmly established throughout Illinois.

Some said the Hennepin Canal's annual operating costs could be met by shipping coal. But in a weird coincidence, central Illinois coalfields shut down most operation within months of the opening of the canal! It was chiefly used for grain transit . . . and for hauling the materials used in canal maintenance.

During its active era, from 1908 to 1951, some 50 men were employed as lock tenders, patrolmen and canal workers. They existed in a kind of linear "extended family," living at points and places along the canal. A private telephone line was built to help with operations, and you can still see some of the short concrete posts of the canal phone line as you go along the route.

The U.S. Army Corps of Engineers generated some extra cash by selling permits for ice-harvesting on the canal and by selling pasture rights to canal lands. For a time, a passenger excursion line even operated along the Hennepin Canal, taking sightseers from Rock Falls down the feeder canal to the main canal line, head west to the Quad Cities and then return to Rock Falls by the Rock River. It was a bucolic pleasure in a slower era.

Just eight years after the canal opened there was talk about closing it down to commercial traffic. The Hennepin Canal reached its all-time highest use in 1929 when just over 30,000 tons of cargo were shipped on the canal—out of a total possible capacity of 18 million tons. A 1937 Rock Island District Corps of Engineers study proposed the building of a much larger canal, but Washington killed the idea. By 1951 it was closed to commercial traffic.

In that very same year, the Izaak Walton League proposed that the canal should become a state park. It has always been a favorite recreation spot. And Illinois Governor Adlai Stevenson and U.S. Senator Everett Dirksen worked to make the park happen. Government paperwork, negotiation and revision, taking its normal course, meant that it was not until 1970 that a new state park could be dedicated: the Hennepin Canal State Parkway.

The Hennepin Canal State Parkway is 5,400 acres of linear park, with a visitor's center just northeast of Sheffield and a number of smaller day-use parks along its length. The Sheffield Visitor's Center features prairie restorations, a wetlands, picnic areas and a boat launch. It also makes a good access point for the towpath. The Visitor's Center also has displays on the canal. It is easy to reach, located just one mile south of Interstate 80 (Exit 45) and near the intersection of U.S. Routes 6 and 34, and U.S. Route 40.

Travel the Hennepin today and you will find ancient cottonwoods, huge and undisturbed fish, and a large moving collection of shimmering butterflies. For years the Hennepin Canal has been a great rallying cause for area fishermen, and the Better Fishing Association has been the Hennepin's best friend for years. They have a reciprocal relationship: the better the canal, the better the fishing. And fishing is good here. There are bass, bluegill and crappie. There are also walleye, catfish and carp in the canal. The Hennepin stretch offers some nice undisturbed spots and fish shelters. We owe some thanks to the Better Fishing Association for helping to make the Hennepin Canal a fine natural resource in Illinois.

The Hennepin Canal is an easy pedal and a splendid ride in the sun. It is a great chance to take in the Illinois tall corn country. The entire canal route is 70 miles, and runs from Bureau Junction (near Princeton) through Tiskilwa, Wyanet, Sheffield, and Geneseo before reaching the Quad Cities. The western trailhead is at Timbrook Field near Lock 29 in Colona, Illinois.

You have give credit to the Illinois Department of Natural Resources for reclaiming the Hennepin Canal. The IDNR recently plowed $12 million into building an asphalt-over-gravel path along the canal route. It is an ironic situation, with one government agency turning another agency's project from a cast-off coal into a diamond. Unfortunately, in recent years local counties forced the replacement of all the fabulous old structural steel truss bridges with cheap, low, culvert bridges and this makes hiking, biking, and boating a tad tight at road intersections.

This western part of the Grand Illinois Trail makes you remember a little Illinois heritage. Some of the old settlers here came from Belgium, and even today some of these communities (Manlius, Sheffield, Annawan, East Moline) near the Hennepin Canal maintain the fine sporting tradition of rolle bolle. Rolle bolle is kind of like horseshoes, except that beveled-edge wooden wheels are used rather than steel horseshoes—a good game to play on a sunny day with a cool beverage.

Following the Hennepin Canal Trail

The Hennepin Canal trail surface is oil and chip, not asphalt, and not limestone screenings. The entire route is paved. The surface accommodates both road bikes and mountain bikes.

Bureau Junction, Illinois, population 368, was incorporated in 1901, and it is often just called "Bureau." The name for the town and for Bureau County comes from Jean-Pierre Buro, an early French fur trader who settled in the area. The "Junction" part of the name comes from being a railroad junction between lines heading west to the Quad Cities and south to Peoria along the river. It is at this point that the Illinois River takes its big swing south and through the middle of Illinois.

Locks 1, 2 and 3 of the Hennepin Canal are at Bureau. Lock 1 has been submerged for years in the Illinois River. Lock 2 is right in the middle of town, forming a small park. There is a new parking lot trailhead installed just off Illinois Route 29, a mile or so south of the Illinois Routes 26 and 29 intersection—the perfect place for the trek west. Trailhead parking is next to Lock 3.

To reach Bureau Junction from Interstate 80, take Exit 61 south on Interstate 180. Travel about five miles to the Interstate 180 intersection with Illinois Route 26. Take Illinois Route 26 east for one mile and you reach the intersection of Illinois Routes 26 and 29. Take Illinois Route 29 south for two miles and you reach the Hennepin Canal trailhead at Lock 3.

From Lock 3 continue west to Tiskilwa. This is a distance of just over nine miles. Tiskilwa is one of the few towns directly adjacent to the Hennepin Canal.

Tiskilwa is a few miles south of Princeton, Illinois, at Exit 56 on Interstate 80. From Exit 56, take Illinois Route 29 through Princeton and follow Main Street through town. Princeton's Main Street runs through town south into Tiskilwa. Lock 11 on the Hennepin Canal is about a half-mile north of Tiskilwa. Princeton itself is noteworthy. Ichabod Codding, an early founder of the Republican Party lived here in the 1840s and 1850s and the town was also home to Owen Lovejoy, minister and congressman. Lovejoy was the brother of the martyred abolitionist Elijah Lovejoy. The city was once known for its elms and called "Elm City."

Tiskilwa, Illinois, population 787, was incorporated 1890. The "Gem of the Valley" is a fine small town immediately south of Princeton, Illinois. While you are in Tiskilwa, be sure to see the Justus Stevens House at 140 E. Main Street—a brick Italianate house that was given an overhaul by noted Chicago architect George Washington Maher. Tiskilwa is home to a Mennonite community, and you may be able to sample fresh farm strawberries locally raised if you come in early summer.

This area, according to the 19th century historian Nehemiah Matson was once "a rolling prairie as far as the eye could see, intermingled with groves of timber. Here, too, ran streams of water." Illini Indians had a village in this area, and it was later home to Chief Senachwine's Potawatomi tribe.

The route between Tiskilwa and Wyanet goes past Lock 13, which has a nice park access. Just about a half mile or so ahead is the trail/aqueduct over Bureau Creek. The distance from Tiskilwa to Wyanet on the Hennepin Canal route is about 6.5 miles.

Another decent trail access is about a half mile west of Wyanet, Illinois, population 1,028, incorporated 1891, on Illinois Route 6, a village seven miles west of Princeton. Wyanet is 15.5 miles from Lock 3 in Bureau. The IDNR has developed a nice park area around a Locktender's House at Lock 19 just south of town, and another country park just west of Wyanet one mile. The Hennepin Canal Day Use Park at Lock 21 contains campsites with running water. It has concrete piers of a canal boat repair station, lined up like rows of ancient dragons teeth. There is also a rusty-red relic lift bridge that spans the canal. This interpretive park is cited on the National Register of Historic Places.

The geological reason the Hennepin Canal could be built is found in the Wyanet region. This is the land where massive glaciers roamed eons ago, creaking and groaning their weight into the ground and towering a half-mile into the sky. The glaciers moved about one mile every 15 years.

During the Ice Age, the site now occupied by Princeton was the junction of two great rivers, the Rock and the Mississippi. Both rivers were pushed out of their course by the earth-flattening Shelbyville glacier. Later glaciers came in and as they melted they filled the ancient riverbeds with silt, sand and gravel.

Foundation stones for a boat repair station on the Hennepin Canal outside of Wyanet.

Just outside of Wyanet is the westernmost ridge of the Bloomington morainal plain, and the land shouts it! There are long ripples and ridges of glacier sediment. Geology cognoscenti call these landforms "knob and kettle" and "swell and swale" moraines. As glaciers melted, their rivulets carried sand and gravel away from the ice mass, and this material was deposited along their courses. This glacier outwash is seen throughout the Green River Lowland in Bureau, Whiteside, Lee and Henry counties. These lumps and bumps of glacial till are sand and rock, and parts of the land cannot be farmed at all. In some areas of glacial outwash, long and spindly irrigation pipes wheel through the fields, delivering water to a thirsty soil.

The area just *east* of this ridge is prime farmland. Bureau County regularly rates in the top 100 agricultural counties in the U.S. The black soil of the Bloomington plain is deep, rich and fertile. Fortunately, many local farmers know its value and worth, and no-till farming is often done in order to reduce the amount of topsoil lost to erosion.

Moving along the canal route, the <u>Hennepin Canal State Parkway Visitors Center</u> is south of Interstate 80 at Exit 45, at the Rock Falls/Illinois Route 40 exit. The Hennepin Canal State Park is a large and significant park area, quiet, with well-developed prairie grass, an oak savanna and houses the canal superintendent's office.

The Hennepin Canal Visitor's Center is about 21 miles from the Lock 3 access point, and about 39 miles from the west end access at Colona, Illinois.

The Visitor's Center is northeast of Sheffield, Illinois, a village with a population of 946 that was incorporated 1883. Sheffield was platted by the Rock Island Railroad in 1850. The <u>Old Danish Church</u> at the corner of Cook and Washington streets dates to the 1880s and is a National Register landmark. The church has historic significance as the site of the oldest Danish Lutheran congregation in the United States, formed in 1865. The congregation was important to early Danish immigration to America.

The point where the Hennepin Canal is highest above sea level is the summit basin. This is a wide, watery spot. The feeder canal meets the summit basin just 4.5 miles west of the Sheffield Visitor's Center. Before this point, the Hennepin Canal Trail dips under Interstate 80, making for an interesting contrast.

The Hennepin Canal Trail continues west and reaches the Illinois Route 78 intersection just north of Annawan about 32.5 miles from the Hennepin Canal Lock 3 starting point.

Annawan, Illinois, population 868, was incorporated 1869. It is about one mile south of the trail. Annawan was laid out as a railroad town in 1853. There is a small boat launch on the Hennepin Canal located one mile north of town. Annawan is right off Interstate 80 at Exit 33. The town has the Purple Onion restaurant downtown and the Olympia Flame Family Restaurant

just off the interstate. During summer months, the Sugar Shack offers ice cream and fast food.

Annawan offers camping facilities, restrooms, parking and an established picnic area. In the early part of the 20th century the land between Annawan and Atkinson was mined for coal, strip-mined by the Peabody Coal Company. So that helps explain why some of the land is sculpted and covered with light trees and brush. The Izaak Walton League operates <u>Giant Goose Conservation Area</u> just outside of Atkinson.

Atkinson, Illinois, population 1,001, was incorporated in 1867. Atkinson is about six miles west of Annawan. This is a basic feed-n-seed kind of town. Its notable structures include <u>St. Anthony's Church</u> at 204 W. Main Street, a downtown rolle bolle court, and a fascinating local historical society museum downtown at 402 N. State Street. The town still ships cattle out by rail. Atkinson at one time was a hustling hog-shipping terminal with daily market prices cited on WGN's farm radio shows.

The Hennepin Canal route passes about a mile north of Geneseo. The first thing to notice is the <u>Lock 24 Day Use Area</u>, a good access point with drinking water and restroom facilities. The road arcing over the canal runs directly south into Geneseo. Geneseo is about 46 miles from the Lock 3 start point.

The Hennepin Canal in action.
(Photo courtesy of the Illinois State Historical Library).

Geneseo, Illinois, population 6,480, was platted in 1829 and settled in 1836, and the town was incorporated in 1855 Geneseo is one of the larger communities along the Hennepin Canal route. The city was formed just about the same time white settlers in Northern Illinois stopped fearing Black Hawk and his dissatisfied Sauk and Fox bands.

Geneseo is easy on the eyes. The town has great old architecture, across a range of 19th and 20th century styles, and there is an ongoing community interest in preservation. Two roads run from the Hennepin Canal into town. North Chicago Street is at the eastern side of town, and you should try to use this instead of Illinois Route 82, which is much busier and has no road shoulders. It is about a mile south into town from the canal trail. Illinois Route 82 becomes College Avenue once it is inside the city limits, and you can reach downtown Geneseo by taking First Street east for two blocks.

If you decide to enter Geneseo by heading south on Chicago Street, pick up Ogden Avenue and go west to State Street.

The Geneseo Historical Museum at 205 S. State Street, right downtown, is a treat and worth a stop. It is a good introduction to Geneseo and Henry County. The town was settled by a group of courageous Congregationalists from Geneseo, New York. They were strong abolitionists and wanted to come out west to make sure the prairie state would stay free.

The museum's prize piece is the original town plat, writ with dark black ink on rag paper looking still fresh after 173 years. "It was found in the city dump in 1974," says Angie Snook, museum curator, "and resurrected and given to the historical society. It's probably the most valuable, most historical, piece in the museum." The museum building is more than house to a collection. It's also an historic house, worth a tour on its own merits. The 40,000-piece museum collection is just so much more gold on top of this.

The museum building was originally the Geneseo House hotel. It was actually a spot on the Underground Railroad, with runaway slaves hidden away deep in the basement. In 1867, the hotel was purchased and expanded by banker brothers Hiram and George Wilson. The building has 27 rooms, so you get the feel of life in

Victorian times. It has a military room, with uniforms and photos and gear. It has a doctors/dentists office. It has a children's room crammed with antique toys, and a "country store" room filled with old grocery tins, scales, bins and boxes. And of course it has a classic Victorian parlor, containing a fabulous crystal chandelier that originally hung at Hull House in Chicago. Years ago, before the house became a museum, rooms in the basement served as temporary housing for Hennepin Canal workers. The museum gets some 7,000 visitors a year, each getting a brush of yesteryear in some way or another.

The First National Bank of Geneseo building on State Street features splendid examples of terra cotta building ornament. This is in downtown Geneseo, which is home to a nice variety of shops. Be sure to visit The Cellar at 137 S. State Street, which is a long-established eatery. The Geneseo Chamber of Commerce at 100 W. Main Street has a self-guided walking tour of Historic Geneseo.

On the northern bank of the canal is the Geneseo Campground, mainly a private outdoor campground for RVs and there are several cabins available for rent. The Geneseo Campground also operates a highly useful store stocked with drinks, snacks, ice and other gear. Canoes and kayaks can be rented here. On the southern side of the canal is a fine public park area maintained by the Izaak Walton League. The Izaak Walton League park is a good place for fishing and camping. It has a playground and meeting space, restroom facilities and parking. Adjacent to the Izaak Walton League grounds is the Geneseo Prairie Park. This is a local nature preserve with hiking trails and picnic spots.

The Green River aqueduct spans the shallow Green River, bringing the canal trail onward to Colona.

Colona, Illinois, population 5,173, was incorporated 1905. Colona is a village outlying the Quad Cities just east of Moline. The town of Green Rock, Illinois was incorporated into Colona in 1996, although the Green Rock name still appears occasionally on various maps.

The western trailhead for the Hennepin Canal towpath is at Timbrook Field on the west end of the Green Rock Memorial Parkway. The canal trail runs as a parkway through Colona. The parkway has a useful parking lot, playground equipment and a shelter for picnicking. The actual canal trail routing ends by joining the Rock River. This is now a park area, <u>Timbrook Field</u>, containing a baseball field and a boat ramp.

It is a fine spot on the Grand Illinois Trail, knowing that during the active years of the canal, commercial boats would take to the Rock River and the Milan Section on a brief run before reaching the Mississippi River.

The distance from Bureau Junction to Colona on the Hennepin Canal route is a total of 60 miles. Local streets take the Grand Illinois Trail further west into East Moline and to Empire Park in Hampton, Illinois. At Empire Park, the Grand Illinois Trail route picks up the Great River Trail.

To Reach the Great River Trail from the Hennepin Canal

The Grand Illinois Trail uses local roads to link the Hennepin Canal Trail with the Great River Trail. To connect to the Great River Trail at Empire Park:

Take Fifth Street north to Fifth Avenue, then go west two blocks to pick up Seventh Street. Turn right, heading north, on Seventh Street and continue to First Avenue/Illinois Route 84. This is a busy street. Use caution.

Take First Avenue/Illinois Route 84 over the Rock River. There is a good shoulder on the bridge, but fast traffic, moving perhaps 50 mph.

Take the very first road after the bridge, and get on Tenth Street heading north. Immediately pick up First Avenue. Stay on First Avenue. This loops around and gets renamed "172nd Street," and as it turns west it gets yet another name, Barstow Road.

Illinois Route 5 is a busy intersection with Barstow. Keep your eyes open when you cross. Barstow quickly ends at County Route 52. Turn right on Route 52 and head north to Morton Street. You should see historic Arnold's Auto Salvage around this point.

Turn left on Morton Street and go west to pick up 36th Street. Take 36th Street north to Fourth Avenue. Here, the GIT route goes through the East Moline Industrial Park. Fourth Avenue in East Moline goes past a few playing fields and the East Moline correctional facility. Stay on Fourth Avenue, even though it takes a jog and gets renamed Third Avenue.

Third Avenue runs into 20th Street. This is Illinois Route 84. Take Illinois Route 84 north to Empire Park in Hampton. The Great River Trail begins right here, and here you can see the Mighty Mississippi!

Additional Trail Connection

Hennepin Feeder Canal

The Hennepin Feeder Canal now runs 26 miles from Rock Falls to the canal feeder basin west of the Hennepin Canal Visitor's Center. This canal supplied water to the main canal.

The feeder also has a sound trail on its west side, which runs south to the summit basin. About half of the feeder canal trail is asphalt pavement, and the remainder is graveled. Several historic canal structures are maintained at the mouth of the canal on the Rock River, making for a very pretty sight. A new pedestrian bridge crosses the Rock River at Rock Falls/Sterling, and leads to the historic Dillon House in Sterling.

Jumping into the canal makes for cool summer recreation.

Hennepin Canal MILEPOSTS

Lock 3 Access in Bureau	0 miles
Tiskilwa	9.1 miles
Wyanet Lock 21 Day Use Area	15.5 miles
Sheffield Visitor's Center	21.1 miles
Summit Basin/Feeder Canal Trail Access	26 miles
Lock 22 (water)	27 miles
Geneseo Lock 24 Day Use Area (water)	46.2 miles
Timbrook Field trailhead in Colona	60 miles

Hennepin Canal LANDMARKS

Bureau Creek Aqueduct
Wyanet Lock 21 Day Use Area/Historic Canal Structures
Sheffield Visitors Center
Hennepin Canal Summit Basin, west of Sheffield Visitors Center
Geneseo Lock 24 Day Use Area
Green River Aqueduct

HENNEPIN CANAL / GREAT RIVER TRAIL

FROM THE HENNEPIN CANAL TO THE GREAT RIVER TRAIL

Fifth Street north to Fifth Avenue
Fifth Avenue west to Seventh Street
Seventh Street north to First Avenue/Illinois Route 84
First Avenue/Illinois Route 84 west to Second Avenue/Illinois Route 84
Second Avenue/Illinois Route 84 north to Tenth Street
Tenth Street east to First Avenue
First Avenue/172nd Street north to Barstow Road
Barstow Road west to the County Route 52 T-intersection (cross Illinois Route 5)
Route 52 north to Morton Street
Morton Street west to 36th Street
36th Street north to Fourth Avenue
Fourth Avenue west to 20th Street/Illinois Route 84
20th Street/Illinois Route 84 north to Great River Trail at Empire Park

FROM THE GREAT RIVER TRAIL TO THE HENNEPIN CANAL

Illinois Route 84 south to Third Avenue
Third Avenue/Fourth Avenue east to 36th Street
36th Street south to Morton Street
Morton Street south to County Route 52 T-intersection
Barstow Road east (cross Illinois Route 5) to First Avenue/172nd Street
First Avenue/172nd Street south to Tenth Street
Tenth Street west to Second Avenue/Illinois Route 84
Second Avenue/Illinois Route 84 south to First Avenue/Illinois Route 84
First Avenue/Illinois Route 84 east to Seventh Street
Seventh Street south to Fifth Avenue
Fifth Avenue east to Fifth Street
Fifth Street to Hennepin Canal

Southern Section Resources

EMERGENCY

ILLINOIS STATE POLICE, DISTRICT 5
(Lockport)
(815) 726-6291 for Will and
Grundy counties.

ILLINOIS STATE POLICE, DISTRICT 17
(La Salle)
(815) 224-2250 for Bureau and
La Salle counties.

LOCAL TOURISM CONTACTS

CHICAGO SOUTHLAND CONVENTION
AND VISITORS BUREAU
2304 173d Street
Lansing, Illinois 60438-6006
(888) 895-8233
www.visitchicagosouthland.
com

GENESEO CHAMBER OF COMMERCE
100 W. Main Street
Geneseo, Illinois 61254
(309) 944-2686
www.geneseo.org

HERITAGE CORRIDOR CONVENTION
AND VISITORS BUREAU
81 N. Chicago Avenue
Joliet, Illinois 60432
(815) 727-2323
www.heritagecorridorcvb.com

HERITAGE CORRIDOR CONVENTION
AND VISITORS BUREAU/WESTERN
OFFICE
I-80 & Rt. 6
Utica, Illinois 61373
(815) 667-4356

PRINCETON TOURISM AND VISITORS
BUREA /PRINCETON CHAMBER OF
COMMERCE
Prouty Building
435 South Main Street
Princeton, IL 61356
(815) 875-2616
www.princeton-il.com

QUAD CITIES CONVENTION AND
VISITORS BUREAU
2021 River Drive
Moline, Illinois 61265
(563) 322-3911
(800)747-7800
www.visitquadcities.com

ILLINOIS TOURISM BUREAU
(800) 2-CONNECT

BED & BREAKFASTS

Marseilles
ANNIE TIQUE'S HOTEL
378 Main Street
(800) 582-7436
(815) 795-5848

STAIN GLASS INN B & B
2820 E. 2559th Road
(815) 795-4471
www.stainglassincc.com

Ottawa
PRAIRIE RIVERS B & B
121 E. Prospect Ave.
(815) 434-3226
www.prairieriversbandb.com

Utica
PATTI'S SLEEPOVER INN/ B&B
304 Clark Street
(815) 667-4151

LANDERS HOUSE B & B
115 E. Church Street
(815) 667-5170
www.landershouse.com

BRIGHTWOOD INN AT MATTHIESSEN
STATE PARK
2407 N. Illinois Rt. 78 (Oglesby)
(888) 667-0600
www.starved-rock-inn.com

Princeton
PHOENIX INN
1930 South Main Street
(815) 872-0282

Tiskilwa
MAPLE MANOR B & B
320 First Street
(815) 646-4135

Sheffield
THE CHESTNUT STREET INN
301 E. Chestnut Street
(800) 537-1304

Geneseo
HARMAN HOUSE B & B
401 S. Center Street
(309) 944-0288
(800) 228-2800

HOTELS & MOTELS

CHICAGO SOUTH

Lansing
BEST WESTERN
2505 Bernice Road
(708) 895-7810

COMFORT SUITES
2235 173rd Street
(708) 418-3337

DAYS INN
17356 Torrence Avenue
(708) 474-6300

SUPER 8
2151 Bernice Road
(708) 418-8884

HOLIDAY INN
172nd and Oak Street
(800) 465-4329

Chicago Heights
CIARA SUITES & CONFERENCE
    CENTER
1040 Dixie Highway
(708) 754-5700

THE STAR MOTEL
400 W. 14th Street
(708) 481-3050

Matteson
BAYMONT INN & SUITES
5210 Southwick Drive
(Lincoln Highway and I-57)
(800) 301-0200

COUNTRY INN & SUITES
950 Lake Superior Drive
(Lincoln Highway and I-57)
(800) 456-4000

HAMPTON INN AT MATTESON
5200 W. Lincoln Highway
(Lincoln Highway and I-57)
(800) HAMPTON

HOLIDAY INN AT MATTESON
5200 W. Lincoln Highway
(Lincoln Highway and I-57)
(800) HOLIDAY

MATTESON MOTEL
211th Street and Kildare
(708) 748-2280

Joliet
COMFORT INN SOUTH
135 S. Larkin Avenue
(815) 744-1770

EMPRESS CASINO & HOTEL
2200 Empress Drive
(815) 744-9400

FAIRFIELD INN SOUTH
1501 Riverboat Center
(815) 741-3499

HAMPTON INN SOUTH
1521 Riverboat Center Drive
(815) 725-2424

HARRAH'S JOLIET CASINO HOTEL
151 N. Joliet Street
(800) HARRAHS

SOUTH SECTION

Ottawa
HOLIDAY INN EXPRESS
900 Holiday Street
(815) 433-0029

HAMPTON INN
4115 Holiday Lane
(815) 434-6405

SUPER 8 MOTEL-OTTAWA
500 E. Aetna Road
(815) 434-2888

OTTAWA TRAVELODGE
I-80 and Rt. 23
(815) 434-3400

SANDS MOTEL
1215 La Salle Street
(815) 434-6440

COMFORT INN
510 E. Aetna Road
(815) 433-9600

Utica
STARVED ROCK LODGE
Rts. 178 & 71
(800) 868-7625
(815) 667-4211

La Salle
ECONOLODGE
I-80 & Rt. 251
(815) 224-2500

Peru
RAMADA LIMITED
4389 Venture Drive
(815) 224-9000

Geneseo
OAKWOOD MOTEL
Jct. Routes 82 & 6
(309) 944-3696

SUPER 8
754 W. Main Street
(309) 945-1898

CAMPING

Channahon
CHANNAHON STATE PARK
I&M Canal State Trail
Two West Story Street
(815) 467-4271

Morris
GEBHARD WOODS STATE PARK
402 Ottawa Street
(815) 942-0796
(815) 942-9501

Marseilles
ILLINI STATE PARK
2660 E. 2350th Road
(815) 795-2448

Utica
LASALLE PERU KOA KAMPGROUND
756 N. 3150th Road
(815) 667-3034

STARVED ROCK STATE PARK
Illinois Route 178
(815) 667-4726
www.dnr.state.il.us

WHITE OAKS CAMPGROUND AT
    STARVED ROCK
Illinois Rt. 178
(815) 667-4758

Sheffield
HENNEPIN CANAL PARKWAY STATE
    PARK VISITORS CENTER
16006 875 E. Street, Illinois
    Highway 40
(815) 454-2328

HICKORY GROVE CAMPGROUND
7478-1745 North Avenue
(815) 454-2338

Geneseo
GENESEO CAMPGROUND
22978 Illinois Hwy. 82
(309) 944-6465
www.fulltiming-america/
geneseo/

SPIRITS IN THE OAKS CAMPGROUND
27430 E. 1350th Street
(309) 944-3889

BIKE STORES/ REPAIR CENTERS

PLANK ROAD CYCLERY
20 W. Elwood
Frankfort, Illinois 60432
(815) 469-3594

DAVE'S BIKES, ETC.
1416 N. Broadway Street
Joliet, Illinois 60435
(815) 723-2204

DAYS GONE BICYCLE COMPANY
207 Ruby Street
Joliet, Illinois 60435
(815) 726-0282

SUMBAUM CYCLE COMPANY
114 N. Larkin Avenue
Joliet, Illinois 60435
(815) 744-5333

BILL'S BIKE SHOP
227 W. Maple Street
New Lenox, Illinois 60451
(815) 463-9708

PEDAL POWER CYCLERY
534 E. Illinois Highway
New Lenox, Illinois 60451
(815) 485-7188

TULLIO'S BIG DOG CYCLERY
Third Street
La Salle, Illinois 61301
(815) 223-1776

SMITTY'S
1410 Guion
Ottawa, Illinois
(815) 434-0717

GLEASON & CO.
385 Main Street
Marseilles, Illinois
(815) 795-5541

GRAND SCHWINN CYCLERY
711 Liberty Street
Morris, Illinois
(815) 942-1510

B & B CYCLERY
820 S. Chicago Street
Geneseo, Illinois
(309) 944-2660

BIKE WORKS
1659 N. Main Street
Princeton, Illinois
(815) 872-0161

Did You Know?

The Grand Illinois Trail runs through or near major Illinois cities such as Chicago, Rockford, the Quad Cities and Joliet. It also is within an hour's drive of the metropolitan areas of Milwaukee and Madison, Wisconsin, by Gary, Indiana by Peoria and Bloomington-Normal, Illinois.

All told, the GIT can be easily reached by over 11 million people.

West

Great River Trail
★
Savanna to Galena Road Routes

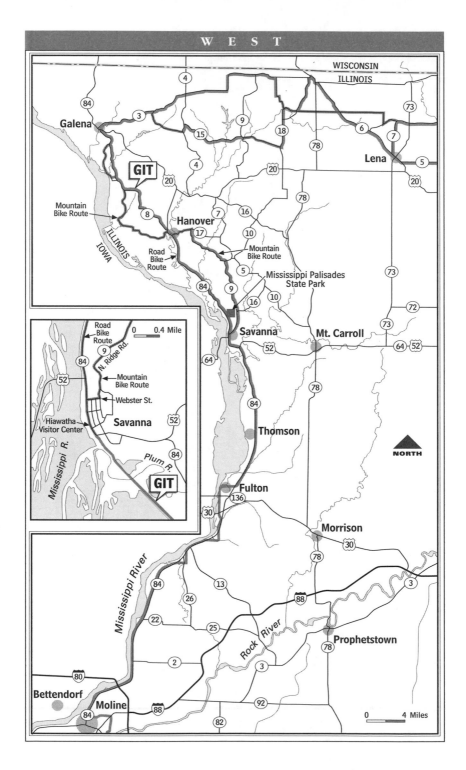

Overview _____

The West Section is all about the Mississippi River and its mark on the land. Here the Great River Trail tours through river bottoms and through towns and cities that burst up and grew fast because of river commerce. The Great River Trail runs near and along the river, through major nature preserves and wildlife areas as well as Albany Mounds, an important site of Hopewell Indian culture.

The Great River Trail runs from East Moline to Savannah, and road routes pass by Mississippi Palisades State Park and Hanover, Illinois on their way to Galena. Carroll and Jo Daviess counties offer a great road workout as well as plenty of natural beauty.

The Great River Trail also links into the extensive bi-state trail paths in the Quad Cities. The Quad Cities is a great place for in-town cycling with a beautiful riverfront path system.

John Deere Commons is a mega-sized museum of agricultural history in downtown Moline.

The Mississippi River At-A-Glance

The Mississippi River is 2,350 miles long, from its source at Lake Itasca in Minnesota to the Gulf of Mexico. (The actual distance always changes as the riverbed moves and shifts).

Major tributaries include the Missouri and Ohio River systems.

The Mississippi drains an area 1,243,700 square miles, across 31 states and two Canadian provinces.

The river has three separate stages. It is a clear stream from Lake Itasca to St. Paul. Then it grows into a powerful river from St. Paul to the mouth of the Missouri River. Finally, the Mississippi is a broad and flat river south of this point, especially after the Ohio makes its connection: at times the river is a mile and a half wide.

The source of the Mississippi River was discovered in 1832 by Henry Schoolcraft and his Indian guide Oza Windib.

Commerce blossomed before the Civil War, the heyday of steamboating on the Mississippi.

Railroads took the commercial advantage after that. The *Effie Alton* case was pivotal in this. The steamboat *Effie Alton* slammed into a Rock Island Railroad bridge pier in the Quad Cities. Owners sued, claiming the piers were an obstruction to navigation. The Rock Island line hired Abraham Lincoln to defend them, and like a good lawyer, Lincoln claimed the bridge piers actually improved navigation by channeling river currents, and that the *Effie Alton* had lost power and steering ability on her own accord. A hung jury in the case meant the bridge stayed, affecting the course of commercial life on the Mississippi for decades.

World War I proved the nation needed the Mississippi River. Railroads could not handle all the needed traffic. By the 1920s, the river trade was reestablished. And the U.S. Army Corps of Engineers began their decades-long work on the Mississippi.

Great River Trail (1)

East Moline to Thomson

"The face of the water, in time, became a wonderful book—a book that was a dead language to the uneducated passenger, but which told its mind to me without reserve, delivering its most cherished secrets as clearly as if it uttered them with a voice. And it was not a book to be read once and thrown aside, for it had a new story to tell every day."

—MARK TWAIN, *Life on the Mississippi*

It is a thrill to see the Mississippi River no matter how old you are, or how many times you've seen it. If such a thing can be said, the Mississippi River has a strong and very real character. It is the kind of thing that makes you think of expressions such as "Force of Nature" or "Act of God." It has a big and definite personality that clearly directs the land and the people around it. Even when it looks quiet, you sense its deep power.

This great river is an inland ocean. The Mississippi River runs for 2,350 miles along its length, and for 550 miles it courses along Illinois banks. Crossing the Mississippi River was a big deal in the 1830s and 1840s. It was a difficult thing to do, accomplished by flat-bottomed ferryboats operating at only the safest and narrowest spots. Trading villages formed at these crossing spots.

This includes the communities of Davenport and Moline and Rock Island, which were sited at a point where the Mississippi River has a shallow, bedrock bottom. These cities were a transfer point between steamboats with a deep draft, and the smaller, lighter steamboats that could navigate the shallow waters of the upper Mississippi.

Steamboats ruled the Mississippi River Valley from 1815 right up to the Civil War. They were marvelous belching contraptions. Steamboats sat high on the water and could be operated in very shallow rivers and pilots would run their boats right up to the riverbanks. Some steamboat captains even boasted that they could run their boats on a heavy dew!

The boats hauled furs, hogs, settlers, whiskey, cowhides, leather, grain, finished goods and even circuses into the "West." Competition for passengers led to steamboats getting tricked up with fancy woodwork, mirrors and crystal and becoming floating palaces.

The hand at the wheel had to have skill. Low water, snags and sandbars were great dangers. It was the smart captain who could keep his boat afloat and working beyond the average five-year lifespan. In its peak year, there were some 1,900 steamboat landings in the Quad Cities. Steamboat captains made good money, and you can see how they spent it in Port Byron and Hampton. Here there are fine old Victorian houses built along the river bluff each decked out with fancy gingerbread and "bargeboard" trim.

The Mississippi River has always been a major commercial route. When the first railroad bridge spanned it, there were enormous economic consequences. Chicago, the rail hub, began taking commercial precedence over St. Louis, the river port. Cities along the river that were centered on river commerce had to adapt. In the end, Rail was triumphant. Railroads offered more regular schedules and more dependable shipping. And farmers could send their grain and produce directly east to Chicago, instead of the longer route to New Orleans and the eastern seaboard.

Commerce on the river remains important. Barges take grain downriver and haul up other commodities: coal, gravel, salt, corn. The Upper Mississippi waterway was improved in the 1930s, in a grand Depression era public works project, and the Lock and Dam 13 area has become a major place for sportsmen. The Upper Mississippi waterway was a lot more than civil engineering projects in the river. The system includes 194,000 acres of land that stretch along both banks of the Mississippi River in Minnesota, Wisconsin, Iowa and Illinois. The Rock Island District of the U.S. Fish & Wildlife Service manages over 93,000 acres of river bottoms and bluffs. This is a great public patrimony, loved by sportsmen and conservationists. Even more so by waterfowl and wildlife.

The Quad Cities actually began with Rock Island. This was the site of Fort Armstrong, a military outpost and trading center built in 1816. Moline was soon established thereafter, and the city flourished with the fortunes of the John Deere and other factories. John Deere, the man who broke the prairies with the remarkable self-scouring steel plow, came here in 1848 after his early experiments and great success in Grand Detour, Illinois. The river gave him great transportation, carrying his finished products out to markets and bringing in steel and other supplies.

The Quad Cities were a staging point for immigrants and native sons traveling west. Here came the prairie farmers as they headed toward Iowa, Minnesota and the Dakotas in the 1850s. It was a steamboat and rail town, with a heavy German and Swedish presence. It was a significant German presence. By 1854 over a third of Davenport was German. They were educated and skilled—refugees from the failed 1848 liberal revolution.

The Civil War era brought the Rock Island Arsenal into being. At the Quad Cities, the Mississippi River takes a hard 90-degree turn and

The Rock Island Arsenal operated at a high pitch during World War I. This 1918 factory line made rifle stocks for the Springfield rifle. (Photo courtesy of the Illinois State Historical Library)

runs East-West. In the middle of the river is Arsenal Island, a liver-shaped, 946-acre jut of bedrock. Arsenal Island was one of the earliest settled areas here. The federal government established a trading post here, managed by Col. George Davenport. Rock Island became a federal arsenal in 1863, and it also became a prisoner of war camp. Some 13,000 Rebs were held here during the war. Over 1,900 small white headstones mark out quiet rows of Confederate dead planted here in a special prisoner of war cemetery on Rock Island.

The Rock Island Arsenal is a National Historic Landmark District, a huge military installation with many points of interest. Ten massive stone buildings define the main arsenal manufactories, and it is here that the arsenal has produced most of its goods. This may not sound like much, but the main buildings on Arsenal Island are huge. In its history, the arsenal has produced small arms, artillery carriages, tin cups, small-lot ordnance, howitzers and rocket launchers. The arsenal has specialized in the repair of damaged tanks. Its staff has made pistol holsters, spurs and machine guns. You name it and it's been built here. Real boom times came during World War I, when arsenal employment shot up from 2,000 to 14,778. The Rock Island Arsenal is still a custom order shop for specialty ordnance and research into artillery recoil and machine gun systems.

These are all impressive and monumental buildings, made of durable stone. But perhaps the most important structure on Arsenal Island is the Colonel Davenport House. This is the heart of Quad Cities history. The Colonel Davenport House, home to the great settler, fur and lead trader and army quartermaster. A roving band killed him on his doorstop.

It is a handsome facility. And it is an active arsenal, the largest in America, and parts of Arsenal Island are open to the public. A reconstruction of the first Fort Armstrong is here, a stout blockhouse. The Rock Island Arsenal Museum contains a wide-ranging and impressive assortment of small arms and a children's discovery museum.

The Rock Island Arsenal was the creation of a unique engineer-soldier, Brigadier General Thomas Rodman. He built the ten main arsenal manufactories and other structures, and lined them up along a central avenue running the length of Arsenal Island. Rodman's plans for the massive arsenal complex originally surprised Congress, but it supported his vision. The main road through the arsenal is Rodman Avenue and he is buried at the east side of the island.

There is a Mississippi River Visitor Center open seven days a week, from 9 A.M. to 5 P.M., on Arsenal Island. The Mississippi River Visitor Center offers bicycle tours of Arsenal Island and is a good place for watching Mississippi River boat activities at Lock and Dam 15 and for watching eagles in season.

The Clock Tower Building, the Old Gatehouse and the Commanding Officer's Quarters ("Quarters One") are some of the noteworthy features of the arsenal. The Commanding Officer's Quarters is a spacious and imposing 19,000 square foot residence across two and a half stories, built in the High Victorian Italian Villa style in 1871. This is the largest federally owned domestic building; larger than the White House.

Railroads have always been important here. Silvis in Illinois was created when the Rock Island railroad expanded in 1903 and needed a new freight yard. Bettendorf was also formed as a railroad town in the early part of the 20th century.

Turn the pages of old newspapers and the names leap out: Moline Plow Company, Moline Wagon Company, Moline Malleable Iron Company, Bettendorf Wheel Works, Sylvan Steel Mills, Frank Foundries. The farm machinery business has always been the key to the Quad Cities. Moline is home to world-renowned John Deere & Co., and the company's exquisite Eero Saarinen-designed headquarters is placed in a magnificent park setting. Case International Harvester was here, along with Caterpillar.

This intensity of heavy industry led to early interest in the automobile. Several companies churned out cars—the Velie Carriage Company that built "the Velie," the Meteor Auto Company and the Moline Automobile Company, which made a large and expensive vehicle called, "The Dreadnought."

Local historian Roald Tweet (of Rock Island's Augustana College) notes that the Quad Cities is "an encyclopedia of 19th Century American settlement patterns which sprinkled the midwest with villages and towns. Here is the mill town (Moline), the river town (Davenport), the mining community (Rock Island), the military

Here the Hennepin Canal joins the waters of the Rock River just a few miles from the Mississippi.

reservation (Arsenal Island), the factory town (Bettendorf) and the planned city (East Moline)."

And, says Tweet, the Quad Cities is also "an ethnic mosaic of Germans, Irish, and Swedes who came in the 1840s and 50s; of Belgians, Greeks, and Eastern Europeans who came in the 1890s; of Blacks and Mexicans who came after the turn of the century; of the Chinese and Native Americans of the 1960s, and the Asian Indians, Laotians and Vietnamese who began arriving in the 1970s."

It is fun exploring the Quad Cities. There is a lot going on along the river front, with weekend festivals and events and unusual public art. And there are fine views of the river. One favorite place is Lindsay Park in East Davenport, and a new park here includes a children's playground stocked with a veritable history of grand historical forms, the "Architectural Park." It is an easy walk from here to the National Register Historic District of East Davenport, an area filled with small boutiques, restaurants, pubs and a fine local bike shop.

The Great River Trail is more than the Quad Cities. You get a glimpse of life along the river as you tour through the Upper Mississippi Fish & Wildlife Refuge. Here there are habitats for a great range of Midwest waterfowl and wildlife.

The Great River Trail includes a number of small towns along the way—Port Byron, Fulton, Thomson and Savanna—and these are all highly accessible and enjoyable to tour. Each town has something interesting to offer. While the Great River Trail ends at Savanna, two road routes push north into Jo Daviess County and Galena. The first route, along Illinois Route 84, is for road bikes and cyclists able to ride with traffic passing at higher speeds. The second route is more leisurely and less traffic-stressed. Both routes access the natural lands of the Savanna Army Arsenal, a site which is currently being decommissioned and which will be returned to a more natural condition.

Following the Great River Trail from East Moline to Thomson

The Great River Trail has this one real asset—it is easy to find and easy to travel on. The trailbed is an eight-foot asphalt strip that runs for 62 miles from Hampton to Savanna, Illinois, except for portions of the route that follow city streets in Cordova and Albany, and a brief hop on Illinois Route 84. The Great River Trail is almost entirely flat for its whole route, as flat as an old railroad bed might be.

The Great River Trail was mainly built on the old railbed of the Burlington Northern railroad. It is immediately adjacent to Illinois Route 84, a relatively busy road that is also a designated National Scenic Byway. There are camping and lodging opportunities along the way. The best parts of the Great River Trail take you right next to Old Man River. The worst are sections next to the busy, blasting highway corridor. Illinois Route 84 is a tight, two-lane with gravel shoulders, and on weekends it carries a lot of recreational traffic: trucks with boats, vans, recreational vehicles and SUVs.

The Great River Trail runs through basic river valley terrain. Between Thompson and Savanna, the Great River Trail goes directly through the Upper Mississippi National Wildlife & Fish Refuge administered by the U.S. Fish & Wildlife Service. The trail ends in Savanna, landing in town from a high box bridge.

Empire Park is a big new local park in East Moline, and it makes a great trailhead for starting north. There are playgrounds and picnic areas, a boat launch and viewing points along the river. There are restrooms and water. It's easy enough to find Empire Park, since it's just off Illinois Route 84. (If you're coming in on I-80, take Illinois Route 84 south to the park entrance).

The park is host to a large Heritage Center, and this is about a half mile down the walk that heads east from the parking lot.

The trail route quickly segues into city streets and you reach First Avenue, a riverfront road in a quiet, established neighborhood. Nice river views. First Avenue has some noteworthy sites to see. There is a fabulous river rock monument to the veterans of the War of 1812, the Black Hawk War, the Civil War and the Spanish-American War. It comes with cannon and cannonballs garnish. The monument is next to a fine and quaint Federal style building.

At 1.2 miles is Black's Hardware. This building, on the National Register of Historic Places, is a strong sample of old-time

A balloon captures a gentle summer breeze above Fulton.

An unusual war monument found along the trail just north of Empire Park.

commercial architecture. They once packed pork here, and Black's was a stagecoach stop on the road to Galena. Then turn right on Eighth Street, and this takes you through a neighborhood of restored (and being restored) brick houses. At 1.4 miles you cross railroad tracks and turn north onto the Great River Trail's exclusive pathway—an eight-foot asphalt strip running mainly along Illinois Route 84. This originally was Burlington Northern Railroad right-of-way.

Head north, turn right to cross railroad tracks and pick up the trail. Almost two miles from Empire Park is the intersection of Twelfth Street/State Avenue/Route 84 near the Illiniwek Rock Island County Forest Preserve.

Now turn left, cross the tracks, and pick up the road through the park. Follow this road toward the river, and turn north. The park office is at 2.3 miles. Just a little way ahead is a kind of artwork, a kind of native stone council ring with a Paleolithic feel to it.

Continue through to the north side of the parking lot to pick up the trail.

The Great River Trail leads out of the campground. At 2.7 miles you cross the tracks and return to the path. At 2.9 is Lock and

Dam 14 on the Mississippi, a place for shady picnicking and fishing. Great water lilies crowd the shoreline just north of the dam.

Fisherman's Corner is at 3.4 miles, a spot for camping and fishing. After another mile or so, the local road is the trail. For the next mile the trail and road are joined as neighbors through a rushing "transportation canyon" where the speed limit is 55 mph. There is road/trail separation at 4.8 miles, and the trail returns to a standard eight-foot asphalt strip.

Interstate 80 thunders overhead at five miles from Empire Park. You are in Rapids City, Illinois, population 953, incorporated in 1875, at 5.5 miles from Empire Park. There is a family restaurant up ahead just off the trail. Through Rapids City there are driveways to local houses cutting across the path. And at 6.2 miles is the intersection of Second Avenue and Twelfth Street. The route here turns left, crosses the railroad tracks, and picks up the trail again at 6.3 miles.

Turn on Twelfth Street to Schuler's Shady Grove, a local park campground with a nice view of the Mississippi River. At 6.7 miles from Empire Park is another fine overlook, and just ahead the trail dips back to Illinois Route 84 and crosses Illinois Route 84.

The city of Port Byron, Illinois is a half-mile ahead. Port Byron, Illinois, was founded in 1828, incorporated in 1876, and has a population 1,535. Port Byron was home to several riverboat

The Quad Cities can boast of a well-developed network of local trails along the river. Some are directly atop river levees.

captains. This was originally the location of a fueling station for steamboats, rough wood firing the boat boilers. And at one time the Overland Stage crossed the Mississippi River at Port Byron, in the course of its run from Des Moines to Chicago.

It is currently the location of a major nuclear reactor. At 7.6 miles the trail turns toward the river, following short but steep Buchanan Street. Be careful here—this is an ornery turn, a tight twist downhill—and a convex mirror is even mounted at the intersection to help visibility. The Great River Trail goes through Port Byron at riverbank level and you can ride along Main Street.

The route dips for a couple of blocks through a city park and boat launch along the river. Travel though the park if you wish and return to Main Street. At 8.6 miles is Stone's Country Market and a very nice, heavily-decorated, two-story Second Empire house. A miniature of it would make a great Christmas ornament!

Main Street dead ends at Agnes Street, and runs into a neighborhood road. Continue on this as the trail. There is a jog to the right (east) at 9.3 miles. Just ahead you should see the familiar Route 84 corridor.

At 11.6 miles from Empire Park is Camp Hauberg campground. At 13.2 miles the trail turns left (west) on 13th Avenue South, and at 13.3 miles turns north on Second Street, through a residential subdivision, the route running along a neighborhood street.

This is Cordova, Illinois, a town with a population of 633, that was incorporated 1877.

At 13.6 miles, take 10th Avenue South up one block, and follow on Fourth Street. There are no bike signs on this part of the road, but this is the right route. At 14.0 miles there is a fine one-story gothic style brick structure, and just ahead you should turn right onto Third Avenue. Continue uphill to the Third Avenue intersection with Sixth Street. Here atop the hill is the 1858 First Baptist Church. It is a refreshing but short downhill to Main Avenue in Cordova. You should see the Boathouse bar and grill. Just past this is the large and rambling Leisure Inn Bed & Breakfast, a nicely restored country Victorian in a wonderful setting in the original town area.

At 14.5 miles you turn left on North Street. Here the road turns and curves, and becomes Third Avenue in the twisting.

Close by is the <u>Diamond Jo Warehouse</u> lookout and there is a good river viewpoint. Here, between 1870 and 1890, were large grain warehouses owned by Diamond Jo Reynolds. The warehouses kept grain from Minnesota, Wisconsin and Illinois, to be shipped by barge to the Fulton, Illinois rail terminal of the Chicago & Northwestern railroad. And here, off in the distance, you can still see barges of grain taking the long trip downriver.

Third Avenue gets the name River Road, and at 15.6 miles you turn off onto 171 Avenue North. This jogs across the rail tracks and puts you back to the familiar Illinois Route 84 corridor.

Just outside of Cordova is the Cordova drag strip, "where the great ones roar," and this is the actual place at 17.4 miles. Here you turn left to the Exelon Quad Cities Generating Station's South Entrance; this is another nuclear power plant along the Grand Illinois Trail route. Cross the tracks and then turn right. The trail travels through company property here, and you cross two railroad spurs that serve the plant. At 18.5 miles you can get a great view of the power plant. Here there are great power line structures that look for all the world like creatures from H. G. Wells' *War of the Worlds.*

A bit after this, turn right and follow the company road back to Illinois Route 84. About 20 miles from Empire Park you should see the Westway Trading Corporation, and at 20.5 miles the vale is filled by a 3M plant. CF Industries, Inc. has its Albany Ammonia and UAN Terminal here, along with its massive phosphate warehouse.

At 23.9 miles, you cross Illinois Route 84 and grab onto Meredosia Road, a winding uphill twist of a road. The country road wraps up and around to the top of the bluff.

<u>Albany Mounds Village Site</u> is here, and it has been here for over 2,000 years. This was the place to be in 200 B.C. Albany Mounds is one of the larger Hopewell Culture sites in Illinois, and there are several other major sites in the state: Cahokia Mounds, Dickson Mounds and Oakwood Mound near Joliet. Smaller mounds still line the banks of the Mississippi and Illinois Rivers. Early European settlers just could not believe

that these mounds were created by the forebears of Native American tribes.

The Hopewell era saw a high point in Native American culture, a point that subsequent generations never met. There is no obvious connection between the Hopewellian culture and modern era Native Americans. Anthropologists know the origins of Hopewell culture, but still hope to understand the end of the era.

It lasted from 500 B.C. to 1200 A.D. Well-developed continental trade routes brought to Illinois items such as mica, copper, seashells and alligator teeth—items found in the mysterious mounds. The mounds themselves were sites of mass and individual burials. Hoes and milling stones found show that Hopewell-era Indians had a well-developed agriculture, one that supported the growth of real cities with settled populations and specialized crafts. Fieldwork shows that the large earthen mounds were frequently oriented to astronomical features, and were the site of seasonal religious ceremonies.

The Albany Mounds is planted today in wild prairie and it really gives you the feeling of actually being surrounded in a sea of prairie. You can hear Eliza Steele's 1841 exclamation:

I was in the midst of a prairie! A world of grass and flowers stretched around me, rising and falling in gentle undulations, as if an enchanter had struck the ocean swell, and it was at rest forever. . . . What a new and wondrous world of beauty! What a magnificent sight! How shall I convey to you the idea of a prairie?

Albany Mounds is not the small, contemporary prairie-garden that you may have already seen alongside the Grand Illinois Trail—it is exactly the kind of thing that takes you to the Illinois landscape of 1673 A.D. or 300 B.C. This is what Illinois looked like—and you're in it! Here you find shooting stars, coneflowers, compass plants and high swaying prairie grasses. The trail wanders through the site, and it is moderately hilly. There is a nice trailhead park with a restroom, water and a nice picnic area, and this is all about 25 miles from the Empire Park starting point. Albany Mounds was purchased by the state in 1971 and it is held by the Illinois Historic Preservation Agency.

From the trailhead park take Cherry Street north; turn left on Eleventh Avenue South. Follow this road up to Church Street and turn right. You are in Albany, Illinois, population 895, incorporated 1869. Oddly enough, the town was decimated—flattened—by a tornado in 1860 and townspeople since then have spent the past 150 years rebuilding, and admiring great flocks of mallard ducks and geese. At 25.6 miles there is a dramatic but short downhill—an *emphatic* downhill—that ends by a shady town park. At 26.1 miles, turn right on Bluff Street. There is a nice, long descent down Bluff Street and it's enjoyable.

The Tri-Township Heritage Museum is an Albany attraction at 306 Lime Street.

Bluff Street becomes Waller Road, and it runs north out of town. Waller Road closely parallels Illinois Route 84, and eventually runs into it. At this intersection, turn right onto Palmer Road. This becomes Kennedy Road.

At 29 miles, cross Illinois Route 84 and head to the river. Take a right on Ebson Road. Continue on Ebson. It is kind of pleasantly rural here, and, in fact, Ebson Road becomes a graveled country lane.

At 30.6 miles, turn left, crossing a dirt road, and then you return to an eight-foot asphalt trail. This runs atop a levee for a stretch. At 31.4 miles you are at Cattail Slough Recreation Area, a boat launch park. Turn right (east) on the access road, head down off the levee to the road below and turn left. This is winding Ward Road. Watch for traffic.

At 31.9 miles, turn left at the Ward Road/Dakin Road intersection. Turn left and take Dakin Road north. Use caution—Dakin Road is marked at 50 mph. Go under the U.S. Route 30/Lincoln Highway bridge just ahead, and at 32.1 miles, take an immediate left onto the Great River Trail's Great Asphalt Pathway.

At Fulton you have two options. If you continue and go straight you will run directly into Fulton, Illinois. Or if you cross Dakin Road and follow the path heading east you will take a trail bypass around Fulton. If you take the Fulton bypass, you will see a neat sight: a Massey Ferguson dealer on one side of Illinois Route 84 and his competitor, John Deere, just across the road. Red versus Green.

At 33.7 miles from Empire Park is the Fulton Industrial Park. A half-mile ahead the trail turns onto city streets in Fulton. Fulton, Illinois,

The Fulton windmill plies the prairie sky on a late summer evening.

population 3,881, incorporated 1859, took its name from Robert Fulton, the American inventor of the steamboat. Believe it or not, Fulton was a planned community, a town created by real estate speculators and developers in 1839 at the site of a good river crossing. The town has been a river port and a terminus for four different railroad lines and for the Diamond Joe Steamboat Line.

After the Civil War, Fulton was home to the Illinois Soldiers' College, an institution offering low-cost degrees to returning veterans. The college became Northern Illinois College in 1873 and finally closed some twenty years later.

Today, Fulton is a pleasant residential town, at the intersection of two designated National Scenic Byways, the Great River Road (Illinois Route 84) and the Lincoln Highway (U.S. Route 30). Fulton is directly across the river from Clinton, Iowa. It is worth taking your camera out to get a snapshot or two of the Fulton windmill, "de Immigrant," an <u>authentic Dutch windmill</u> that celebrates the city's Dutch heritage. The windmill was built in the Netherlands and put in place by Dutch craftsmen. It is tall—a real skyscraper.

The <u>Martin House</u> at 707 Tenth Avenue contains the Fulton Historical Society's collections. <u>Heritage Canyon</u> at 515 N. Fourth Street shows the elements of an historic working village.

<u>Lock and Dam 13</u> on the Mississippi River is a huge attraction here. This is a good place for birdwatching, along with fishing and boating. The tailwaters of the dam are a good place for fishing walleye and sauger in the fall and spring, and white bass

and drum in the summer. Fishermen also find plenty of crappie, bluegill, catfish and bullheads in all the backwater lakes and sloughs along the Mississippi.

When you leave the Great River Trail pathway, go past the old white depot building and head directly toward the new, low brick building, the Central Bank of Fulton. You should be picking up Fourteenth Street here, and at 34.3 miles you turn right onto Fourteenth Avenue—at the Fourteenth Street/Fourteenth Avenue intersection. At the Schafer Road intersection you pick up the eight-foot asphalt path again.

Penrose intersects the trail at 36.4 miles. Just over a mile from this, turn left (west) on to Lock Road, then take a quick jog and the first right onto Railroad Lane. The Great River Trail follows here just next to a huge prairie planting. Prairie plantings usually can look kind of dry: this stuff looked lush, with a great variety of colors and plants. At 38.9 miles is Mickelson's Landing—a boat launch area popular for fishing. And then you arrive at the entrance to Thomson-Fulton Sand Prairie State Preserve. This is next to the Thomson Causeway Recreational Area.

This is an odd and beautiful thing. Sand prairies are weird ecosystems. Here you find typical prairie plants living side-by-side, root-by-root, with plants out of the far West. These sandy species migrated into the Midwest over 10,000 years ago, when climactic conditions were much drier. As our climate changes, they could yet find a niche at Fulton.

The sand matters. Sandy soil drains quickly. Plants with small or narrow leaves reduce the amount of moisture they give off. Plants with deep roots that can seek out moisture tend to do well. So do plants with roots that mat together over the surface area, like beach-heath and rocky spikemoss, since these are able to quickly catch whatever water appears.

The pride of Fulton is the Prickly Pear Cactus. These low-lying cacti live in clumps—large, spiky lobes—and send forth a gorgeous yellow flower in June. The park holds such unusual plants as butterfly weed, birds' foot violet, blazing stars, sand phlox and New Jersey tea.

About a mile down the road you turn off the road and onto an unusual sand and gravel trail surface. Believe it or not, this is high-tech, low-tech stuff. This is an experimental trail surface. It uses natural materials (crushed stone) and binds them together with a special type of cactus gum. This combination makes the trail environmentally friendly, something especially important to the sand prairie. You can tell from the surroundings, though, not to strew gum wrappers here.

At 42.2 miles out, the trail turns into visitor parking at the Thomson Causeway Recreational Area, and this is an excellent trailhead point. Here is plenty of parking, restrooms and water. And the park also contains boat launches, areas for fishing, and camping sites.

The U.S. Army Corps of Engineers runs the Thomson Causeway Recreation Area. The <u>Indian Mound Day Use Area</u> is here, as well as Potter's Marsh, an area good for watching waterfowl. The Recreation Area is open from April through October. The Thomson Causeway is a good access point for the West Section of the Grand Illinois Trail, whether you are heading south to the Quad Cities or north to Galena.

Additional Trails

The Quad Cities area boasts a strong network of local trails. These all tied into the Great River Trail, and the Grand Illinois Trail, at Empire Park in East Moline.

The Quad Cities are remarkably bike-friendly. The Ben Butterworth Parkway ranks among the finest such riverfront pathways in the Midwest. The Quad Cities along with their neighboring towns have made a great network of connecting local trails. These allow great access throughout the area, and they are a great part of the riverfront. Even though a river runs through it, the Quad Cities trails in Iowa and Illinois are connected by Channel Cat Water Taxi!

Ben Butterworth Parkway

The Ben Butterworth runs through Moline and East Moline, starting near the Interstate 74 bridge and ending at Empire Park in Hampton, Illinois. A portion exists in Rock Island. The parkway follows a riverfront route, and includes riding on levees alongside the Mississippi River and passing by the Case and Deere plants.

Long-term plans call for stretching this two-mile route further west into Rock Island.

Duck Creek Parkway

This runs for 13.5 miles from Emis Park in Davenport to Devils Glen Park in Bettendorf. It began life as a scenic parkway through local parks. There are bridges galore as the trail passes back and again over Duck Creek.

River Way Trail

This 6.6-mile trail is a high-impact trail. It gives a great introduction to the river. The River Way Trail stretches from Davenport to Bettendorf all along the riverfront and it runs through neat parks, downtown Davenport, Lock and Dam 14 and the village of East Davenport. It is here at the village landing in Lindsey Park that you can pick up the Channel Cat Water Taxi and ferry over to the Illinois side. There is interesting art all along the way.

Rock Island Arsenal Trail

This is a short trail, only 3.9 miles long. But it is packed with things to see. It begins at the U.S. Army Corps of Engineers Visitor Center, follows King Drive and ends at Rodman Avenue at the east end of the island. Arsenal Island is a federal military installation, and it may on occasion be closed to the public.

Channel Cat Water Taxi

But one fascinating thing for bicyclists is the Channel Cat Water Taxi. This is a light packet boat that ferries bicycles, bicyclists and walkers across the river every hour in season for a modest fee. It carries up to 40 passengers and 20 bikes!

It is possible to board the Channel Cat Water Taxi in Moline, at Celebration Cruises dock; in Bettendorf at Leach Park dock; in Davenport at the Lindsay Park dock; and in downtown Moline at the John Deere Commons dock.

Tour of the Mississippi River Valley

A cycle tour of the Mississippi River valley is held each year in the early part of June. This overnight adventure runs up from East Moline to Galena and Dubuque, Iowa on the Great River Trail, and then returns to the Quad Cities on the Iowa side of the river. The ride is sponsored by the Quad Cities Bicycle Club.

Quad-Cities POINTS OF INTEREST ————————————

Black Hawk State Historic Site
1510 46th Avenue, Rt. 5
Rock Island
This is Saukenuk, ancient home of the Sauk and Fox tribes, and home to Black Hawk and his followers. Includes a 200-acre nature preserve and the Hauberg Indian Museum.

Celebration Belle
18th Street
A fine river cruiser, an authentic paddlewheeler.

Channel Cat Water Taxis
2501 River Drive, Celebration Belle Dock
A unique QC attraction: passenger ferries that take passengers (and bikes) across the broad Mississippi. A wonderful idea worth trying.

Davenport Museum of Art
1737 W. 12th Street
Davenport, Iowa
Fine local collection of art, the first art gallery in Iowa, holding more than 3,500 works.

Deere-Wiman House and Butterworth Center
1105 8th Street
Moline, Illinois
Beautiful mansions owned by the Deere family, with fine gardens and grand interiors.

Deere & Company Administrative Center
John Deere Road/Rt. 5
Moline, Illinois
World-famous architecture by Eero Saarinen, the corporate headquarters and grounds of John Deere are an amazing sight. The HQ feature product displays open to the public.

John Deere Pavilion and John Deere Collectors Center
17th Street and River Drive
Moline
A great 1950s-era John Deere dealership, with special displays and vintage equipment.

Family Museum of Arts and Science
2900 Learning Campus Drive
Bettendorf, Iowa
A children's educational complex, filled with arts and science displays and experiences.

Lagomarcino's
1422 5th Avenue
Moline, Illinois
The place to visit in the QC: authentic old-fashioned ice cream parlor featuring homemade chocolate and ice cream.

Niabi Zoo
13010 Niabi Zoo Road
Coal Valley, Illinois
Large, rambling zoo home to 700+ animals. The big cats, elephants, zebras, etc.; a regional attraction.

Putnam Museum of History and Natural Science
Davenport
A center for exploring the natural world, with displays of the Upper Mississippi River ecosystems. Featuring an Asian/Egyptian gallery and an IMAX theater.

Quad City Botanical Center
2525 4th Avenue
Moline
A huge and unique conservatory, focusing heavily on tropical plants. With waterfall, reflecting pools, outdoor conifer garden, art exhibits and special events.

Rock Island Arsenal
Arsenal Island in the Mississippi River
Guarded by the Army, Rock Island Arsenal is a working arsenal, but certain portions are open to the public. Includes the 1833 Col. Davenport homestead, reproduction buildings of the Ft. Armstrong site, the famous arsenal workshop buildings and clock tower, and the John Browning firearms museum. The island also holds the Mississippi River Visitors Center at Lock 15. Note Confederate burial grounds, a silent testament to the POW camp set up on the island during the Civil War.

Rock Island Arts and Entertainment District
"The District"
Great entertainment district, with restaurants, bars, unique shopping opportunities.

Rock Island Historical Society House-Museum Complex
822 11th Avenue
Moline, Illinois
Great collections of local history; come into touch with 19th century Americana.

Village of East Davenport
The whole tiny village is a historic site, filled with unique boutiques.

Great River Trail (2)

Thomson to Savanna

From Thomson to Mississippi Palisades State Park in Savanna, Illinois you must rely for the most part on local, low-volume roads. The Great River Trail ends at Savanna.

Following the Great River Trail from Thomson to Savanna

Thomson, Illinois, population 559, was incorporated in 1865, and it is the <u>Melon Capitol of the World</u>. Sandy river bottom land here produces great watermelons. The <u>Thomson Depot Museum</u>, containing railroading memorabilia, is at 907 Main Street.

From a starting point at the <u>Thomson Causeway</u>, take Main Street in Thomson west to Sandridge Road. Follow Main Street west. It quickly curves north. This is now called Sandridge Road.

Heading north on Sandridge Road you arrive at the site of the <u>Thomson State Penitentiary</u>.

This is a brand-new state facility for holding high-security convicts. The penitentiary has never opened, due to a lack of funding. It is a shiny boondoggle sprawled out under the sun.

At about one mile from the Thomson Causeway, turn left and take Ideal Road west. This is just up from the penitentiary. The very next road that you come to is Sandpatch Road. Note that Sandpatch Road is also called Riverview Road. There is mostly only local residential traffic here. You should be able to see the Mississippi River at points as you travel along.

Riverview Road runs north to <u>Big Slough Day Use Area</u>, a boat launch with a beautiful view of the river. This is about five miles north of the Thomson Causeway. Continue on Riverview and you see plenty of examples of "weekend architecture," small residences built mainly for weekend retreat. One favorite is the "Hodge Podge Lodge."

Riverview Road goes directly through the Upper Mississippi Fish & Wildlife Refuge, at about 6.5 miles from Thomson. Sloane Marsh is here, and while it may not be lovely and beautiful in a classic sense, this kind of wetlands is a habitat teeming with important wildlife resources.

Just above the marsh flat, perched on a hill, is the Upper Mississippi Fish & Wildlife Refuge Visitors Center. Here you can find some good information about the wildlife protection being done here, and about the river ecology and its wildlife. The staff is knowledgeable. This is a good place to begin a birding trip to the area, and a number of important bird types have been seen here. The Visitors Center has restrooms and water.

Just ahead Riverview Road sways back toward Illinois Route 84. You cross a set of railroad tracks. This is an active line.

Here, at this point in its development, the Grand Illinois Trail route runs on Illinois Route 84 for just under a mile and a half. At the intersection of Riverview Road and Illinois Route 84, turn north on Illinois Route 84. Watch the traffic!: this is a road that really begs for a good widening project from IDOT. It has only gravel shoulders, so keep well to the right. Ride the paint.

Stay on Illinois Route 84 for about a mile and a half.

Railroad rails cut a diagonal across Illinois Route 84 at a potentially dangerous angle. So watch your wheels.

Just past the railroad tracks at the west side of the road is a tiny bit of pavement. It is not well marked. This is the tail end of the new trail route into Savanna. Exercise caution in stopping and in crossing Illinois Route 84. This former Sioux Lines railbed now carries the Great River Trail directly into Savanna. The trail passes through some scenic wetland areas, across a nifty box steel bridge, and then one of the small delights of the Grand Illinois Trail: the enormous box bridge that conveys the trail up and over and into Savanna!

At the end of the path, just cross the railroad tracks and you will find the restored 1950 passenger coach. This is about 11 miles from the Thomson starting point. The train coach is the Hiawatha Train Car Museum, a visitors center that recalls the time when up to 100 trains would pass through Savanna each day.

Savanna, Illinois, population 3,542, was incorporated in 1874. The first settlers here came from Kentucky in 1838. It is a handsome town along the Mississippi, a sportsmen's paradise and a good place for antiquing—check out the 24,000 square foot Pulford Opera House Antique Mall downtown.

The town's early settlers worked the river, especially in the lumber trade. Prosperous riverboat captains built their houses along the river bluff and they enhance the historic appeal of Savanna.

The Mississippi River bridge in Savanna is a local attraction of sorts. Called the Savanna-Sabula Bridge, the massive steel truss bridge is 520 feet long. It was built in 1932, the fruit of fifty long years of political lobbying.

Mississippi Palisades State Park, at Savanna, is the end of the Great River Trail. The park, named after the magnificent Palisades of the Hudson River, gives commanding views of the river. Established in 1934, the park has 2,500 acres of bluffs, cliffs and woodlands. The U.S. Department of Interior deemed the park a National Landmark in 1971 and its wildlife and plant life range is impressive.

This is the confluence point for the Apple River and Mississippi River.

There are ten internal trails, five running through the south end of the park and five through the north part of the park. These provide access to river overlooks and campgrounds. The park has a boat launch, primitive and trailer/tent camping, showers and restrooms. There are 1930s CCC shelters throughout the park.

To reach Mississippi Palisades State Park, stay on Illinois Route 84 heading north. There are several entrances to the lower park along the way. An upper entrance is reached by getting on Scenic Ridge Road. This road is reached by taking Clay Street from Main Street and connecting with Fifth Street, going uphill it becomes Scenic Ridge Road.

Mountain Bike vs. Road Bike

There are two ways to get to Galena from Mississippi Palisades State Park. The first, for mountain bikers and more casual riders, uses low-volume roads. The second route, along Illinois Route 84, is better for road bikes and experienced cyclists and it is the more direct route.

The Mountain Bike Route

To continue to Jo Daviess County and Galena by mountain bike, you need to get to Scenic Ridge Road at the top of the river bluffs. Access Ridge Road by taking Webster Street (it intersects Main Street at the north side of Savanna) east and upward to Fifth Street. Heading north out of town, the road becomes Ridge Road. There are several entrances into <u>Mississippi Palisades State Park</u>.

Ridge Road gets renamed Scenic Ridge Road and then South Derinda Road. It wiggles and turns. South Derinda Road intersects with South Heer Road at about 10 miles from Savanna. Take South Heer Road and then take an immediate right onto South Curtiss Hill Road.

Continue on South Curtiss Road to South Gamble Hill Road, then take a left on West Hanover Road. West Hanover Road takes you into Hanover, Illinois. In town, the road gets called Monroe Street, but stay on it. It then is renamed Plateau Street before becoming Jefferson Street. Jefferson Street is Illinois Route 84 through Hanover. It is about 18.3 miles from Savanna.

Stay on Illinois Route 84 through town, and cross the bridge over the Apple River. Take the very first left onto Fulton Street, take this a block to Madison Avenue. Madison Avenue curves out of Hanover and gets called Fulton Road. Stay on this; it gets renamed West Blanding Road.

Take West Blanding Road to Blanding; from Hanover this is about 7.5 miles. At Blanding, take South River Road north. (It is possible to reach Blackjack Road—the road into Galena—by picking up North Sand Hill Road just a short stretch). South River Road leads to Aiken, and then this same road gets renamed South Pilot Knob Road. Continuing on this, it becomes North Pilot Knob Road, and this road rejoins Blackjack Road about a mile and a half south of Galena. Blackjack Road then leads into Galena, joining U.S. Route 20 just before downtown Galena.

The total distance for the mountain bike option is 39 miles from Savanna to Galena.

The Road Bike Route

To continue to Jo Daviess County and Galena by road bike, stay on Illinois Route 84. This might sound dangerous, but consider: up ahead is Hanover (a pretty small town) and Galena. There can be heavy tourist traffic through this way, taking Illinois Route 84 to Galena. The speed limit is 65 mph on this road.

But much of the traffic on Illinois Route 84 simply gets up to the Savanna-Sabula Bridge and crosses the river at this point. So Illinois Route 84 gets a bit quieter and a bit safer past this point.

At 19.3 miles from Thomson is the entrance to the old <u>Savanna Army Depot</u>. It is here that the army tested generations of artillery shells, blasting them off and measuring how they scattered and fell. A large cleanup has been in progress for some time, and it is expected that the land will become open for more recreational purposes. At present, the U.S. Fish & Wildlife Service is doing some guided tours. The site, by the way, is also a place of some entrepreneurship: Eagles Landing development is to bring in some commercial development.

Continue on Illinois Route 84 to Hanover.

Hanover, Illinois, population 836, was incorporated in 1849. This is the "Mallard Capital of the World," and Illinois Route 84 goes directly through town, turning at Ivensys appliance controls factory and crossing the Apple River. Hanover is actually a very pretty little town, kind of like an undiscovered but miniature Galena, with some fascinating old houses. There is a bit of a hill, and just at the edge of town is a three-way crossroad. This is about 26.5 miles from Thomson. Here you can continue on Illinois Route 84 north (and into Galena) or take Speer Road.

Or you can take Blackjack Road (known to maps as Rt. 8). This is the road heading off at an angle. Take Blackjack Road—this is the Grand Illinois Trail route into Galena.

Yes, there are hills on Blackjack Road and in Jo Daviess County. There are easy hills and tough hills. There are scenic points and places. You should bring a camera. And at times the GIT route is high above much of the county!

But Blackjack Road also conveys speeding SUVs and monster trucks, propelling at high speeds around tight curves. Despite a number of small and pathetic roadside crosses, indicating highway deaths, automobile travelers here disregard the warnings. Keep an open eye, and hang close to the edge of the road!

If you like, try imagining wagons filled with lead bars following this route, with their ox teams heaving and straining uphill and then careening downhill.

Roughly 33 miles from Thomson is the intersection of Blackjack Road and Blanding Road. Chestnut Mountain Ski Resort is just down Blanding Road. For the Grand Illinois Trail, it is an important crossroad. Here the mountain bike portion rejoins the road bike route, and the trail goes singly into Galena.

Just ahead is a sharply dropping hill. A bicyclist can easily go over 40 mph on it. So use your brakes as you go. This is the steepest drop on the route.

At 42 miles from the Thomson Causeway access point is Galena. Blackjack Road enters Galena and it quickly ties into U.S. Route 20. This is a busy road filled with tourists and trucks. Head down toward the Galena River and downtown Galena by turning left and heading west.

The Black Hawk War

A rich part of Illinois' Indian heritage is in northern Illinois, scene of the skirmishes and blunders that made up the Black Hawk War of 1832. By strange coincidence the war brought together men who were to become famous in American history— Jefferson Davis, Zachary Taylor, Abraham Lincoln and Colonel Robert Anderson, the defender of Fort Sumter.

The Black Hawk War all began with treaties and political alignments just too confused for the average Indian, and white settler, to understand. Indian history in Illinois is complicated by the many tribes, both Indian and white, who contested for the land, sometimes against each other, sometimes against themselves. The war itself was a scramble of maneuvers and feints, of skirmishes and follies.

If there ever was a man between a rock and a hard place it was the Sauk warrior Black Hawk.

Black Hawk was a distinguished warrior and medicine man who had sided with the British cause in the War of 1812. He was the leader of the "British band" of the Sauk tribe, a splinter band of the Sauk tribe with as many as 7,000 members. The advance of the Americans into northern Illinois brought Black Hawk's leadership into question.

It was in 1804 that a one-sided, rum-laced treaty bought 50 million northern Illinois acres for a mere $1,000 a year annuity to the Sauk and Fox. The treaty called for the tribes to move west of the Mississippi River. In 1816, the treaty was re-ratified at Fort Armstrong at

Black Hawk

Rock Island, and was signed by Black Hawk.

Sauk and Fox tribes often set up camp close together. They were cousin tribes, both of Algonquin stock originally from Canada. They lived along the Rock and the Mississippi rivers. Like other tribes in Illinois, they planted corn and hunted game. They would move village sites on a seasonal basis. Pressure from white settlers, and also some fear of the mighty Winnebagos, led to the Sauk and Fox leaving Illinois in 1829. They finally fulfilled their agreement to head west even though it meant moving into enemy territory held by the fearsome Sioux.

But some wanted to stay, especially at Saukenuk, their village located near the junction of the Rock and Mississippi rivers. Black Hawk later recounted that, "we had about 800 acres in cultivation. . . the land around our village, uncultivated, was covered with blue-grass, which made excellent pasturage for our horses. Several fine springs broke out of the bluff, nearby, from which we were supplied with good water. The rapids of Rock River furnished us with an abundance of excellent fish, and the land, being good, never failed to produce good crops of corn, beans, pumpkins, and squashes."

In 1830, white settlers began wanting this land near Saukenuk. To underscore their claim they destroyed Indian cornfields and lodges. Black Hawk asked settlers to leave, and his warriors burned a few cabins and killed some cattle to emphasize their concern. The Illinois Governor called out the troops, and Black Hawk and his band returned to Iowa after signing an accord acknowledging guilt in crossing the river contrary to the terms of the treaty.

But the very next year, low of food but full of resolve, the Sauk returned. Black Hawk announced his intention to plant corn with a friendly Winnebago band fifty miles up the Rock River at Prophetstown. There Black Hawk joined up with White Cloud, a half-Sauk, half-Winnebago, who also was known as The Prophet. Apparently Black Hawk thought he had found an ally in his fight with the Americans, and hoped for his confederacy of tribes to take shape.

The Illinois Governor again alerted the militia. Black Hawk tried to enlist other tribes in his fight for their ancestral home. None would join.

Pursued up the Rock River by 3,000 soldiers, Black Hawk scored a "victory" that only meant a worse defeat. At "Stillman's Run," near present-day Stillman Valley, a desperation charge by 40 Sauk braves sent Stillman's 275 inexperienced white troops running for their lives down the river valley.

The Indian threat quickly blew out of proportion. Fear went through the Illinois country. More troops, 4,000 in all including U.S. Army regulars, assembled to fight the Sauk. Black Hawk, and his 300-some warriors and their families, headed north to seek refuge among the Winnebago. He found none. His band went west, to cross the Mississippi. But by then, the U.S. Army caught up to them.

At the Battle of Bad Axe the army killed two braves carrying the truce flag. Out of control gunners on the army gunboat "Warrior" slaughtered women and children as they tried the river crossing. Those Sauk and Fox who made it across the river were slaughtered by their ancient foe, the Sioux Indians, that were waiting for them on the Iowa side.

In the end, up to 600 Indians and 72 soldiers died. Black Hawk was caught a little while later, taken on a grand tour of the eastern states. He died six years later, in 1838, a man who had lived through a total transformation of native life. As he remarked in his autobiography, "Rock River was a beautiful country. I like my towns and my cornfields, and the home of my people; it is now yours. It will produce you good crops."

Today the Saukenuk site is Black Hawk State Park. Travellers on the Grand Illinois Trail can easily reach Saukenuk and explore its great setting, along with the Hauberg Museum, which holds a valuable collection of Sauk and Fox artifacts.

Black Hawk State Park is itself a wonder to visit, and it includes some choice specimens of Civilian Conservation Corps architecture: a grand lodge building and several cabins. It is a wonderful place to hike in the fall.

The Thomson-Fulton Sand Prairie

One of the most unusual natural features of the Grand Illinois Trail is the Thomson-Fulton Sand Prairie.

This 262-acre state nature preserve boasts some of the most exotic and beautiful plants in Illinois.

A sand prairie is a rare environment. The Thomson-Fulton Sand Prairie was formed by sandy glacier outwash as the western edge of the Wisconsonian glacier melted over 10,000 years ago. This really is the dividing line between flat as a pancake, glaciated Illinois and the topsy-turvy hills of unglaciated Jo Daviess County.

In the spring you find sand phlox and bird's-foot violet. Late spring brings violet spiderwort and puccoon. Plants flowering in the summer include dwarf dandelion, black-eyed Susan and butterfly weed. Pink blazing star makes its showy appearance in late summer.

Prickly pear cactus, all yellow and spiny, makes a dramatic and showy appearance in June. According to experts, "the flora of the sand prairie is composed of plants common to the tallgrass prairie of Illinois mixed with plants of open habitat that probably arrived in Illinois over the past 10,000 years." These open habitat plants arrived in Illinois during a dry period and were widely distributed. The plants in the Thomson-Fulton Sand Prairie are still here today even after changes to a moister modern climate because the sand allows for fast water drainage and dry conditions. Sand plants have smaller, narrower leaves, and they have leaves with protective coatings. They often have either deep roots that reach down to moisture, or matt-like fibrous roots spreading out after water.

The ground underfoot here is sandy and the trail is made of an environmentally friendly composite. And even though the temperature may be pleasant, you'll still feel like you should be hot and thirsty. It's a desert scene, but it's all Illinois.

Cactus colonies thrive in the dry soil of the Thomson-Fulton Sand Prairie.

Western Section Resources

EMERGENCY

ILLINOIS STATE POLICE, DISTRICT 1
(Sterling)
(815) 632-4010 for Carroll and
Whiteside counties.

ILLINOIS STATE POLICE, DISTRICT 3
(East Moline)
(309) 752-4915 for Rock Island
County.

ILLINOIS STATE POLICE, DISTRICT 16
(Pecatonica)
(815) 987-7156 for Jo Daviess
County.

LOCAL TOURISM CONTACTS

QUAD CITIES CONVENTION AND
VISITORS BUREAU
2021 River Drive
Moline, Illinois 61265
(563) 322-3911
(800) 747-7800
www.visitquadcities.com

GALENA/JO DAVIESS COUNTY
CONVENTION AND VISITORS
BUREAU
101 Bouthillier Street
Galena, Illinois 61036
(815) 777-4390
(800) 747-9377
www.galena.org

FULTON CHAMBER OF COMMERCE
Post Office Box 253
Fulton, Illinois 61252
(815) 589-4545
www.cityoffulton.us/chamber.
html

SAVANNA CHAMBER OF COMMERCE
25 Main Street
Savanna, Illinois
(815) 273-2722

ILLINOIS TOURISM BUREAU
(800) 2-CONNECT

BED & BREAKFASTS

Moline
WE SHARE B & B
1860 25th Avenue
(309) 762-7059

Rock Island
POTTER HOUSE
1906 Seventh Avenue
www.qconline.com/potterhouse
(800) 747-0339

TOP O' THE MORNING B & B
1505 19th Avenue
(309) 786-3513

VICTORIAN INN B & B
702 20th Street
(800) 728-7068
(309) 788-7068

Port Byron
OLDE BRICK HOUSE GUEST HOUSE/
B & B
502 N. Hight Street
(309) 786-3513

Cordova
LEISURE HARBOR INN
701 Main Avenue
(309) 654-2233

Thomson
LYNN WOOD LYNKS AND LODGE
5020 Illinois Route 84 South
(800) 596-6966

Lanark
THE STANDISH HOUSE B & B
540 W. Carroll Street
(800) 468-2307

Savanna
GRANNY O'NEILS RIVER INN
31 Third Street
(815) 273-4726

HOTELS & MOTELS

Galena
BEST WESTERN MOTEL
9923 Hwy. 20 West
(815) 777-2577
www.quiethouse.com

CHESTNUT MOUNTAIN RESORT
8700 W. Chestnut Rd.
(800) 397-1320
www.chestnutmt.com

COUNTRY INN & SUITES
11334 Oldenburg Lane
(866) 268-7946

THE DESOTO HOUSE HOTEL
230 S. Main Street
(800) 343-6562
www.desotohouse.com

EAGLE RIDGE INN & RESORT
Hwy. 20 East
(815) 777-2444
www.eagleridge.com

GRANT HILLS MOTEL
9372 Hwy. 20 West
(815) 777-2116

Barstow
LUNDEEN'S LANDING
21119 Barstow Road
(309) 496-9956

Thomson
THOMSON HOUSE VILLAGER LODGE
800 One Mile Road
www.thomsonvillager.com
(800) 328-7829

CAMPING

Savanna
LAKEWOOD RESORT
6577 Mill Hollow Road
(815) 273-2898

MISSISSIPPI PALISADES STATE PARK
16327A Illinois Route 84
(815) 273-2731

SEVEN EAGLES CAMPGROUND AND
RESORT
9734 Illinois Route 84 South
(815) 273-7301
www.goseveneagles.com

Hampton
FISHERMAN'S CORNER
I-80, Illinois Route 84 South
(309) 794-4524

Fulton
MAPLE LANE MOTEL AND CAMPING
18920 Frog Pond Road
(815) 589-3038

Thomson
UPPER MISSISSIPPI RIVER NATIONAL
WILDLIFE AND FISH REFUGE
7071 Riverview Road
(815) 273-3302

U.S. ARMY CORPS OF ENGINEERS/
THOMSON CAUSEWAY
Recreation Area
Lewis Avenue
(815) 259-3628

**BIKE STORES/
REPAIR CENTERS**

P & B LAWN EQUIPMENT AND
CYCLERY
820 S. Chicago Street
Geneseo, Illinois 61254
(309) 788-2092

BIKE & HIKE
3913 14th Avenue
Rock Island, Illinois
(309) 788-2092

ARNOLD'S BICYCLE REPAIR
210 Walnut Street
Savanna, Illinois 61074
(815) 273-7789

The Rambling Mississippi River Trail

Still a work in progress, still being planned and developed, is the Mississippi River Trail.

The trail will start at the headwaters of the Mississippi, at Lake Itasca in Minnesota, and run through ten states on the way to the Gulf of Mexico. It will have a length of over 2,000 miles. It is a chance to see the whole Mississippi River culture, North and South, and get better acquainted with the single most outstanding feature of the North American landscape.

The Mississippi River Trail was first envisioned by the Lower Mississippi Development Commission in the early 1990s. It has relied on collaboration between many local partners. For more

contact the MRT office in St. Paul at (651) 698-4568 or check www.mississippirivertrail.org.

North

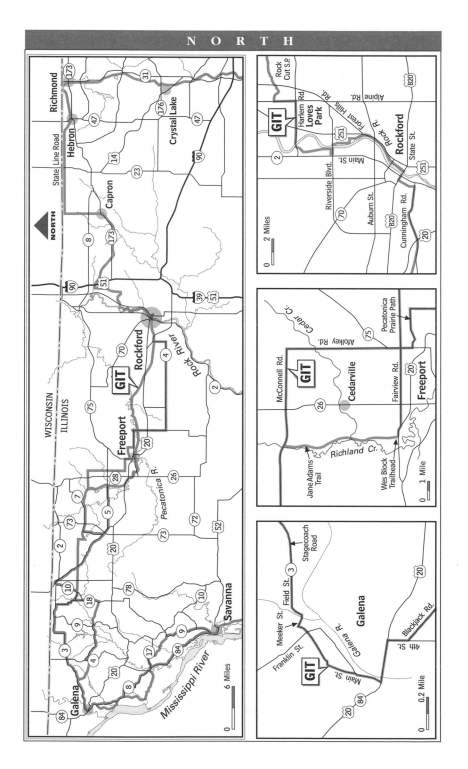

Overview _____

The North Section of the Grand Illinois Trail runs from Galena through Rockford to Richmond, Illinois. This section offers many fine road touring opportunities. The unglaciated Jo Daviess County is a land of beautiful vistas and broad green hills. Its hills tell the tale of what Illinois looked liked long before the glaciers. Boone and McHenry County provide classic farm views.

Galena in the Northwest corner of Illinois is a charming town filled with historic charm. Much of the town is on the National Register of Historic Places. Its downtown shopping district is packed with antique stores, craft shops, gift shops, art galleries and restaurants. Main Street in Galena is a bustling place and a major Midwest tourist destination.

At Freeport, the Jane Addams Trail runs toward Wisconsin on a railbed once used by the Illinois Central. Both local roads and the Pecatonica Path connect Freeport and Rockford. Rockford's exceptional city trails let you explore much of the city, and especially highlight scenic Sinnissippi Park along the Rock River.

Road biking through McHenry and Boone counties, on backroads and on the Long Prairie Trail, is a pleasure of the North Section of the Grand Illinois Trail.

Galena's architecturally resplendent Belvedere Mansion.

127

NORTH SECTION POINTS OF INTEREST

Old Market Square, GALENA
The Belvedere House, GALENA
Ulysses S. Grant House, GALENA
Main Street GALENA
Galena River
Apple River Canyon State Park
Lake Le-Aqua-Na State Park
Richland Creek
Pecatonica River

Rockford Rec Path
Rock River
Jefferson Street Bridge, ROCKFORD
Rock Guardians of the Rock River
Sinnissippi Park Lagoon, ROCKFORD
Rock Cut State Park
Caledonia water tower
Main Street CAPRON
Stateline Road

Find Me A Place

Find me a place, safe and serene,
Away from the terror I see on the screen.
A place where my soul can find some peace,
Away from the stress and the pressure's released.
A corridor of green not far from my home
For fresh air and exercise, quiet will roam.

Summer has smells that tickle my nose
And Fall has the leaves that crunch under my toes.
Beware, comes a person we pass in a while
With a wave and hello, and a wide friendly smile.
Recreation trails are the place to be,
To find that safe haven of peace and serenity.

— Beverly Moore
Capron, Illinois
Illinois Trails Conservancy

Northwest Corner Routes

Galena and Jo Daviess County

Galena, Illinois, population 3,460, was established in 1826 and incorporated in 1835. Everyone in Illinois, and much of the Midwest, gets a positive vibe from Galena. The town is quaint, historic, scenic and precious. The countryside in this northwest corner of the state is markedly different. There are rolling hills and valleys.

Charles Mound, at 1,235 feet above sea level, is the highest point in Illinois. And it's true that you feel you can see forever on a clear day from Long Hollow Tower near Elizabeth. Just about everywhere is a broad, green vista. No one can go through Jo Daviess County without appreciating its beauty.

Tucked away in the corner of the state, set above the Galena River, is the city of Galena. Galena is a city preserved in amber. Some 85% of the townsite is actually on the National Register of Historic Places. This place is a dream for antique-lovers and architecture buffs, and it has been recognized as such for decades.

The route of the Grand Illinois Trail, like everything else that's here, is set by topography, the lay of the land.

Here the Grand Illinois Trail is forced onto local roads and state routes. These provide access into the area.

The key to the secret of Galena's appearance and her rise to prominence in the 19th century can be found in geography. The secret itself is lead.

Galena (a Latinate term for lead sulphide) was the center of the nation's most prodigious lead mine district. Jo Daviess County never experienced the flattening crunch of glaciers, the way the most of Illinois did. It retains the ancient geographical lineaments of the Pliocene age, features that were wiped away in the rest of the state. Curiously enough, in Galena we can see a glimpse of what the Illinois terrain looked like before this great leveling.

Without the glaciers and their sediments, Jo Daviess County lacks a thick layer of topsoil. Because of this, it is possible to scrape for lead deposits appearing close enough to the earth's surface to be mined.

The first white men, the French explorers, to travel through the area noted the presence of lead. This caused a great sensation. Maps were printed in Paris describing the deposits. By 1717, feverish speculation in stocks of the state-authorized mining company went overboard, and led to the "Mississippi Bubble," a great scandal that almost bankrupt the French government. At the height of speculative frenzy, a French observer said, "Everybody speaks in millions. I don't understand it at all. But I clearly see that the God Mammon reigns an absolute monarch in Paris."

Actual on-site mining was sporadic. A hole here, a dig there. But the strategic value of Galena was recognized in international politics during the 1767 French & Indian War, the Revolutionary War and the War of 1812. French, British and American forces all claimed the region at one time or another during its early days.

Galena as a town dates only to about 1818. It has been linked to river trade with Davenport. It was a frontier boomtown, the sort of place where 14 year-old girls were married off to grizzled miners. The miners, of course, were hard drinking guys, many of them from England, Ireland or Wales, where they had worked the famed Cornish tin mines. (There are reports of bloody "Cornish duels" in Galena: each combatant would build a pile of rocks in front of him, and hurl them at the other man until he was dead).

The U.S. Government held title to the mine country, and mining rights were leased to mining companies under the supervision of the Secretary of War. The mine operators could sell their ore only to registered smelters. New mine owners had to post $5,000 bond (a lot of money back then), for each square half-mile of land to be mined. They also had to pledge to employ at least 20 men and pay the government 10% of their lead. Smelters had to post $20,000 bond and pay 10% of their smelted lead to the government. At crest, there were 23 smelters operating in Jo Daviess County!

The town was a great marketplace. After 1823, steamboats arrived from Davenport or St. Louis filled with finished goods. Oxcarts and wagons would arrive in town with lead to be shipped south. Stagecoach lines ran to Peoria and Chicago. It was about as much of a Wild West frontier that Illinois ever mustered.

In 1823, the mines of Jo Daviess County and adjacent lands produced 425,000 pounds of lead. By 1829, production reached 13,000,000 pounds!

The top year of lead production was in 1845 when 54,500,000 pounds were extracted from the rolling hills. This represented 83% of total U.S. lead production in that year.

It never got any better. The 1848 Gold Rush in California predictably drew off plenty of miners, itching to match their skills to more lucrative rewards. By 1855, the town's river trade declined as the Illinois Central's railroad terminus in Dunleith (East Dubuque) took away much of the regional trade. The Galena River, always getting filled with silt from farming and the mining, was finally made impassable even to light-draft steamboats in 1863. The peak years, the good years, for Galena were in the 1840s and 1850s.

The architecture shows this.

The Belvedere Mansion, at 1008 Park Avenue, was built in 1857 by J. Russell Jones, a steamboat captain and one-time ambassador to Belgium. Its beautiful belvedere, or cupola, has pretty much symbolized Galena tourism for the past four decades.

The Dowling House, downtown at 220 Diagonal Street, is the oldest standing residence in town, built of native limestone. It was once a trading post.

DeSoto House Hotel, 230 S. Main Street, should be on the National Register. It was opened to business in 1855. The hotel has provided hospitality to presidents Lincoln and Grant, and countless other dignitaries over the years, and the DeSoto House remains a top place to stay when in the area.

The Old Stockade, 208 Perry Street, was the local shelter and defense during the Black Hawk uprising of 1832.

Washburne House State Historic Site, 908 Third Street, is a Greek Revival house built by Elihu Washburne, the region's congressman in the 1850s and 1860s. Washburne was a friend of Lincoln, and an early advocate of U. S. Grant. Built in 1843, subsequent additions to the structure were made in 1859 and 1860.

Old Market House State Historic Site, 123 N. Commerce Street
Right downtown on Commerce Street, the Old Market House is a fine Greek Revival structure, built in the 1845-46. It was multi-purpose in its functions, and the Old Market House was a combination city council chamber, city jail, public market place and meeting hall. In almost every way, it was the focal point of community life in bustling Galena.

Galena's lead heritage can be found at Vinegar Hill Lead Mine and Museum, outside of town at 8885 N. Three Pines Road. Tours go down into a typical 1822 lead mine. For general history, check in at the Galena/Jo Daviess County History Museum, at 211 S. Bench Street, for a look into Galena's past. The museum contains a wide-ranging collection on local mining, steamboating, the Civil War, period furnishings, clothing, dolls and toys.

Beyond these highpoints are the many smaller reminders of Galena's exceptional heritage. The long and curving Main Street is a fine vista, the views from points in and around the city, the remarkable beauty of smaller brick houses.

Galena doesn't owe her architectural beauty to the sophisticated tastes or foresightedness of her town founders. The city has benefited

An early drawing shows the beauty of Galena's location, nestled in the rolling hills of Jo Daviess County. (Photo courtesy of the Illinois State Historical Library).

from "preservation by default." Galena lost population over the years, with one result being that there was very little need to build new structures. During its boom years, there were 14,000 residents; now there are fewer than 4,000.

There is a fitting coincidence in the fact that just as Galena began her decline, U.S. Grant became the nation's leader. Grant had been a captain in the 1847 Mexican-American War, where he had served and known such army officers as Jefferson Davis and Winfield Scott. He spent 15 years with the army as a captain. He tried to be a math teacher, and finally moved his family to Galena, where he worked in his father's leather goods store.

He was—and perhaps this is why there is a smoky-real flavor to him—a completely, totally ordinary man. He walked the up-and-down streets of Galena as an ordinary man, nothing special, a clerk in a leather store. Grant's prewar dwelling is at 121 S. High Street. His townsmen may well have ignored him or looked down on him before the war.

Ulysses S. Grant was a reluctant general. He began his Civil War greatness with a simple speech to Galena men who were organizing a military unit. His sensible talk led to an offer to train volunteers, and later, an offer of unit command. Grant accepted it and took the unit to Springfield. There, Illinois Governor Yates offered him adjutant generalship of Illinois' troops. He was then commissioned as Colonel of the 21st Illinois Infantry Regiment.

Grant returned, after battles, campaigns and other exploits, to Jo Daviess County in 1865. In order to commission him appropriately, Congress had to give George Washington a posthumous five-star commission, so that no man would ever outrank the Father of our Country.

Here Grant lived until 1868, when he accepted the presidency. It's true he was not much of a president and he even acknowledged this. But Galenans loved the man. Grant's friends became his trusted generals, and this small Illinois town boasts a whopping nine Union generals: John Rawlins, Ely Parker, William Rowley, Augustus Chetlain, John Eugene Smith, Jasper Maltby, John C. Smith, and John Duer.

Townspeople gave Grant the massive U.S. Grant Home, at 500 Bouthillier Street, in 1879, after his presidency and after a world tour. It is on the National Register. Here he lived, cigar and all, until 1883 when he moved to New York. Ulysses S. Grant was buried in Grant's Tomb, in Riverside Park in New York City.

Today Galena is a major summer vacation destination, a routine subject for *Midwest Today* and other such magazines. People are drawn not only by history and architecture but by endless shopping opportunities along Galena's Main Street, by fine and decorative arts, by local wine and food, and by festivals and other occasions. As a Grand Illinois Trail destination, Galena is a bit of a treat along the way.

This northwest corner of Illinois is unlike any other place in the state. It is unlike any place in the Midwest. Jo Daviess County (named after an heroic Kentucky lawyer) is a place where roads curve and wander, where cattle grace the hillsides and barns look picture-perfect. It is simply—amazingly and breathtakingly—scenic. It makes you start wondering what all it would take to become a farmer. Jo Daviess County is a visual relief if you have gotten tired of always viewing a flat Illinois, and it is a chance to fly a bit closer to the cloud line.

An old-time Galena newspaper writer noted: "On rambling through Galena I have been particularly struck with the unique, wild, picturesque appearance which it presents, unlike that of any place I ever visited."

Circumnavigating Jo Daviess County is a skill to be learned. The only significant automobile traffic in the county comes and goes along U.S. Route 20 or Illinois Route 84 along the Mississippi River. God calls the shots when it comes to local geography. Highway engineers can only do so much when it comes to straight and level roadways.

The west side of Stephenson County is the west edge of the glacier field, and so you start finding the countryside getting flatter as you head east.

The terrain in Jo Daviess County presents no easy solutions for trail builders and trail users. The Grand Illinois Trail here is routed so that the high-volume roads are generally avoided. On a map, you see few straight roads. County blacktops make up the trail here. And they can be steep and challenging, so dismounting may make sense along the way.

There are two official Grand Illinois Trail routes from Galena to Rockford, one for mountain bikes and one for road bikes. Both routes are exceptionally hilly and present plenty of fine opportunities for cardio workouts. This is a little bit of Switzerland in the Midwest; the Illinois Alps. Feel strong (and unusual) if you do not dismount and walk at least a few of these hills. The positive thing here is the high speed you can achieve going downhill!

Following the Trail to Rockford

The Road Bike Route

From Galena take West Stagecoach Trail Road (also called County Route 3) east. This can be found in Galena by taking Main Street east to Meeker Street, and then turning south on Meeker and picking up Claude Street. This is a short street, and it gets renamed Field Street. And outside of town, Field Street gets called West Stagecoach Trail Road.

Continue on West Stagecoach Trail Road (County Route 3) all the way to the town of Apple River, Illinois. You should see some "Stagecoach Trail" signs along the way.

County Route 3 runs 13 miles east to Scales Mound and then another 11 miles to Apple River, Illinois. This road is an old stagecoach road, where miners and mine workers would take wagons of lead ore to be melted down in Galena. This is the route of the old Frink & Walker Stagecoach Line, formed in 1829 to take lead from these hills to Chicago. It used to take a wagon and mule team about 11 days to cart the lead to Chicago, and only eight days for the return trip, a little richer, a lot lighter.

One-way passenger tickets were $10, and passengers would sometimes have to walk alongside the wagon as it went through tough spots on the route. A ferry operating in Rockford shuttled wagons across the Rock River.

Scales Mound is just south of Charles Mound, the highest elevation in the state of Illinois, at 1,235 feet above sea level. The whole town of Scales Mound is on the National Register of

Historic Places. Scales Mound, population 401, was established in 1855, and the town, along with another local mound, was named for town founder Samuel H. Scales.

Apple River, population 379, was incorporated in 1876, and the town is proud of its quality of life. It was settled in the 1830s and became a fully established farming center once the Illinois Central railroad came to town in 1854. It is possible to take an authentic stagecoach ride in Apple River at Stage Coach Trails Livery.

In town limits, East Stagecoach Trail Road is Hickory Street. Follow this east for about 1.6 miles to reach North Canyon Park Road. North Canyon Park Road joins East Stagecoach Trail Road for just a short distance until it again bends south directly to Apple River Canyon State Park.

This extremely scenic state park packs a pretty big punch. It ranges across 297 acres of dolomite bluffs, pretty streams and hills. You can find plenty of wildflowers here. The 523-acre park was bought by the state in 1932—one of many developed during the Depression years and Roosevelt's conservation interest. The park was formed when a glacier lake on Apple River burst. The pounding of lake water ripped through the riverbed, tore out a canyon and diverted the course of the Apple River.

The park is home to a broad carpet of spring wildflowers. Come in early spring, around April or early May, and you can find up to 165 different kinds of wildflowers here, tiny concentrations of color and form, delicate bits of grace. It is possible to even find the rare bird's-eye primrose at Apple River State Park. There are some 500 different herbaceous species here. The park includes five short trails, a concession stand and 47 Class C campsites here, without water.

A tiny town, Millville, was here at the park location many years ago, a stop on the stagecoach trail. Bypassed by the Illinois Central, the town clung here until 1892 when it was scattered by a flood.

From Apple River Canyon State Park, take East Canyon Road (County Route 18) east all the way to the Jo Daviess/Stephenson County line. At the county line, all of a sudden East Canyon Road gets renamed West Fisher Road. Stay on West Fisher Road and go east until you come to North Five Corners Road/Route 176.

At this point, head south on Five Corners Road. You can access Lake Le-Aqua-Na State Park off of Five Corners Road, but the main entrance is at the east side of the park. The lake here is 40-acres in size, with a swimming beach, and it is a good place to spend an outdoor weekend. There are 178 Class A and B campsites here, with showers and electricity available.

From Five Corners Road, the Grand Illinois Trail route turns onto West Pin Hook Road. Take West Pin Hook Road to West Lake Road. This blacktop reaches Illinois Route 73, and then it gets a name change: West Lake Road is now West McConnell Road.

West McConnell Road takes you places. Out in Stephenson County, you can get on West McConnell Road and continue east, past the town of McConnell and onward to Buena Vista, Illinois. (McConnell Road is County Route 19).

Just south of the park is Lena, Illinois. Lena has two local cheese manufacturers, good places to visit, along with the Lena Area Historical Museum, a site featuring a blacksmith shop, a log schoolhouse, a barn exhibit and a chapel.

From Lake Le-Aqua-Na State Park, take West Lake Road east to McConnell Road. McConnell Road runs through McConnell. In order to stay on McConnell Road, be sure to take a hard right turn just past the McConnell Fire Department at the east end of town. Ahead is Buena Vista, Illinois.

Buena Vista was a stop on the Illinois Central spur that ran north to Madison picking up milk, delivering southern Illinois coal, and occasionally taking football fans up to see the Badgers in action. It is now a bedroom community to Freeport. Buena Vista has trailhead parking here for the Jane Addams Trail. Here you pick up the Jane Addams Trail and head south if you are on a bike with durable tires. The Jane Addams Trail is a limestone-screened surface running south to its trailhead at U.S. Route 20 just north of Freeport.

If you are on a road bike or racing bike with very thin or lightweight tires, you can avoid the perils of the limestone path by continuing east on McConnell Road. After crossing Illinois Route 26, pick up North Henderson Road. This road is a straight shot into Cedarville and then Freeport. Visit the Cedarville Historical Museum on Cherry Street to see a permanent exhibition on Jane Addams. Her burial site is at Mill Street in the Cedarville Cemetery. Her father's house, the <u>John Addams House</u> (1850), is at 425 N. Mill Street. It is on the National Register.

The Mountain Bike Route

The Mountain Bike Route mainly gets its name because a couple of parts run on gravel country roads. These roads, though, are not difficult for touring bikes since they are fairly hard packed. Most of the roads are in excellent and above average condition. Some of the roads have hard shoulders, and most have gravel shoulders.

From downtown Galena, take Meeker Street south to Claude Street. Claude becomes Field Street. Take Field Street east out of town, and it becomes West Stagecoach Trail.

Take West Stagecoach Trail/County Route 3 to North Miner Road and head south. This is about five and half miles from Galena. Pick up West Heller Lane. This road becomes West Guilford Road and leads into Guilford.

As you go through the county, cows in the shade will gravely observe your procession. The traffic along the way can be heavy on weekends along this route, at least until you past the <u>Galena Territory</u> resort area about eight miles outside of Galena.

Heading east from Guilford, West Guilford Road becomes West Rawlins Road. Take Rawlins to North Elizabeth Scales Mound Road/County Route 4. Get on this road and head north to West Schapville Road/County Route 15. West Schapville Road runs into Schapville at about 15 miles from Galena. The road then gets a new name, East Schapville Road, as it heads east. It intersects with North Scout Camp Road/County Route 9 about four miles east of Schapville. Here turn south and then quickly pick up East Townsend Road. This road runs to North Canyon Park Road/ County Route 18.

North Canyon Road runs directly north to <u>Apple River Canyon State Park</u> (see park description above). North Canyon Road is an improved road with fast traffic. This is about 28 miles from Galena. Right near the park—just uphill from the park area by the river—is East Canyon Road.

East Canyon Road becomes gravel about five miles from the state park. It is graveled from North Mammoser Road to Crossroads Road for a distance of about nine miles.

At the county line, East Canyon Road gets renamed West Fisher Road. Note that Fisher Road takes a quick jog south on Crossroads Road, returning quickly to Fisher Road. Stay on Fisher until it reaches North Five Corners Road. Here you will see the red arrowhead sign announcing the <u>Stephenson-Black Hawk Trail</u>.

Head south on North Five Corners until you reach West Pin Hook Road. <u>Lake Le-Aqua-Na State Park</u> is just past this point.

Take West Pin Hook Road (a gravel road) east about a mile and a half to meet Lake Road/County Route 7. After crossing Illinois Route 73, the road is called West McConnell Road. This road, West McConnell, will take you through McConnell and on to the Buena Vista trailhead of the Jane Addams Trail. McConnell is almost 47 miles from Galena.

Note that McConnell Road takes a hard right at the McConnell Fire Station at the end of town, and McConnell Road runs past the local feed store. Run McConnell Road for about 2.5 miles out to the Jane Addams access point at Buena Vista (pronounced *Boon-a* Vista).

The total distance of the Northwest Mountain Bike Route is 49.9 miles.

GALENA TO JANE ADDAMS TRAIL (ROAD BIKE ROUTE)

Main Street/Galena north to Meeker Street
Meeker Street east to Field Street
Field Street west to West Stagecoach Trail Road
West Stagecoach Trail Road/County Road 3 east to Hickory Street/Apple River
Hickory Street east to East Stagecoach Trail Road
East Stagecoach Trail Road east to North Canyon Road
North Canyon Road south to East Sweet Home Road
East Sweet Home Road east to North Canyon Road
North Canyon Road south to Apple River Canyon State Park/East Canyon Road
East Canyon Road east to County Road 10
County Road 10 north to County Road 13/Warren
County Road 13/North Stagecoach Trail Road south to North Lake Road/Lena
North Lake Road north to West Lake Road
West Lake Road east to West McConnell Road
West McConnell Road east to Jane Addams Trail access at Buena Vista

Or to avoid using the Jane Addams Trail:

West McConnell Road east to North Henderson Road
North Henderson Road south to Freeport

From Jane Addams Trail to Galena

Jane Addams Trail/U.S. Route 20 to Buena Vista Trailhead/ West McConnell Road
West McConnell Road west to West Lake Road
West Lake Road west to North Lake Road
North Lake Road south to West Galena Road/County Route 6
West Galena Road/County Route 6 northwest to North Stagecoach Trail/County Route 13
North Stagecoach Trail northwest to South Railroad Street/Warren
South Railroad Street northwest to Francis Street
Francis Street west to Pearl Street
Pearl Street south to East Jefferson Street
East Jefferson Street west to South Water Street
South Water Street north to Galena Avenue
Galena Avenue west to Morse Road
Morse Road south to North Fiedler Road/County Route 10
North Fiedler Road south to East Canyon Road
East Canyon Road west to North Canyon Road/Apple River State Park
North Canyon Road north to East Sweet Home Road
East Sweet Home Road west to North Canyon Road
North Canyon Road north to East Stagecoach Trail Road
East Stagecoach Trail Road west to Hickory Street/Apple River
Hickory Street west to West Stagecoach Trail Road/County Route 3
West Stagecoach Trail Road west to Field Street/Galena
Field Street west to Meeker Street
Meeker Street northwest to Main Street in Galena

GALENA TO JANE ADDAMS TRAIL
(MOUNTAIN BIKE ALTERNATE ROUTE)

West Stagecoach Trail Road east to North Miner Road
North Miner Road south to West Guilford Road
West Guilford Road east to West Rawlings Road
West Rawlings Road east to North Elizabeth Scales Mount Road
North Elizabeth Scales Mount Road north to West Schapville Road
West Schapville Road east to East Schapville Road/Schapville
East Schapville Road east to North Scout Camp Road
North Scout Camp Road south to East Townsend Road
East Townsend Road east to North Canyon Park Road
North Canyon Road north to East Canyon Road
East Canyon Road/West Fisher Road east to Crossroads Road
Crossroads Road south to West Fisher Road
West Fisher Road east to North Five Corners Road
North Five Corners Road south to West Pin Hook Road
West Pin Hook Road east to West Lake Road
West Lake Road east to West McConnell Road
West McConnell Road east to Jane Addams Trail Access at Buena Vista

From Jane Addams Trail to Galena

Jane Addams Trail Access at Buena Vista west on West McConnell Road
West McConnell Road west to West Lake Road
West Lake Road west to West Pin Hook Road
West Pin Hook Road west to North Five Corners Road
North Five Corners Road north to West Fisher Road
West Fisher Road west to Crossroads Road
Crossroads Road north to West Fisher Road/East Canyon Road
East Canyon Road west to North Canyon Road
North Canyon Road south to East Townsend Road
East Townsend Road west to North Scout Camp Road
North Scout Camp Road west to East Schapville Road
East Schapville Road/Schapville west to West Schapville Road
West Schapville Road west to North Elizabeth Scales Mound Road
North Elizabeth Scales Mound Road south to West Rawlings Road
West Rawlings Road west to West Guilford Road/Guilford
West Guilford Road west to North Miner Road
North Miner Road north to West Stagecoach Trail Road
West Stagecoach Trail Road west to Field Street/Galena
Field Street west to Meeker Street
Meeker Street north to Main Street in Galena

Jane Addams Trail

If you were a (Hull House) resident, it would not be at all unusual to move over the course of a day from reading George Eliot, to debating Karl Marx, to washing newborns, to readying the dead for burial, to nursing the sick, to minding the children.

—Jean Bethke Elshtain

The North Section of the Grand Illinois Trail leads to the Jane Addams Trail just north of Freeport.

Abraham Lincoln called her father "the Addams with two 'ds.'" At that time, John Addams was a state senator and a local leader in the new Republican Party and he ran a flourmill on the Cedar River. His daughter Jane was a leader as well, organizing and operating Hull House in Chicago over a hundred years ago. Hull House became internationally known as an innovative community-based provider of education and social services to Chicago's burgeoning immigrant population. Most people talk about doing it, but Jane Addams really made the world around her a better place.

She was born in the northern Illinois town of Cedarville in 1860. Her father was a miller and he operated a wheat and corn mill on the Cedar Creek. Jane attended Rockford College and made the grand tour of Europe after graduation. She developed Hull House with Ellen Gates Starr in 1889 after having seen London settlement houses. A world-famous pacifist, she received the Nobel Prize for Peace in 1931.

Jane Addams, Chicago's great philanthropist and social leader, was born and buried in Cedarville, Illinois just north of Freeport. Addams' work at Hull House promoted democratic values in the new industrial age. (Photo courtesy of the Illinois State Historical Library).

Addams died in 1935, world famous for her great philanthropic labors, and she is buried in the Cedarville Cemetery.

Dedicated in 2002, the Jane Addams Trail runs for 12.4 miles along a former spur of the Illinois Central railroad. The trail is ten-foot wide limestone screening. Several roads cross at grade level. There are many wooden bridges along the way. Most of the route is pleasantly shaded by trees with plenty of good sun blocking overhead.

The Jane Addams Trail has strong scenic values. Here we find prairie plants along the way, some planted, some growing wild. The actual trail route was developed as roadbed for the Illinois Central. The IC ran freight trains loaded with coal and cattle-feed to points in Wisconsin and Freeport, Illinois was a regional headquarters for the railroad. One railroad retiree has recalled 60 unit trains would haul coal to the University of Wisconsin, and that at times there would be special excursion trains into Wisconsin.

You could easily be in southern Wisconsin, and, in fact, the Jane Addams Trail may soon be continued north into Monroe, Wisconsin where additional connections lead to Madison. Planning has been completed for a continuation of the Jane Addams Trail into Wisconsin called the "Badger Trail". This trail connection is awaiting funding.

Overall, the Jane Addams Trail seems ready-made for family outings and recreation riding. The trail runs through beautiful farm country, a level roadbed through a gently rolling hillside. Farmers here raise hay as well as corn and beans. Richland Creek makes an appearance at points along the trail, a modest and quiet stream. The trailbed has a few adjacent wetland areas.

Following the Jane Addams Trail

The Jane Addams Trail runs North-South through the Richland Creek greenway. It is a ten-foot limestone screened path. It runs through a number of small towns up to Orangeville, Illinois. It meets the Grand Illinois Trail routing at Buena Vista, Illinois.

The Freeport Park District built the Wes Block trailhead for the Jane Addams Trail to be north of town just off U.S. Route 20. This trailhead is easily seen from the road, on the south side of U.S. Route 20, and it is about two miles east of the U.S. Route 20/Illinois Route 26 intersection. There is parking for over 20 cars at the trailhead.

Plans call to join the Jane Addams Trail directly to the Freeport, Illinois trail system. This would be done by pushing the trail route south along the Pecatonica River corridor to Tutty's Crossing just north of downtown Freeport near Taylor Park.

Starting from the Wes Block trailhead, it is just over a half mile to a scenic little rock outcropping of the ancient Pennsylvanian dolomite that underlies the countryside.

At 1.2 miles, there is a road crossing, with Winneshiek Road. A quarter-mile west on Winneshiek is a scenic little slough, Duck's Misery Slough, which, a child on the trail suggests, is the place where pike bite off the duck's feet as they paddle in the water.

This stretch is reasonably well shaded, running through established trees.

A wood bridge comes up at 1.6 miles out, a simple bridge over a country streamlet. Just past this, at 1.8 miles, is a road crossing, at grade, with Iris Hill Road.

The tiny hamlet of Scioto Mills is right on the trail at about two miles out. There is a fine relic grain elevator here, wood planking with a native stone foundation, and corrugated steel peeling from its sides. It is around this point that you will encounter Richland Creek, a meandering stream that wiggles and worms its way south from Wisconsin. In straight miles, it is perhaps ten miles to the Illinois-Wisconsin border. But Richland Creek could easily be twice this in length, if its silly string of a streambed could be picked up and pulled straight.

Three miles past Scioto Mills is a good view from the bottom of the morainal valley. A backwaters here has large, bold frogs popping up to look around.

The Cedarville Road appears at 3.2 miles. It is a busy road. Cedarville, Jane Addams' hometown, is about 1.5 miles east on the Cedarville blacktop. The John H. Addams Homestead, at 425 N. Mill Street, is on the National Register of Historic Places. The Cedarville Historical Society is at the corner of Mill and Cherry Streets, and it keeps a permanent Jane Addams display.

At around 4.5 miles, there is a pair of wooden bridges. Just ahead is Beaver Road, with the trail passing through the crossroad community of Red Oak. There are a few houses making up the town, a quiet place of its own.

Continuing north, a trail rider will encounter another wood bridge and just pass this, Elassar Road. Here, adjacent to the trail is "the Bottoms". Note the <u>Illinois Central caboose</u> placed next to the trail and converted to a new use.

Richland Road crosses the Jane Addams Trail at 6.5 miles from the Wes Block trailhead. This area is good for nature study. At 7.6 miles out is a road crossing to the right, with a bit of Richland Creek on the left. At 7.9 miles out is one of the most scenic portions of the trail—a section carved through native bedrock. Here it is cool and damp in spots, with tree branches forming a high canopy over the trail. This is a hard-to-find microenvironment, and ferns do well in it.

There is another bridge at eight miles out. And just a half-mile ahead, more exposed rock. At 9.2 and 9.6 miles are more wood bridges running the route over prairie low spots. There is a fine valley view. A blacktop road crossing at 9.7 miles is McConnell Road, and this is Buena Vista, Illinois.

Note: The official Grand Illinois Trail route takes off at this point, taking McConnell Road and leaving the Jane Addams Trail and heading west toward Jo Daviess County and Galena. McConnell Road is moderately traveled two-lane county road. Ten miles west on McConnell Road is Le-Aqua-Na State Park.

Further on, past the Grand Illinois Trail junction, the Jane Addams Trail runs north to Orangeville, Illinois.

About ten miles from the Wes Block trailhead there is a rock outcrop at the left side of the trail. Past this are interesting prairie plants. These are thriving, and include coneflowers and cup plant. Birds pick at the chokeberry. You can pull back the leaves of a cup plant and see that, true to its name, a large amount of water is held by its leaves. You will notice a golf course, <u>Brush Creek</u>, to the immediate west of the trail.

Be careful and exercise caution at the trail intersection with Illinois Rt. 26. This is a busy, slightly curving road through the valley. Give yourself plenty of time to get across.

Just past this intersection, at 11.1 miles, is a good place to view that hillside to the west. This large exposed rock face is a reminder of an early stone quarry. The Jane Addams Trail continues north, crossing over a few more wood bridges. Note the old wood telephone poles that follow alongside the trail at

Opening day on the Jane Addams Trail brought out local leaders to enjoy the ribbon-cutting.

some points—this was a private telephone line used by the Illinois Central.

At 12.4 miles from the Wes Block Trailhead, the Jane Addams Trail comes to Orangeville, Illinois. You are merely 2.5 miles as the crow flies from the Wisconsin state line. The trail ends here at the Richland Creek trailhead, a large site donated by Harry Bowen at 1850 N. Orangeville Road/1415E/Ewing Street intersection. The trailhead has enough parking for perhaps 30 cars and is near a convenient store/gas station.

Freeport to Rockford

By Road and Pecatonica Path

The Jane Addams Trail is located immediately north of Freeport, with the Wes Block Trailhead along U.S. Route 20. From here local roads access Freeport. Long-term planning envisions an off-road connection through the Pecatonica River greenway to Tutty's Crossing and downtown Freeport.

Freeport, Illinois, population 26,443, was first established in 1835 and incorporated in 1855. It is the county seat of Stephenson County.

Freeport will always be remembered for the "Freeport Doctrine" elaborated by Abraham Lincoln. It was on a warm August day in 1858 that Lincoln made this famous challenge in the second of seven debates with Stephen Douglas. Where the Ottawa debate had no clear winner, in Freeport it was all Lincoln. Here Lincoln pressed the crucial point: "Can the people of a United States territory, in any lawful way, against the wish of any citizen of the United States, exclude slavery from its limits prior to the formation of a State Constitution." Douglas' reply, affirming that people could choose or reject slavery lost him support in the North and South: neither much liked the idea that slavery or complete freedom could be merely a choice to be voted up or down.

The energy and excitement in that Senatorial election was unbelievable. The Little Giant, Stephen Douglas, was a national leader of the Democratic Party. He was a long-time genius of Illinois politics, and he was critically wounded. The political firmament was rattled as well. Freeport recalls this critical event with the Leonard Crunelle statue, *Lincoln the Debater*, in Taylor's Park. This was dedicated by Teddy Roosevelt in 1902.

Freeport was a major stop on the Chicago to Galena stagecoach run, and the town was settled just as the Black Hawk War was over. The Grand Illinois Trail route is slated to be pushed through to Tutty's Crossing. This is the location of a ferryboat operated by Tutty Baker, one of the area's early settlers. Tutty would ferry people and wagons across the Pecatonica River for free. He was an innkeeper and expected his grateful passengers would stay for supper.

Many of the houses in Freeport retain their historical character, and the Oscar Taylor House at 1440 S. Carroll Avenue is on the National Register, along with the fascinating Soldiers' Monument at 15 N. Galena Avenue. The Old River School Historic Neighborhood, at Galena's Northeast side, contains Tutty's old inn.

The town is also known as the original home of the Newell Companies (now Newell Rubbermaid), a major conglomerate of household fixtures and office supply companies. A Honeywell microswitch division is here, along with Kelly Springfield Tire Company, Sauer-Danfoss and the C.J. Vitner Company, makers of great potato chips.

Freeport's downtown is jammed with charm and antique and gift shops.

The Trail from Freeport to Rockford

There are two different routes that make up the Grand Illinois Trail between Freeport and Rockford. Current Grand Illinois Trail routing sweeps around the northeast corner of Freeport and leads to two trail route options.

The road section takes low volume county roads east into Rockford. The Pecatonica Prairie Path is a pleasant off-road trail useful for hikers and mountain bikers. The Pecatonica Path is an abandoned Chicago & Northwestern railbed that is now used as a utility and nature corridor, and it runs through Ridott, Pecatonica and Winnebago. The Pec Path is 21 miles long and is great for viewing wildlife. Especially cottontail rabbits.

Pecatonica Path

Beginning at the Jane Addams Trail's Wes Block trailhead, ride up and cross U.S. Route 20. The visibility is good but the traffic is fast, so watch before crossing.

Take Fairview across and follow the road as it takes an immediate right. This takes you up a good-sized hill that leads in and through a rural subdivision. At two miles out, you cross Illinois Route 26. The road here snakes around a bit and a small quarry is near this point. The Henderson Road intersection is three miles out, and at around five miles from the Wes Block trailhead is the Illinois Route 75/Alfolkey Road intersection. Take Alfolkey Road south to Maize Road (Maize is the fourth road on the left side, heading east, in a small country subdivision). Maize curves around a bit, and you should pass by a United Steel Workers of America union hall.

Eight miles out is Dakota Road. This is the road that you are looking for, since it heads south right to the Pecatonica Path. Just over a mile down Dakota is the start of the Pec Path. It is just exactly what a green, grassy utility corridor should look like.

Get on the Pecatonica Path and just about two miles later you will cross the Pecatonica River on an old iron truss bridge. The Pecatonica River is a funny kind of brown creek. It wiggles its way from Wisconsin, drips through Illinois and then squirms right back north to Badgerland. It is shallow and shy, with a north-flowing stream.

At 12.6 miles from the Wes Block trailhead is Ridott, Illinois, with a population of 159 and incorporated in 1874. At 15.5 miles out you come to Farwell Bridge Road. Just ahead are the <u>Winnebago County Forest Preserve</u> lands that are adjacent to the trail, making this a decent birding spot.

Pecatonica, a lovely little northern Illinois town, is 18.6 miles from the trailhead. With a population of 1,997, Pecatonica was incorporated in 1869. You will enter town through the fairgrounds. <u>Summer Park</u> in Pecatonica just past this makes a good stop, with restrooms and water available. Proceeding through town you may notice that the old grain elevator is now the Pec Playhouse Theater. The <u>William H. Roberts House</u> at 523 Main Street is on the National Register of Historic Places. The path through town runs the risk of turning into backyard space and could use formal definition. At Third Street, take Taylor Street to pick up the Pec Path.

At almost 23 miles from Freeport on the Pec Path is an unavoidable danger—crossing busy U.S. Route 20. The road is posted at 65 mph, but real-life traffic moves much faster than this. It is a separate four-lane with whizzing cars and trucks. Take your time crossing it. Cross the first two lanes, then wait again to cross the last pair.

On the Pec Path, continue east for about 1.5 miles and you come out on a staggered country road intersection. Directly across the roads is the Pec Path, so jump on the roads merely to make the connection. Continue into Winnebago, Illinois.

Winnebago, Illinois has a population of 2,958 and it was incorporated in 1855. It is a bedroom community to Rockford. The town boomed as the railroad was built, attracting settlers from New England, Canada, England and Scotland. The town was named for the Winnebago Indian tribe. There is a nice park downtown, with water and restrooms about 26 miles from the Wes Block trailhead.

At 29.9 miles from Freeport is Meridian Road. This busy North-South is at the very west edge of Rockford and to travel into Rockford, take Meridian Road south for about a quarter mile to its intersection with Cunningham Road. Cunningham runs directly into downtown Rockford.

A 1.2 mile-long Davis-Pecatonica Path is planned to provide an off-street connection between the Pecatonica Path and the Rock River Recreation Path.

Road Route

The road route between the Jane Addams Trail and Rockford is the easier trek.

Starting at the Wes Block trailhead, cross U.S. Route 20, get on Fairview Road and follow it east through a hilly rural subdivision. Two miles out, you cross Illinois Route 26. An intersection with Henderson Road is three miles from the Wes Block trailhead, and two miles further from this point is the Illinois Route 75/Alfolkey Road intersection. Take Alfolkey south to Maize Road. Turn left heading east on Maize Road, and about eight miles from the Wes Block trailhead is Dakota Road.

Follow Dakota Road south to River Road. Take River Road east for three miles (it winds a bit) to Rock City Road. Rock City Road goes south through Ridott, and crosses U.S. Route 20.

At 17.4 miles from the Wes Block trailhead in Freeport, pick up Edwardsville Road. This is an 15.5 mile-long East-West blacktop that takes you directly to Rockford, right up to Meridian Road on the city's west side.

At Meridian Road, turn north and go about two miles up to reach Cunningham Road. Follow Cunningham into Rockford.

JANE ADDAMS TRAIL / ROCKFORD ROAD ROUTE

JANE ADDAMS TRAIL TO ROCKFORD ROAD ROUTE

Jane Addams Trail/Wes Block Trailhead north and east on Fairview Road
Fairview Road east to Alfolkey Road
Alfolkey Road south to Maize Road
Maize Road east to Dakota Road
Dakota Road south to River Road
River Road east to Rock City Road
Rock City Road south to Edwardsville Road
Edwardsville Road east to Meridian Road
Meridian Road north to Cunningham Road
Cunningham Road east to Cunningham Street/downtown Rockford

ROCKFORD TO JANE ADDAMS TRAIL

Cunningham Street to Cunningham Road
Cunningham Road west to Meridian Road
Meridian Road south to Edwardsville Road
Edwardsville Road west to Rock City Road
Rock City Road north to River Road
River Road west to Dakota Road
Dakota Road north to Maize Road
Maize Road west to Alfolkey Road
Alfolkey Road north to Fairview Road
Fairview Road west to Jane Addams Trail Wes Block Trailhead

A War, A Canal, and A Plow. . .

Three things opened up Northern Illinois to settlement. First came the Black Hawk War, a final effort by Native Americans to resist American settlers. When the war was over, the federal government made the land available for purchase.

The Erie Canal, the wonder of the world in upstate New York, opened up the Midwest to the Atlantic seaboard. You could ship Michigan lumber and Illinois wheat to New York and Boston markets. The Erie opened in 1825 and it was an immediate success. Along with freight heading east came passengers heading west. Many passengers were native New Englanders, sons of farmers of rocky soil. Many were immigrants who had heard of the West and its opportunities. Both groups came to Illinois eager to farm the boundless prairies.

But John Deere provided the final and essential ingredient in this mix. His self-scouring, blade-cleaning steel plow was tough enough to cut through the dense prairie soil. This earth was black and rich from thousands of years of prairie grass growth. It took Deere's "path-breaking" technology to bust the sod and allow for farming on the high prairies of Illinois.

The Prairie Ecosystem

The Illinois Country is the furthest east edge of the prairie system that extends across the west, and pioneers had their first experience of prairie in Illinois. At one time a great swath of prairie waved and swayed in Illinois, covering about 60% of its land area. Times change. The first farmers in Illinois avoided farming prairie ground. Not only did they think it was not very fertile, but their plows simply could not cut through the thousand-year growth of prairie grass roots.

The Grand Illinois Trail runs through some of the best and largest prairie areas in Illinois. The Illinois Prairie Path has many prairie gardens. Prairie grasses wave along the Long Prairie Trail, and the Goose Lake Prairie is near the Illinois & Michigan Canal Trail. The Midewin National Tallgrass Prairie is under development outside of Joliet.

Prairie has its own charms. A typical prairie offers a changing selection of flowers. Recent "re-prairie-station" efforts try to revivify dormant seeds, some of which are more than fifty years old. This is done in wetland areas by restoring natural water flows to the area. In uplands, the seedbank can come to life simply by turning over the very top layer of soil in order to get rid of existing weeds.

There are three main types of plants found in prairies and prairie plantings. These include:

Grasses
Prairie is best known, and for most people is defined by, the tall and exotic prairie grasses. These are grasses of the *poaceae* family. It is the grasses that make Illinois soil rich and black. Prairie grass has a high silicon oxide level, to keep the grass stiff enough to resist high winds. And grass can reproduce sexually, through seeds, and asexually, using rhizomes to spread.

Grasses reach to seven or eight feet high. Their roots penetrate up to 12 feet deep in the ground. Prairie grasses are either "cool season" or "warm season." Cool season grasses grow earlier in the year, beginning in the spring and maturing in April. Warm season grasses, such as big and little bluestem, grow in late spring and mature in the fall.

Legumes
Legumes are nitrogen-fixing plants, so they provide nutrition to the topsoil. Legumes that appear in prairies include prairie clovers, peas, gentians and indigos.

Composites
Composites are usually asters, or members of the *aseraceae* family. Asters make up more species than any other plants in a prairie. They range across many different kinds of soil conditions, in a variety of habitats. Some asters are colonizers and move into new territory, while other varieties stay put.

Rockford City System

Rock Cut State Park to the Pecatonica Path

Rockford, Illinois, seat of Winnebago County, was first settled in 1835 and chartered in 1852. The city has a population of 150,115 in a metropolitan area of 371,236.The Rock River runs through it and the river made the city. Rockford is exactly that—a fording place across the Rock River. Here the river water rushes along a bedrock channel bottom. You can see the yellow dolomite sticking out in places along the trail here.

The Chicago to Galena stagecoach road ran here, heading from Lake Michigan shores to the mining boomtown of Galena. Initially, there were two towns at Rockford, the first, by Germanicus Kent, called "Kentville" was formed in 1834, as soon as white settlers would brave living out in the open in lands formerly prized by the Sauk and Fox and the Winnebagos. The next year, Mr. Daniel Shaw Haight built his very own "Haightville." There was an initial rivalry between the two townsites. Eventually, the first name for Rockford was "Midway Village," because the town was halfway between bustling Galena and Chicago.

A massive bronze tribute to the Founders' spirit is found in downtown Rockford. This is a sculptural grouping of Germanicus Kent, Thatcher Blake and Lewis Lamon located downtown at the intersection of Main, Wyman and Green streets.

The river provided waterpower in a serious fashion. Soon enough there were local milling operations along the river—sawmills, gristmills—and the city-built Rockford Water Power Company. Rockford became a manufacturing center.

There was talk and plans for improving the Rock River, scraping the rocky bottom and making it better for commercial river traffic. And in the early days there was some bright-eyed speculation about building a canal ninety miles east to Chicago.

The city of Rockford was incorporated in 1852 but not without misgivings. Dissatisfied with South-sympathizers in the rest of Illinois, and certainly not a part of Chicago, Winnebago County voted in 1842 to secede from Illinois and join the Wisconsin Territory.

It was from the start a heavily Scandinavian and German community. The Galena and Chicago Union Railroad brought them. The railroad ran from Chicago out to a Rockford terminus in 1852. And at the same time there was heavy Swedish immigration to America. The Swedes would simply go west as far as they could to the end of the line. They were carpenters and craftsmen and their highly-skilled labor and no-nonsense tack built the town.

Reenacters portray classic battles in Rockford during Civil War Days. Rockford was a bastion of Union support. (Photo courtesy of the Illinois State Historical Library).

The Scandinavian political impact was immediate then and it can still be felt now. Rockford was abolitionist in the Civil War. It developed a moderately progressive social tradition, and the city once elected a socialist mayor. It was home to John B. Anderson, the moderate who ran as an Independent for president in 1980. Lynn Martin represented Rockford in Congress, and became Secretary of Labor during the Reagan era.

There was also an upstate New York presence among these early settlers. These groups all held a natural sympathy for the Union cause during the Civil War. In fact, before the war the young bucks of Rockford established a military drill team, the Rockford Zouaves, which won national merit. The Zouaves were led by Elmer Ellsworth, an athletic guy who was Lincoln's bodyguard for only a short while before becoming the first official Union casualty of the Civil War.

Rockford became an industrial city chiefly because of the Swedish influence. The growing river city made farm implements, hosiery and furniture (a "Rockford Side-by-Side" is a combination writing desk with side bookcase). The city had a peculiar magic—local capital invested locally, combined with a talented and well-motivated workforce, met with great success and economic growth for the community. The town exploded. It tripled in size from 1850 to 1860. There were factories like mad—everywhere there were factories.

The list of industries doing business in Rockford is impressive. John H. Manny brought his Manny reaper company to Rockford in 1853. The 1870's saw an explosion of furniture companies, large and small, all taking Wisconsin lumber and making new furniture for burned-out

A look at early downtown Rockford. Today the city celebrates its architectural history at Midway Village. (Photo courtesy of the Illinois State Historical Library).

Chicago households and for a national market. Nelson Knitting Co. developed seamless socks (a technological wonderment in those days) in 1880. Ingersoll Milling Machine Company, a great maker of machine tools, moved here from Cleveland in 1891 and was a long-time star of the Rockford establishment. Other companies arrived with the turn-of-the-century. Elco Tool was formed in 1918. Sundstrand also was formed in 1918, built around a simple adding machine product. In 1928, Borg-Warner was formed here.

Rockford leaders built Camp Grant as a regional training center for World War I, and tens of thousands of doughboys hustled through town on their way to France.

Rockford is home to Rockford College, a small liberal arts school that began as a female-only seminary attached to male-only Beloit College. Old-time accounts tell of pleasant wintertime sleigh ride parties between the schools.

An amazing early business leader was Pehr August Peterson, a smart Swede who by the end of his life was president of nine companies and owned parts of 50 other companies.

Phillip Wrigley, owner of the Chicago Cubs, formed the Rockford Peaches in 1943, a women's baseball team that played professionally for 12 years and remembered in the movie *A League of Their Own*. Perhaps Wrigley built on the city's keen interest in baseball. Her "Forest City Nine" were the self-declared Amateur Champions of the World in 1867 and 1869.

In the 1960s Rockford outstripped Peoria to be Illinois' second-largest city. This was a great era for Rockford, a time when Rockford could call itself the metal fastener capital of the world, or as some joked, "the screw capital of the world."

Rockford was called the Forest City due to a great concentration of residential street trees. Due to its ethnic communities and their settlement, the city for many years had five distinct commercial regions.

Global competition in the 1970s and 1980s hit Rockford manufacturers hard. The city rated low on *Money* magazine's annual "Best Places to Live" list because of this. But the past decade has shown real improvement for Rockford.

Rockford today is home to Airguard Industries, Barnes International, Bergstrom, Cincinnati Tool Steel Company, Danfoss Drives, Dasco Pro, Dean Foods, Ello Furniture Manufacturing, FPM-DB Metals, Greenlee Textron, Gunite Corporation, Hamilton Sundstrand, Liebovich Brothers, Pacific Scientific, Rockford Products Corporation, Valspar and the W.A. Whitney Company, among others. The Dodge Neon automobile plant in nearby Belvidere is a major area employer. The city supplies world markets with precision cutting tools, fasteners, aerospace components, and machine parts. Rockford businesses make valves, gaskets, screws, bolts, castings and fasteners.

Rockford developed its first recreation path in 1976 as part of the city's Bicentennial celebration. The Rec Path was popular from the start and it is the town's great promenade. Everybody goes there. This core path runs from the Jefferson Street Pedestrian Bridge to the Auburn Street bridge, chiefly along the river. This is the finest portion of the Rockford city system since it runs next to the Rock River and along the riverside Sinnissippi Park.

Sinnissippi Park is the kind of city park that made up old-time postcard memories. It is a grand municipal park in the naturalistic, "Frederick Law Olmstead" manner, complete with floral plantings and winding roads with scenic vistas. The Rock River itself is busy in the summer with recreational boaters, fishermen and water skiers. You can walk through a formal rose garden, complete with porticoes and pergolas—and a quaint sundial contributed in 1923 by the white-gloved Daughters of the American Revolution. Or you can pause next to the park lagoon, observing the proud, cantankerous and very territorial white swans.

And here, too, are botanical displays at Sinnissippi Gardens and Greenhouse, along with the oddly beautiful "Rock Guardians of the Rock River" stone Vikings statue group next to the river. An actual old-time trolley, Trolley Car #36, takes people through the park; fun transportation at a reasonable pace and price.

The Rock River is the real star. It is a gorgeous, picture-perfect river, beautiful and sparkling on a summer's day. Founder's Landing at Davis Park is the site of the original river fording point.

Future plans for the Rockford City System call for more fully developing the path along the Rock River, as opportunities come up. There is a desire to take the trail to the Wisconsin border, where it can join with the existing Beloit, Wisconsin city trail system along the Rock River. The existing Perryville Path, running north and south through Rockford on the city's east side, may be extended up to, and beyond, Rock Cut State Park. Other pathways being considered will form a usable local transportation network.

Local planners are projecting an off-road trail that will run east through Rock Cut State Park and connect to the Long Prairie trail.

Rockford City System Trail

Much of the Rockford City System is along a ten-foot wide asphalt strip. It passes through several quiet, well-kept neighborhoods on local streets. These street routes are well marked.

Planners in Rockford have routed the city recreational path through city parks. The trail goes through Sinnissippi, Shorewood, Martin and Sportscore parks, as well as near the Winnebago County Forest Preserve District headquarters.

Start at Rock Cut State Park just northeast of Rockford in Loves Park. Rock Cut State Park is a 3,092-acre state park with attractive woodlands, a fine 162-acre recreational lake, Pierce Lake, and 50-acre Olson Lake for swimmers. You can find over 100 kinds of wildflowers here in the spring. There are accommodations for camping. Rock Cut has 14 miles of trail, including a 4.25-mile long main trail that circles Pierce Lake. There is a variety of camping options here, especially the rent-a-camp program.

Rock Cut State Park is accessed by Highway 173 or Harlem Road. From the Highway 173 entrance wind south to the Lakeview Day Use area. This has good parking (for about 20 cars) and trail access. It is next to the Willow Creek bike trail that will take you west into Rockford.

Rock Cut is a pretty state park, with a gorgeous blue main lake, ringed by heavy woods. You find sailboats gliding on the lake surface, and fishermen working the waters as well. Plenty of kids adventure along the lake, some checking out the wood ducks paddling by the lake spillway.

The <u>Willow Creek Trail</u> is asphalt and it winds alongside the creek. This makes for a fun, twisty ride through the woods. You can find some prairie plantings along the way as well as woodchucks.

The Willow Creek Trail goes under four-lane Perryville Road and enters residential subdivisions. Plans call for hooking up the Perryville Path with Willow Creek Trail just next to the trail underpass. It is expected that the Willow Creek Trail will be extended further west toward the river.

Just after the Forest Hills Road underpass you enter <u>Dennis Johnson Park,</u> a nice little subdivision park. There is drinking water available here.

At about three miles from Rock Cut State Park, you get to Harlem High School. From here, take Alpine Road (a main north-south road in Rockford) south to Roosevelt Road. Roosevelt is just after Sunset Memorial Chapel. Alpine is a busy street. Roosevelt is not.

Heading west on Roosevelt, cross North Second Street/Route 251 after another mile. You are now at Machesney Park Mall. Roosevelt Road is now called Machesney Road. Take this west to Victory Avenue, passing by Machesney Park Village Hall.

At the intersection of Machesney Road and Victory Avenue you should be able to see Marquette Elementary School. You are now about 5.5 miles from Rock Cut State Park.

Turn south (left) on to Victory Lane. The trail here is a striped local road, and follow this for about seven blocks south to the Frank Bauer Parkway. Take the Frank Bauer Parkway west to the river (note the curious colonial-style toll booths). You are now about 6.5 miles from Rock Cut.

The <u>Bauer Bridge Trail</u> is a kind of political landmark. Due to engineering work, and a novel design, the pedestrian/bicycle bridge cost $2 million. There was dismay over the price tag. But it is solid and well-built, and it takes you right across the river to the grounds of the <u>Winnebago County Forest Preserve District headquarters</u>.

At the headquarters is a small prairie restoration, one that lets you get up close to the various plants. The nice things here are the helpful markers that identify the plants. You can either take a path up to the headquarters or continue south along the river.

A short jog through residential streets takes you to the Rockford Park District's <u>Sportscore Park</u>, known officially as the "Greater Rockford Veterans Memorial Park and Sportscore." This is a great set of playing fields, and you can find baseball games and soccer games. Young children and old couples walked the pathway while Johnny played ball. There are permanent restrooms and water fountains in the park. The park has a small fishing lagoon.

The trail continues through the park to the west end, crossing over a set of rails. Here the path is a ten-foot asphalt strip, and it follows south along the west side of the Rock River.

Through this portion of the trail is a fine selection of trees. You can find tulip trees, black walnut, sugar maple and hackberry. There are even patches of raspberries growing wild and free.

Ahead there is exposed native stone, the old dolomite. And also a stone circle rest area in the woods.

A trail switchback brings you back up the river bluff and up to Riverside Boulevard. Across the way is <u>Cliffbreaker's Restaurant and Convention Center</u>. Cross busy Riverside Boulevard at the light just west (at Trilling Avenue) and head east to cross on the Riverside Boulevard bridge. Immediately after the bridge is <u>Peace Park/Martin Memorial Park</u>.

The path continues south along the river and then takes to Loves Park streets for short stretches. Take East Drive south. This street curves a bit and becomes Evelyn Avenue at <u>Shorewood Park</u>. Shorewood Park is one of the many city parks along the <u>Rock River</u>. This is a nice park just to sit in and take a break.

From Shorewood Park, take north-south Forest Grove Street south to Snow Avenue. Check out the stone house here. At the very next street, turn right, heading south, on Arlington Street. Arlington takes you quickly, in two long blocks, down to Illinois Street. And at Illinois Street, you arrive at Illinois Street Park.

Continue south. There are water, telephone and portable toilets here. The path is a 15-foot roadway, so rollerbladers are here.

This is River Park, just next to the Auburn Street Bridge. Just south is the main segment of the Rockford Rec Path.

This is the city's Great Promenade, a place where people meet and see each other. It is enormously popular, and the park amenities add to the mix.

The Rec Path runs through the riverfront side of Sinnissippi Park and it is a busy place. There are good spots to stop here and admire the river scenery.

Just after the Whitman Street Bridge, get on Madison Street, the next street from the river. Take Madison Street south to Prairie Street. At Prairie Street, you can jog back to the riverside trail. Ride past the ice rink and the YMCA. On the other side of the tennis courts is the Jefferson Street Pedestrian Bridge, which is a bridge that has a lower platform built just for pedestrian and bicyclist crossing. It looks great lit up at night.

Once across the Jefferson Street Bridge, follow Winnebago Street south to Cunningham Street. While you are on Winnebago Street, you will pass over a heavy-duty bridge that crosses over some railroad tracks.

Cunningham Street is the very first street at the end of the bridge. Tinker Park and the Tinker Swiss Cottage Museum are to the east. It is also possible at this point to see the Graham-Ginestra House (an 1857 limestone structure with a fine garden and heirloom roses) at 1118 S. Main Street and the Ethnic Heritage Museum at 1129 S. Main Street from this point, by just going through Tinker Park, picking up Kent Street and taking Kent Street east to Main Street.

To continue on the Trail, turn right on Cunningham heading west. The Trail route passes through a basic residential part of Rockford. Take Cunningham out of town. The street sticks fairly well close to the old Chicago and Northwestern Railway railbed.

At Meridian Road, you find the start of the Pecatonica Prairie Path. The Chicago & Northwestern Railroad formerly used this grassy corridor. It currently can be hiked and mountain biked. But it is a work-in-progress, and it will require some muscle and some cash to bring it up to standard.

ROCK CUT STATE PARK / MERIDIAN ROAD

FROM ROCK CUT STATE PARK TO MERIDIAN ROAD

Willow Creek Trail west (under Perryville Road)
   to Harlem High School/Alpine Road
Alpine Road south to Roosevelt Road
Roosevelt Road/Machesney Road west to
   Victory Lane
Victory Lane south to Frank Bauer Parkway
Frank Bauer Parkway to Bauer Bridge Trail/
   Rockford Trail System
Rockford Trail System south to East Drive/
   Loves Park city street
East Drive/Evelyn Avenue south to Shorewood
   Park
Shorewood Park to Forest Grove Street
Forest Grove Street south to Snow Avenue
Snow Avenue south to Arlington Street
Arlington Street south to Illinois Street
Illinois Street south to Illinois Street Park
Illinois Street Park south to Rockford Rec Path/
   Sinnissippi Park
RecPath south to Whitman Street Bridge/
   Madison Street
Madison Street south to Prairie Street
Prairie Street west to Rockford RecPath
Rockford Rec Path south to Jefferson Street
   Bridge
Jefferson Street Bridge west to Winnebago Street
Winnebago Street south to Cunningham Street
Cunningham Street west to Cunningham Road
Cunningham Road west to Meridian Road

FROM MERIDIAN ROAD TO ROCK CUT STATE PARK

Meridian Road to Cunningham Road
Cunningham Road east to Cunningham Street
Cunningham Street east to Winnebago Street
Winnebago Street north to Jefferson Street
Jefferson Street/Bridge east to Rockford
   Rec Path
Rockford Rec Path north to Prairie Street
Prairie Street east to Madison Street
Madison Street north to Whitman Street Bridge
Whitman Street west to Rockford Rec Path/
   Sinnissippi Park
Rockford Rec Path north to Illinois Street Park
Illinois Street Park north to Illinois Street
Illinois Street north to Arlington Street
Arlington Street north to Snow Avenue
Snow Avenue north to Forest Grove Street
Forest Grove Street north to Shorewood Park
Shorewood Park north to Evelyn Avenue/East
   Drive
East Drive to Rockford Trail System
Rockford Trail System to Frank Bauer Parkway
Frank Bauer Parkway west to Victory Street
Victory Street north to Machesney Road
Machesney Road/Roosevelt Road west to
   Alpine Road
Alpine Road north to Harlem High School/
   Willow Creek Trail
Willow Creek Trail west to Rock Cut State Park

Rockford Area Additional Trails

Perryville Path

This is a 14.9-mile bicycle "ring road" bypass around central Rockford. This accesses a lot of the newer subdivisions and Rockford's main bike trails. It follows closely along Perryville Road, a major in-town roadway.

Stone Bridge Trail

This stone-surfaced trail runs 5.75 miles on an abandoned railbed from McCurry Road in Roscoe to the Boone County Line.

Long Prairie Trail

This trail is part of the Grand Illinois Trail, and it is just outside of Rockford. The Long Prairie Trail runs from Roscoe to Capron, Illinois for a distance of 14.6 miles.

Hononegah Recreation Path

This is a 2.75-mile asphalt strip along Hononegah Road running from Hononegah High School in Rockton and Illinois Route 251 in Roscoe.

Rockford POINTS OF INTEREST ————————————

Rockford offers much to visitors, and it makes sense to get familiar with the city. Some of these unique treasures and attractions include:

Anderson Japanese Gardens
318 Spring Creek Road
A great formal Japanese garden, with 12 acres of waterfalls, koi ponds and a 16th century style tea house. Visit the Blue Iris gift shop.

Coronado Theatre
314 N. Main Street
Built in 1927, this wonderful theater's renovation put it back in the public eye.

Erlander Home Swedish-American Museum
404 S. Third Street
In Haight Village, the 1871 Erlander Home is a center for learning more about Swedish immigrant home life.

Klehm Arboretum and Botanic Garden
2701 Clifton Avenue
Over 150 acres of unusual trees and shrubs offer an open invitation to explore. Includes themed flower beds, a children's garden and maze, and 1.5 mile bike trail. There is a busy schedule of sales, events and shows.

Midway Village Museum Center
6799 Guilford Road
The village has 24 restored Victorian houses, shops and businesses on 137 acres. You get a feel for 19th century life. The village includes a blacksmith shop, one-room schoolhouse, church, general store, bank and fire station. There are indoor galleries focused on Aviation, Swedish Singers, the Rockford Peaches and on local industry. The Center has costumed guides and interpreters.

Discovery Center Museum
711 N. Main Street
Great family-oriented museum that explores basic scientific principles through 250+ fun exhibits. The Discovery Center has a working TV studio, robotics lab, a planetarium and an outdoor science park.

Burpee Museum of Natural History
737 N. Main Street
The museum has a fabulous collection of fossils, including a Tyrannosaurus Rex and woolly mammoth. It proudly hosts a rare new Nanotyrannus named "Jane." The museum also has an authentic Pennsylvanian coal forest with simulated thunderstorms.

Riverfront Art Museum
711 N. Main Street
Home of the local arts scene and the Rockford Art Museum, with a strong collection of 19th and 20th century American art.

Sinnissippi Gardens, Greenhouse and Lagoon
1300 N. Second Street
This is a wonderful old-fashioned park along the banks of the Rock River, featuring an established, tranquil rose garden, a great floral clock, a greenhouse complete with aviary, and scenic lagoon. The lagoon has highly-expressive swans.

Tinker Swiss Cottage Museum
411 Kent Street
Swiss-style architectural charm in this quaint 1865 house built by a local businessman, with great interior and special collections. National Register-listed.

Forest City Queen at Riverview Park
324 N. Madison Street
The Forest City Queen offers boat tours with narration on the Rock River; good sightseeing and brunch.

Magic Waters Water Park
7820 Cherry Vale North Boulevard
Cherry Valley, Illinois
Just next to Rockford, this is the largest water park in Illinois and the second largest water park in the country. It has body slides, a wave pool, tube slides, a water roller coaster and other hydro-recreations.

Trolley Car #36 at Riverview Park
Right downtown, this active open air trolley car spins a 45-minute trip through Sinnissippi Gardens along the Rock River.

Trailside Equestrian Center at Lockwood Park
5209 Safford Road
There are 40 acres of woods and meadows here, a good place for horseback riding. The Center offers trail rides and a petting zoo.

A spontaneous wild turkey crossing in northern Illinois!

Boone and McHenry Counties

From Rock Cut State Park to Richmond, Illinois

When all is said and done, the Rockford to Richmond section of the Grand Illinois Trail makes for a nice riding experience. It is a blend of flat and gently rolling farm fields and gradually rising hills. This is really a bucolic part of the state. In terms of agriculture, you can see it all. There is a mix of soybean fields, cornfields and dairy farms. Along with corn, soybeans are top royalty for Illinois farmers.

Dairy farming is important as well. Many of the dairy farms through this part of Illinois came into existence to serve the city market. Railroads like the Chicago & Northwestern would make daily "milk runs" into the city from farm stops in towns like Caledonia.

The terrain in this part of northern Illinois shows the impact of glaciers. This is why the land is hilly. The Grand Illinois Trail provides good upland views of moraine country. The moraine features can be seen around Hebron and around Glacier Park south of Richmond. Moraines are basically long, narrow ridges of glacier debris—gravel and sand—that ran off the glacier as it melted and retreated. Large heaps of glacier stuff, kames, is also in McHenry County. Kames are odd heaps formed from the gravel and sand that slopped from the melting tops of the glaciers. By the way, from a farming perspective, dairying is one of the better uses of morainal land because the soil is usually less productive due to the gravel and sand and rapid soil drainage.

Old glacier outwash plains also have fens, marshes and bogs due to the way the glacier edge, and loose pieces of glacier, melted.

The soil naturally tends to a mix of prairie and oak savannah. The route is along the furthest northern edge of the Illinois prairie, and there are prairie plants suited to gravel hill prairies.

On this northern section of the Grand Illinois Trail, you experience two dedicated off-road trails as well as good road mileage on low volume roads. This Grand Illinois Trail section begins at Rock Cut State Park and proceeds by country roads to the Long Prairie Trail. Some notes about the Long Prairie Trail:

- The Long Prairie Trail contains remnants of prairie plants that are commonly found around oak savannah prairies.

- The Long Prairie Trail runs along a portion of the old Chicago & Northwestern Railroad railbed. This part was known as the Kenosha Division and it continued into southern Wisconsin. The line was first laid out in the 1850s.

- You can find traces of an old train derailment by Beaverton Road.

- The Long Prairie Trail is a total of 14.6 miles at present, and there are plans to extend it beyond the Boone County line into McHenry County. The Grand Illinois Trail runs on about half of the Long Prairie Trail, picking it up at Caledonia and heading east into Capron. The Long Prairie Trail continues northwest from Caledonia into Roscoe.

Boone and McHenry Counties Trail Routing

This section of the Grand Illinois Trail is a tour through the countryside using county blacktops, a portion of the Long Prairie Trail and the Hebron Trail.

Most of the McHenry County section is on low-volume roads kept in reasonably good condition. But this part of the GIT requires keeping in touch with your directions and negotiating the trail route. The routing for this section begins at Rock Cut State Park and takes a few blacktops to reach Caledonia, Illinois and the midsection of the Long Prairie Trail. The Long Prairie Trail is a former Chicago & Northwestern Railroad right-of-way, and it stretches from Roscoe, Illinois north of Rockford east to Capron, Illinois. It will soon be extended further east to Chemung, Illinois.

From Caledonia, head east on the Long Prairie Trail to Capron. The Grand Illinois Trail route picks up Capron Road in Capron, Illinois and heads up to the Wisconsin state line. There, a unique State Line Road straddles Wisconsin and Illinois. Follow State Line Road to Norris Road, which drops into Hebron. At Hebron, pick up the Hebron Trail, which leads to Richmond, Illinois and the Prairie Trail.

Begin at Rock Cut State Park at the west side parking lot (just off Route 173 northeast of Rockford). Take the Willow Creek Trail west and out of the park. The trail is just at the parking lot by the lake spillway. This is a fun ride through the park, an asphalt snake of a trail curling through the woods.

Once you get to the edge of the park, take the path to the sidewalk along Perryville Road. Travel south on Perryville Road to Harlem Road, and then turn left (you should be heading east here). Harlem Road rises and winds a bit, but stay on it for about 3.6 miles to Argyle Road. Turn left and head north on Argyle Road for about one mile to reach Argyle, Illinois.

Be careful at Argyle to make sure that you stop! Argyle is a very small town (or a very large crossroads). Take Beloit Road for about a mile up to Kelley Road and head east on Kelley.

Kelley Road is a pleasant stretch. You can even find wild turkey families lurking in the brush along the roadside and get up close to a Holstein. Stay on Kelley Road for 2.4 miles.

Caledonia Road is another matter. It is briskly traveled. There is a large, rural subdivision outside of Caledonia, and residents rely heavily on using Caledonia Road for travel. There are a lot of fast SUV's running late for appointments and games. Turn left, heading north, and take Caledonia Road for just over a mile into Caledonia, Illinois.

Caledonia, Illinois, population 199, recently incorporated in 1995, is a town built as a stop along the railroad. The Long Prairie Trail can be found simply by heading toward the town water tower in the middle of the village: the trail is just below this landmark. Turn off Caledonia Road onto Randolph Street and you will soon run into the trail.

The Long Prairie Trail is a top-notch trail, an eight-foot asphalt strip that runs for the most part alongside Route 173 to Capron. Along the way are several interesting natural and historical markers, one of which notes the scene of a major railroad derailment. After Caledonia, the Long Prairie Trail takes a slight dip south before heading east. Poplar Grove is ahead 4.1 miles.

Poplar Grove has a population of 1,368 and was incorporated in 1895. The village of Poplar Grove stretches along either side of the trail, and there is an excellent little sandwich shop/ice cream parlor in town. This might be a good fueling station and rest stop along the way.

Capron, Illinois, population 961, incorporated 1873, is named after a railroad official. This was a pretty common thing for towns to do during the 19th century railroad boom. Plenty of Illinois communities feature names taken from prominent railroad officials, as a way of soliciting their favor and their road. Capron is now home to two metal-plating firms, along with Side-by-Side Cyclery, and Capron maintains an active downtown with good rest amenities for trail users.

At Capron, the Long Prairie Trail comes to a sudden end, right at the Boone County line. Bare, rusted rails point the way toward Chemung, Illinois, and plans call for continuing the Long Prairie Trail into Chemung, and thence into Harvard, Illinois.

Even though the Long Prairie Trail continues east through Capron out to the Boone County/McHenry County line, you need to leave the Long Prairie Trail just as you reach Capron, unless you need a stop and want to visit a bike store or restaurant.

From the west edge of Capron, take Wooster Street north. It becomes Capron Road outside of town. Take Capron Road directly north to State Line Road. This is about 6.4 miles from the Long Prairie Trail. State Line Road is exactly on the line between Illinois and Wisconsin. You can square yourself to it, look south, and imagine all the state stretched before you, with Carbondale, Illinois so far off.

State Line Road runs a direct East-West. This is a good thing, because almost all the county roads in Boone and McHenry County run on diagonals. Take State Line Road for about 12.2 miles. You will pass through Sharon, Wisconsin (a few houses) and Big Foot, Wisconsin (a few more houses and an intersection with Route 14, a spot in the road called Big Fork Prairie, Wisconsin). Continue on State Line Road to Nichols Road. Nichols Road is the next road east of Knickerbocker Road. Take Nichols Road as it dips south and east and pick up Hebron Road. Take Hebron Road east into Hebron. It becomes Bigelow Avenue in town.

Hebron, Illinois, population 1,038, incorporated 1895, was another stop on the Chicago & Northwestern dairy run. It is an antique-lover's kind of town, with a fine main drag lined with antique shops and interesting restaurants.

The Hebron Trail runs on an abandoned railbed to Richmond. To reach the trail, take Bigelow Avenue to Illinois Route 47. Take Illinois Route 47 south one block to the Illinois Route 47/Illinois Route 173 (Maple Avenue) intersection. Take Illinois Route 173/Maple Avenue east to Church Street, and then take Church Street north to the Hebron Trail.

The Hebron Trail is an asphalt path built on a railroad bed. It runs from Hebron to a spot just northwest of Richmond, Illinois.

A restful farm scene at the Illinois-Wisconsin state line.

To reach Richmond from the east end of the trail, take Keystone Road south to Broadway Street and continue east on Broadway into Richmond.

Richmond is the northeast corner of the Grand Illinois Trail. It has a fine downtown worth exploring. Try the ice cream. Two National Register houses are in Richmond: the <u>Lucien Bonaparte Covell House</u> (1905) at 5825 Broadway is a Queen Anne gem, and <u>Memorial Hall</u> (1907) located at 10308 Main Street. But the entire Main Street commercial district has great architectural appeal.

Richmond, population 1,091, was established in 1865 and was named by Isaac Reed. Reed won the right to name the town by winning a mill-climbing contest!

BOONE AND McHENRY COUNTIES

FROM ROCK CUT STATE PARK TO RICHMOND

Rock Cut State Park west on Willow Creek Trail
Willow Creek Trail west to Perryville Road
Perryville Road south to Harlem Road
Harlem Road east to Argyle Road
Argyle Road north to Beloit Road
Beloit Road east to Kelley Road
Kelley Road east to Caledonia Road
Caledonia Road north to Caledonia water tower/Long Prairie Trail
Long Prairie Trail east to Wooster Street/ Capron
Wooster Street/Capron Road north to State Line Road
State Line Road east to Nichols Road
Nichols Road south to Hebron Road
Hebron Road/Bigelow Avenue east to Illinois Route 47
Illinois Route 47 south to Illinois Route 173/ Illinois Route 47
Illinois Route 173/Maple Avenue east to Church Street
Church Street north to Hebron Trail
Hebron Trail east to Keystone Road
Keystone Road south to Broadway Street
Broadway Street east to downtown Richmond

FROM RICHMOND TO ROCK CUT STATE PARK

Broadway Street west to Keystone Road
Keystone Road north to Hebron Trail
Hebron Trail west to Hebron/Church Street
Church Street south to Maple Avenue/Illinois Route 173
Illinois Route 173/Maple Avenue north to Illinois Route 47/Bigelow Avenue
Bigelow Avenue/ Hebron Road to Nichols Road
Nichols Road north to State Line Road
State Line Road west to Capron Road
Capron Road/Wooster Street south to Capron/ Long Prairie Trail
Long Prairie Trail west to Caledonia water tower
Caledonia water tower west to Caledonia Road
Caledonia Road south to Kelly Road
Kelley Road west to Beloit Road
Beloit Road south to Argyle Road
Argyle Road west to Harlem Road
Harlem Road west to Perryville Road
Perryville Road north to Willow Creek Trail
Willow Creek Trail east into Rock Cut State Park

Tour the Interactive Grand Illinois Trail

Connect on the internet to www.grandillinoistrail.com for the most recent trail news and to help plan your trip.

Discover new events and places along the way. Trade information about the trail. Learn what experienced hikers and bikers have to say. And you can record your own trip news on the site.

The Grand Illinois website includes wayfinding points, detailed distance charts and lodging and hospitality information. It also contains useful links to additional resources.

The website is headquarters to the Trail Blazers Hall of Fame—a roll call of people who have completed the entire Grand Illinois Trail in a calendar year. Give www.grandillinoistrail.com a tour!

McHenry County Uncommon and Rare Birds

McHenry County has a number of uncommon and rare birds visit each year.

_____ Horned Grebe (rare)
_____ American Bittern (rare)
_____ Cattle Egret (rare)
_____ Yellow-crowned night heron (rare)
_____ Greater Scaup (rare)
_____ Osprey (uncommon)
_____ Bald eagle (uncommon)
_____ Red-shouldered hawk (uncommon)
_____ Peregrine falcon (uncommon)
_____ Gray partridge (uncommon)
_____ Virginia rails (uncommon)
_____ Ruddy turnstone sandpiper (rare)
_____ Sanderling sandpiper (rare)
_____ Long-billed dowitcher (rare)
_____ Forster's tern (uncommon)
_____ Long-eared owl (rare)
_____ Short-eared owl (rare)
_____ Acadian flycatcher (uncommon)
_____ Alder flycatcher (rare)
_____ Carolina wren (rare)
_____ White-eyed vireo (uncommon)
_____ Kentucky warbler (uncommon)
_____ Connecticut warbler (uncommon)
_____ Mourning warbler (uncommon)
_____ Hooded warbler (uncommon)
_____ Yellow-breasted chat (uncommon)
_____ Clay-colored sparrow (rare)
_____ Henslow's sparrow (uncommon)
_____ Lapland longspur (uncommon)
_____ Snow bunting (uncommon)
_____ Western meadowlark (uncommon)

For a complete checklist contact the McHenry County Conservation District.

Northern Section Resources

EMERGENCY

ILLINOIS STATE POLICE, DISTRICT 16
(Pecatonica)
(815) 987-7156 for Boone, Jo
Daviess, Stephenson and
Winnebago counties.

ILLINOIS STATE POLICE, DISTRICT 2
(Elgin)
(815) 224-2250 for McHenry and
DuPage Counties.

LOCAL TOURISM CONTACTS

STEPHENSON COUNTY CONVENTION
AND VISITORS BUREAU
2047 AYP Road
Freeport, Illinois 61032
(815) 233-1357
(800) 369-2955
www.stephenson-county-il.org

ROCKFORD AREA CONVENTION AND
VISITORS BUREAU
211 N. Main Street
Rockford, Illinois 61101
(815) 963-8111
www.gorockford.com

GALENA/ JO DAVIESS COUNTY
CONVENTION AND VISITORS
BUREAU
101 Bouthillier Street
Galena, Illinois 61036
(815) 777-4390
(800) 747-9377
www.galena.org

ILLINOIS TOURISM BUREAU
(800) 2-CONNECT

BED & BREAKFASTS

Rockford
FOX RUN B & B
2815 N. Rockton Ave.
(815) 963-8151
www.foxrunbedandbreakfast.com

CHURCH STREET BED AND BREAKFAST
1003 N. Church Street
(815) 965-6080
(800) 216-2524
www.churchstreetbedandbreakfast.com

RIVER HOUSE B & B
11052 Ventura Boulevard/
Riverfront
(815) 636-1884
www.riverhouse.ws

Richmond
RICHMOND INN
10314 East Street
(815) 678-2505

Lena
SUGAR MAPLE B & B
607 Maple Street
(815) 369-2786

Cedarville
CEDAR CLIFF B & B
5758 Illinois Route 26 North
(815) 563-4296
www.cedarcliffbb.com

Freeport
HIGHPOINT INN
2440 E. River Road
(815) 233-0233
www.highpointbedandbreakfast.com

Caledonia
LEE CREEK B & B
21344 Grade School Road
(800) 815-8360

Winnebago
VICTORIAN VERANDA B & B
8430 W. State Road
(815) 963-1337
www.bbonline.com/il/veranda

Galena
Galena is the absolute center of
the B & B Universe and the
options are endless. If you have
never tried a bed and breakfast
arrangement, this is a great
place to start!

AARON'S COTTAGES AT THE
GOLDMOOR
9001 Sand Hill Road
(800) 255-3925
www.galena-il.com

ALDRICH GUEST HOUSE
900 Third St.
(815) 777-3323
www.aldrichguesthouse.com

ANNIE WIGGENS GUEST HOUSE
1004 Park Avenue
(815) 777-0336
www.anniewiggins.com

AVERY GUEST HOUSE
606 S. Prospect Street
(815) 777-3883
www.averybedandbreakfast.com

BELLE AIRE MANSION
11410 Hwy. 20 West
(815) 777-0893
www.belleairemansion.com

BIELENDA'S MARS AVENUE GUEST
HOUSE
515 Mars Avenue
(815) 777-2808

BRIERWREATH MANOR B & B
216 N. Bench Street
(815) 777-0608
www.brierwreath.com

CAPTAIN HARRIS GUEST HOUSE
713 S. Bench Street
(815) 777-4713
www.captainharris.com

CLORAN MANSION
1237 Franklin Street
(815) 777-0583
www.cloranmansion.com

DEZOYA HOUSE B & B
1203 Third Street
(815) 777-1203
www.dezoya.com

EARLY AMERICAN SETTLEMENT LOG
    CABIN LODGING
Blackjack & Hart John Roads
(815) 777-4200
www.easll.com

FARMERS' GUEST HOUSE
334 Spring Street
(815) 777-3456
www.farmersguesthouse.com

FELT MANOR GUEST HOUSE
125 S. Prospect Street
(815) 777-9093
www.feltmanor.com

FOUR OAKS GUEST HOUSE
6594 Hwy. 84 North
(815) 777-9567

GALLERY GUEST SUITE
202 S. Main Street
(815) 777-1222
www.cjart.net

GRANDVIEW GUEST HOUSE
113 S. Prospect Street
(815) 777-1387
www.galena-bnb.com/grandview

GREENBRIAR COUNTRY INN & SUITES
345 Spring Street
(815) 777-3153

HAWK VALLEY RETREAT
2752 W. Cording
(815) 777-4100
www.hawkvalleyretreat.com

HELLMAN GUEST HOUSE
318 Hill Street
(815) 777-3638
www.hellmanguesthouse.com

JOHN HENRY GUEST HOUSE
812 S. Bench Street
(815) 777-3595

LOGAN HOUSE
301 N. Main Street
(815) 777-0033

MAIN STREET INN
404 S. Main Street
(815) 777-3454
www.mainstreetinn.com

PINE HOLLOW INN
4700 N. Council Hill Road
(815) 777-1071
www.pinehollowinn.com

RENAISSANCE RIVERBOAT SUITES &
    ROOMS
324-328 Spring Street
(815) 777-0123
www.galenarensuites.com

SNOOP SISTERS INN
1000 Third Street
(815) 777-3062
www.snoopsistersinn.com

SPRING STREET GUEST HOUSE
418 Spring Street
(815) 777-0354
www.cfach.com

STILLMAN'S COUNTRY INN
513 Bouthillier
(815) 777-0557

THE CAPTAIN GEAR GUEST HOUSE
1000 S. Bench Street
(815) 777-0222
www.captaingearguesthouse.com

THE GOLDMOOR
9001 Sand Hill Road
(815) 777-3925
www.galena-bnb.com

THE INN AT IRISH HOLLOW
2800 S. Irish Hollow Road
(815) 777-6000
www.irishhollow.com

THE QUEEN ANNE GUEST HOUSE
200 Park Avenue
(815) 777-3849

THE WILD TURKEY B & B
1048 N. Clark Lane
(815) 858-3649

TIERRA LINDA
826 S. Rocky Hill Road
(815) 777-1950
www.beautifulearth.com

VICTORIAN MANSION
301 S. High Street
(812) 777-0675
www.victorianmansion.com

HOTELS & MOTELS

Galena
BEST WESTERN MOTEL
9923 Hwy. 20 West
(815) 777-2577
www.quiethouse.com

CHESTNUT MOUNTAIN RESORT
8700 W. Chestnut Rd.
(800) 397-1320
www.chestnutmt.com

COUNTRY INN & SUITES
11334 Oldenburg Lane
(866) 268-7946

THE DESOTO HOUSE HOTEL
230 S. Main Street
(800) 343-6562
www.desotohouse.com

EAGLE RIDGE INN & RESORT
Hwy. 20 East
(815) 777-2444
www.eagleridge.com

GRANT HILLS MOTEL
9372 Hwy. 20 West
(815) 777-2116

Barstow
LUNDEEN'S LANDING
21119 Barstow Road
(309) 496-9956

Thomson
THOMSON HOUSE VILLAGER LODGE
800 One Mile Road
www.thomsonvillager.com
(800) 328-7829

CAMPING

Lena
LAKE LE-AQUA-NA STATE PARK
8542 N. Lake Road
(815) 369-4282

Loves Park
ROCK CUT STATE PARK
7318 Harlem Road
(815) 883-3311

Pecatonica
PECATONICA RIVER FOREST PRESERVE
7260 Judd Road
(815) 877-6100

Rockford
SUGAR RIVER FOREST PRESERVE
10127 Forest Preserve Road
(815) 877-6100

Galena
PALACE CAMPGROUNDS
11357 US Rt. 20 West
(815) 777-2466

Apple River
APPLE RIVER CANYON STATE PARK
8763 E. Canyon Road
(815) 745-3302
www.dnr.state.il.us

McHenry
HARBOR LIGHTS
1009 West Bay Road
(815) 344-6938

Leland
HI-TIDE RECREATION
4611 E. 22d Road
(815) 495-9032

Lena
LENA KOA CAMPGROUND
10982 W. Highway 20
(815) 369-2612

BIKE STORES/ REPAIR CENTERS

SIDE BY SIDE CYCLERY
142 W. Main Street
Capron, Illinois 61012
(815) 569-2472

KEGEL'S BICYCLE SHOP
120 S. Chicago Avenue
Freeport, Illinois 61032
(815) 235-2014

THE BICYCLE CONNECTION
2412 N. Main Street
Rockford, Illinois 61103
(815) 966-2453

BIKE PATH OUTFITTERS, INC.
843 N. Madison Street
Rockford, Illinois 61107
(815) 968-2453

KEGE'S BICYCLE STORE
2605 Charles Street
Rockford, Illinois 61108
(815) 229-5826

BOB'S BIKE SHOP
7921 Venus Street
Loves Park, Illinois 61111
(815) 633-4263

ROCKFORD BICYCLE COMPANY
6132 E. Riverside Blvd.
Loves Park, Illinois 61111
(815) 636-0664

SHOSIE'S CYCLERY
514 Windsor Road
Loves Park, Illinois 61111
(815) 633-0755

CYCLE M
11604 N. Second Street
Machesney Park, Illinois 61115
(815) 633-4584

VELOCITY SPORTS
11400 W. U.S. Highway 20
Galena, Illinois 61036
(815) 776-9075

Wild things along the trail! Rock guardians stand tall in Rockford's Sinnissippi Park.

East

Chicago and Chicago
Lakefront Path
★
Burnham Greenway
★
Old Plank Road Trail
★
Illinois Prairie Path
★
Fox River Trail
★
Prairie Trail

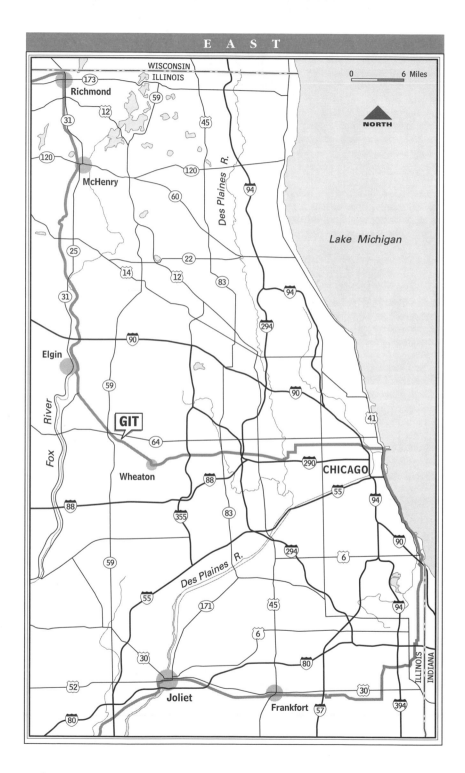

WISCONSIN
ILLINOIS

173
Richmond
59
31
12
45

120
120
McHenry
60

Des Plaines R.
94

Lake Michigan

25
22
14
12
83
31
94

294

90
Elgin

59
41

GIT
64
90

Wheaton
290
CHICAGO
88
55
94
83
355

Des Plaines R.
294
6
90

59

55
171
45
94
6

Fox River

30
80

52
ILLINOIS
INDIANA

Joliet
Frankfort
57
30
394
80

0   6 Miles

NORTH

Overview _____

*An exciting part of the Grand Illinois Trail is visiting the Chicago
Lakefront Path and touring through Chicago neighborhoods. The
Grand Illinois Trail runs along the Illinois Prairie Path, that historic
strip through the western suburbs that formed an early and important
national model for trail development. It takes city streets through
Chicago to the lakefront.*

*The East Section includes the Burnham Greenway through Chicago's
south side and the Old Plank Road Trail through the south suburbs.
It also includes the beautiful Fox River and Prairie Trails from Elgin to
Richmond, Illinois.*

*This part of the Grand Illinois Trail is a moving adventure. There are
well-loved local trails and connecting street routes. The North Section
offers hiking and biking through large and small cities and across a
variety of trail environments.*

*The Grand Illinois Trail runs along Chicago's scenic lakeshore. In the summer, it is refreshingly cooler
near the lake!*

EAST SECTION POINTS OF INTEREST

Glacier Park, RINGWOOD
Veterans Park, CRYSTAL LAKE
Dundee Visitor Center and Park
Haegar Pottery, DUNDEE
Fox River
Trout Park, ELGIN
Voyageur Landing, ELGIN
Grand Victoria Casino, ELGIN
Volunteer Park, WHEATON
Volunteer Bridge, WHEATON
Villa Avenue Station, VILLA PARK
Ovaltine Factory, VILLA PARK
Frank Lloyd Wright's Oak Park
Chicago River
Chicago Water Tower
Navy Pier
Chicago Lakefront

Grant Park
Buckingham Fountain
Shedd Aquarium
Promontory Point
Museum of Science and Industry, CHICAGO
South Shore Country Club, CHICAGO
Jackson Park, CHICAGO
Calumet River
Calumet Park
William Powers Conservation Area,
    CALUMET CITY
Lansing Woods, LANSING
Thorn Creek Forest Preserve
Illinois Central Caboose #9951
Frankfort Depot
Frankfort Bridge

City Streets Riding Tips

Ride in a straight line.

Never ride against traffic.

Watch the dangerous "door-zone" next to parked cars. Look into parked cars to see if anyone may be exiting.

Keep track of the traffic behind you, since you may have to suddenly move to the middle of the road.

Use hand signs. Drivers can't guess. They're driving.

Chicago City System

Maywood to Burnham Greenway

Hog butcher for the World
Toolmaker, Stacker of Wheat
Player with Railroads and the Nation's Freight Handler
City of the Big Shoulders

—CARL SANDBURG

Chicago is the third largest city in the United States, it is by far the largest city in Illinois, and it is the county seat of Cook County. Chicago was first incorporated in 1835 and has a metropolitan area population of 8,370,000. Chicago exploded from 350 to one million people in a mere sixty years. She commanded the railroads and the grain and lumber trade. Through her history, the city has railroads, commodities, steel and auto, consumer electronics and, lately, aviation interests. Her pull is irresistible. You have the lake, a serene blue contemplation.

Chicago actually has a big heart for bikes. The mayor pedals. Bicyclists do not have to be professional messengers to ride through downtown traffic. There are bike lanes and some bike accommodations on buses. Someone has put out bike racks here and there. All of these good things are due to a dedicated cycling community, notably the Chicago Bicycle Federation.

Spokes and wheels have had a long connection to the city. Chicago was home in the 1890's to a bustling bicycle industry—with plenty of manufacturers responding to the bike craze. We all know the Schwinn name, but there were plenty of other manufacturers here as well: Pope Manufacturing Company (run by an old Civil War colonel), A. G. Spaulding, Rothchild & Company, March-Davis Bicycle Company and Armstrong Brothers. At that time West Madison Street was called Bicycle Row, and you would wear knickers when you got on the big wheel.

There were plenty of cycle clubs then, and there are plenty of clubs today. The Chicago Cycling Club holds a wide variety of events and outings for both recreational and serious cyclists. The Chicago Bicycle Federation holds some major bike events as well, along with the City of Chicago. The organization sponsors an annual Bike Month that is packed with cycling-related events and rides.

Chicago also is a place for walkers, hikers and strollers. In fact, one of the city's earliest mayors, Gurdon S. Hubbard, was renowned as an intrepid foot-traveler. The city has many notable walks.

Chicago is a world-class city with all the sights and sounds you would expect of a city of this stature. Skyscrapers romp downtown.

Streets are busy. There are rich people and poor people and all those in-between people. You can fly a kite in Grant Park or purchase egg-sized diamonds on Wabash Street. For $1 you can buy a copy of *Streetwise*. For a few bucks more, you can take in *Sunday in the Isle of Grand J'atte* by Georges Seuratt, the pointillist masterpiece at the Art Institute.

The Grand Illinois Trail route runs through diverse parts of the city. You go through the Austin, River West and River Gallery District neighborhoods before reaching downtown. From Navy Pier, the GIT follows the majestic lakefront trail south to the South Side Cultural Center and runs on low-volume streets to Calumet Harbor. This is a nice one-day trip in itself, exploring much of the Windy City.

The Lakefront Path can be used year-round, but Chicago Park District lakefront facilities "officially close" on Labor Day. Portable toilets are unlikely to be found after Labor Day.

Chicago has a long reputation as a hustling kind of place. Part of the reason for this is the poetry of Carl Sandburg. Part of the reason is the residual impact of the World Fair on the public memory: Chicago is known as the Windy City not because of her climate but because of her great boosterism. And part of the reason is there has always been a steady stream of midwesterners pulled to the city from small towns, and for them and everybody else, there's magic in the hustle and bustle of the big city.

Chicago is associated with all kinds of people: Ernie Banks and Mayor Daley, Oprah Winfrey and Saul Bellow, Mike Royko and Marshall Field. It is where Sears and Roebuck got their start, and Montgomery Ward made his first dollar. Chicago was home to the world's first Ferris wheel, the world's first zipper, the world's first mass production line, balloon frame houses and skyscrapers. Chicago is home to Chess Records and the blues, WLS and the radio barn dance, Bobby Hull and Stan Mikita.

And the fact that the Grand Illinois Trail includes so much of the city is a real plus for the trail experience, Illinois' big feature. The following are some of the chief spots along the route.

The Chicago Watertower and North Michigan
    Avenue
Navy Pier
Buckingham Fountain
The classic view of downtown Chicago from the
    Shedd Aquarium
The 31st Street Beach
Ohio Street Beach
Promontory Point and 63rd Street Beach
Jackson Park Harbor
Calumet Park

From the Illinois Prairie Path to the Chicago Lakefront Path

The Grand Illinois Trail route from the Prairie Path to Navy Pier is just under 14 miles long. For the most part, the routing is along Augusta Boulevard through Chicago's west side.

Maywood, Illinois, population 26,987, incorporated 1881, was settled by New Englanders and was home to a major can manufacturer.

From the Illinois Prairie Path trail access at First Avenue in Maywood, take First Avenue north for about eight blocks to reach Washington Street. You will pass by Proviso East High School. Head east, turn right, and Washington Street takes a bridge across the Des Plaines River. Just continue east once you cross the river and two blocks later you will pick up Keystone Street. At this point, you are in River Forest.

River Forest, Illinois, population 11,635, incorporated 1880, has always been a well-heeled and well-treed community. Two former Governors hail from River Forest, Otto Kerner and Edward Dunne. The town is home to Concordia University and Rosary College. Mainly residential, there are a number of prairie school houses, including five built by Frank L. Wright.

Plans are in place for pushing through the Illinois Prairie Path across First Avenue and down Van Buren Street, entering Forest Park, Illinois and passing along the north side of the Cook County Circuit Courthouse. This short half-mile extension is to connect to the CTA commuter rail and PACE bus center in Forest Park. The IPP extension would cross the Des Plaines River and run through Concordia Cemetery. The unusual brick complex, the large institution, is *Altenheim*, a nursing home. You can see some pauper gravestones in the cemetery to the north side of Van Buren Street.

Take Keystone Street north for two blocks to Hawthorne Street. Keystone is blocked by a railroad embankment, so take a quick jot left on Hawthorne Street and use the railroad underpass to continue on Keystone. It is at the Keystone and Hawthorne Street intersection that you will see an incredibly well preserved (and maintained), three-story Italianate villa towering on the corner, a mansion of some 19th century entrepreneur. Use Hawthorne for its railroad underpass. Once you get through this, you will note Keystone Field. Go north on Keystone Street, and after about five blocks you will find Augusta Boulevard.

This part of the Grand Illinois Trail takes you through some very pleasant neighborhoods. Here there are Victorian mansions, grand master bungalows, and large Craftsman style houses. But I think the best part of these neighborhoods isn't the houses, but the great "street architecture" of large house lots with towering street trees. These create a pleasant and relaxed atmosphere. The traffic here is light and local.

Augusta Boulevard is a main east-west street in Chicago, named for the daughter of the city's first dentist. The Grand Illinois Trail relies on Augusta to cross the city. Augusta goes through River Forest and Oak Park, passing three blocks north of the <u>Frank Lloyd Wright historic district</u>. Concordia University is at Augusta and Monroe Streets in River Forest. Oak Park is also a beautiful suburb, with pleasant and beautiful houses resting under grand old trees. When you cross Oak Park Avenue, you will be in Oak Park.

Oak Park, Illinois, population 52,524, incorporated 1901, is internationally known for its Frank Lloyd Wright houses. Wright, one of the premier modern architects, lived his early years here, and the neighborhoods of Oak Park reveal the Master's Touch. But the Prairie Style was more than just Wright and it is everywhere here, along with splendid examples of many architectural styles.

Ernest Hemingway, the writer, lived at 339 N. Oak Park Avenue. The city was also home to popular writers Bruce Barton and Edgar Rice Burroughs. Oak Park is proud of its architecture, proud of its racially diverse citizenry and proud of its vibrant downtown.

There are points of architectural interest right along the Grand Illinois Trail on Augusta Boulevard:

- 710 W. Augusta, <u>Harry S. Adams House</u>, 1913. This is the last prairie house designed by Frank Lloyd Wright in Oak Park. At the north side of Augusta, just west of Linden.

- 700 N. Linden, <u>William H. Gardner House</u>, 1911. This three-story, poured concrete prairie house is by E. E. Roberts. Edgar Rice Burroughs, "Tarzan" author, lived here.

- 647 N. Linden, <u>C.S. Castle House</u>, 1924. This Italian Renaissance Revival house is by Frederick R. Schock. Note the castle at the Castle house!

- 516 Augusta, <u>Norman S. Smith House</u>, 1927. This is a Tudor Revival by Graham, Anderson, Probst and White. Revival styles after World War I spelled the end of the prairie style. Graham, Anderson, Probst and White was a major downtown firm, builders of the Shedd Aquarium, the Wrigley Building and Union Station.

It's possible to spin off the GIT route for a quick tour of Oak Park and its architectural wonders. For a full map of Oak Park's architectural treasures, stop in at the Oak Park Visitors Center. A good sample can be seen by turning south on Euclid Avenue.

- 637 N. Euclid, <u>George C. Page House</u>, an 1896 neoclassical by Harvey L. Page. The pavilion is a copy from Mt. Vernon.

- 630 N. Euclid, <u>Henry C. Todd House</u>, a 1904 Tudor Revival house by E. E. Roberts. Roberts is a bit of an unsung hero in Oak Park, having contributed 200 buildings to the community.

- 600 N. Euclid, <u>George D. Webb House</u>, a 1910 Prairie style house by Henry K. Holsman.

- 530 N. Euclid, <u>Charles R. Erwin House</u>, a 1905 Prairie house by George W. Maher. Note the water lily motif used by Maher, especially see the windows.

- 507 N. Euclid, <u>E.P. Jennings House</u>, a 1903 neoclassical house by Henry Fiddelke.

- 420 N. Euclid, <u>Charles Ward Seabury House</u>, a 1912 Tudor Revival by Charles E. White, Jr.

- 405 N. Euclid, <u>James Hall Taylor House</u>, a 1912 Prairie house by George W. Maher. A dressy, neatly-tailored building.

- 333 N. Euclid, <u>Paul Blatchford House III</u>, an 1898 eclectic structure by Pond & Pond. Here the English Arts & Crafts style provides inspiration; Pond & Pond do the rest. Blatchford's wife trucked in the front yard boulder from her house in Maine.

- 321 N. Euclid, <u>Charles E. Roberts House</u>, an 1883 Queen Anne house by Burnham & Root. Burnham & Root was a major Chicago firm. Charles Roberts was the inventor of an electric car, and a friend to Frank Lloyd Wright. (Wright redid the house interior).

- 312 N. Euclid, <u>Calvin H. Hill House</u>, a 1903 Colonial Revival house by Patton & Miller.

- 231 N. Euclid, <u>Edward W. McCready House</u>, a 1907 Prairie style house by Spencer and Powers. The McCready House gives you faith in the Prairie Style. Here Spencer and Powers makes a grand display of the style. Note the windows.

- 232 N. Euclid, <u>George W. Furbeck House</u>, an 1897 eclectic house by Frank Lloyd Wright. This is an early experiment by Wright, and shows a Japanese influence with its geometries.

- 220 N. Euclid, <u>Caswell A Sharpe House</u> (Cheney Mansion), a 1913 Tudor Revival by White and Christie.

- 175 N. Euclid, <u>Henry P. Magill House</u>, a 1903 Prairie style house by E. E. Roberts. Another fine monumental Prairie house.

The center of the Frank Lloyd Wright universe is undoubtedly at 951 Chicago Avenue, the <u>Frank Lloyd Wright Home and Studio</u>. Here Wright lived and worked, spreading the geometries of the Prairie Style and proclaiming a New Architecture. It makes a splendid tour. Owned by the National Trust for Historic Preservation, the house is a National Historic Landmark. This part of Oak Park, along Chicago Avenue and down Forest Avenue, is well worth a stroll: it is, in fact, a kind of open air museum to Wright and contains a dense collection of his work.

Downtown Oak Park contains many interesting small shops and boutiques and restaurants. It is only about three blocks south of the Frank Lloyd Wright Home and Studio. Wright's <u>Unity Temple</u>, at 875 Lake Street and the Oak Park Conservatory, at 615 Garfield Street, are worth seeing. <u>Pleasant Home</u>, at 217 Home Avenue, is a George Maher building owned by the park district.

When you cross Austin Avenue, you enter Chicago and the Austin neighborhood. If you keep a sharp eye, you will see the Grand Illinois Trail marker here. It is true that the crime rate in Austin is a problem for the city. But much of this crime is local and involves people looking for trouble. Don't look for trouble. Stick to Augusta Boulevard.

The traffic on Augusta Boulevard can be heavy, but only at times. For the most part, traffic is fairly steady. You should keep an eye out for cars pulling out. Augusta Boulevard is a marked bicycle route in the City of Chicago, and the street is striped for bicycles from Central Park Avenue to Western Avenue. Past Western, there are street signs noting the bicycle route. More importantly, around Western Avenue you can see the John Hancock building and the other skyscrapers of the great city of Chicago.

Along the way, you might want to check out the unusual church bell contraption at the Our Lady of the Angels/St. Francis of Assisi Church at Augusta and Pulaski.

Augusta Boulevard runs into Interstate 90/94 (the Kennedy Expressway). The entrance ramp to Interstate 90/94 is the extreme right. Don't take this. Just continue across the bridge in front of you.

Keep alert for Milwaukee Avenue ahead. Turn left on Milwaukee to Chicago Avenue. The Chicago Academy of Arts is at the intersection of Green Street and Chicago Avenue and you should note here the fine ecclesiastical architecture of the St. John Kanissius Church.

Augusta Boulevard intersects with Milwaukee Avenue, and Milwaukee runs on a long diagonal, so the intersection is not perfectly square. Take Milwaukee Avenue to Chicago Avenue. (You will need to be on Chicago Avenue in order to cross the Chicago River). Chicago Avenue is about three blocks down Milwaukee. Note: this is a troublesome area for bicycle riders, and you should ride cautiously and slowly here.

Once on Chicago Avenue, it is enjoyable riding into downtown Chicago and getting a different, non-motor, view of the area. Go past the Abraham Lincoln Bookstore (note that this is the River North Gallery part of town, filled with interesting art galleries and specialty shops) and the Moody Bible Institute. The Newberry Library, a major private research library, is just two blocks north of Augusta on Dearborn Street. Bughouse Square, the park across from the Newberry, is famous as a site for impromptu public debate over issues great and small.

You will be nicely surprised to arrive at Michigan Avenue, and it is exciting to see the Water Tower and the John Hancock Center. Cross Michigan Avenue on the light, and continue along Chicago Avenue. Once across, you will see the Museum of Contemporary Art, Northwestern Medical Center and the faux-Gothic Northwestern Law School. At the very end of the street, of course, is the blue of Lake Michigan and a nice look over to <u>Navy Pier</u>.

There is a tunnel and stairs access to the <u>Lakefront Path</u>. This is the Chicago Avenue access point. You can find this at the north side of the Chicago Avenue-frontage road intersection, after the Museum of Contemporary Art and across the street from the American Bar Center at Northwestern Law School. Once under and across, you access the Lakefront Trail.

The Lakefront Path

First in importance is the shore of Lake Michigan. It should be treated as park space to the greatest extent possible. The lakefront by right belongs to the people.

—DANIEL BURNHAM

The Lakefront Path is beautiful. On one side is the watery blue wonder known as Lake Michigan. On the other is the grand architectural mountainscape of the city. The Lakefront Path is more than a connector. Here you meet anybody. The trail is home to walkers and joggers, rollerbladers with Burleys, folks walking dogs, mountain bikers and marathoners-in-training. It is a promenade of humanity and human scale motive power. To sit on a sunny day and watch the traffic on the Lakefront Path for only an hour is to get a deep lesson in life and living.

A postcard view along the Grand Illinois Trail.

The Lakefront Path stretches from Ardmore Avenue at Osterman Beach (in the Edgewater neighborhood) south to 71st Street and the South Shore Cultural Center, for a total of 18 miles. This is pretty much the full extent of the city's continuous lakefront parkland. The Grand Illinois Trail runs south from its midpoint to the very end of the Lakefront Path at the South Side Cultural Center, a distance of ten lakefront miles.

It is hard to imagine Chicago without the grand city views. The views go both ways, looking out from the city over Lake Michigan, and looking into the city from Lake Michigan's shore. But no one really wanted it this way—Chicago's business and political chiefs all have had different notions of how to properly "use" the great lakefront parklands. And they all fought against the 1836 decision of the Illinois & Michigan Canal Commissioners that the lakefront be "Public Grounds—a Common to Remain Forever Open, Clear and Free of Any Buildings or other Obstruction whatever."

This noble goal was furthered by the Commercial Club of Chicago's plan for Chicago, created by Daniel Burnham. A brilliant designer and an eloquent speaker, Burnham built the master plan for the city. Chicago was to become a city of grand boulevards and interconnected parks. These were united and invigorated by strong classic architectural design. Perhaps the best place to see his imprint on the city is at the intersection of Congress and Michigan Avenue. It took furious battles to plant the Art Institute, the Field Museum, Shedd Aquarium, Meigs Field, Soldier Field and McCormick Place on the "open, clear and free" lakefront.

It was Montgomery Ward, the rich retail genius, who spent 20 years keeping the lakefront from improper development: "I fought for the poor people of Chicago, not the millionaires. Here is park frontage on the lake, comparing favorably with the Bay of Naples, which city officials would crowd with buildings, transforming the breathing spot for the poor into a showground of the educated rich. I do not think it is right."

There is a delightful mini-park just north of Navy Pier. The Grand Illinois Trail route travels into Navy Pier for a view of the Ferris wheel and sailing ships. There is a children's museum, sightseeing boats and other sights and sounds. The Navy Pier also contains restaurants, water, and restrooms for travelers. A very popular side feature at Navy Pier is the wide-ranging permanent collection of stained glass windows. It is a beautiful display. You should also note the public sculpture scattered here.

Navy Pier is the site of the annual Taste of Chicago and countless other summer events and shows and conventions. Navy Pier was once a navy training center for naval aviators, established after World War I.

Navy Pier—always a place for fun times in Chicago!

And it was home to the University of Illinois at Chicago. It is now a perpetual party. You find kids and parents, young and old couples, friends and even sailors on leave from Great Lakes Naval School taking in the scene. Something is always happening.

Follow the Lakefront Path on the bridge over the mouth of the Chicago River. The path goes past the Chicago Yacht Club at Monroe Harbor. At Grant Park there are spectacular views of city skyscrapers. Quite a collection.

Grant Park is a fine park to tour any time of the year. There are parks within the park: Daley Bicentennial Plaza, a prairie park, the Millennium Park. This is the first place in the city to smell the scent of Spring, the first place to go for a summer picnic, the first place to see the great allees of mature elms and their yellow autumn leaves. With a busy summer schedule of Petrillo band shell music—jazz, gospel, blues, rock, the Chicago Symphony Orchestra—Grant Park has been called "the world's largest free outdoor carnival." Buckingham Fountain is a favorite sight at the south end of the park, a monumental 1927 gift to the city by Kate Buckingham in memory of her brother.

Believe it or not, most of Grant Park was built up from infill, by the dumping of river and canal dredgings.

The lakefront museum campus at Grant Park includes the <u>Field Museum</u>, <u>Shedd Aquarium</u> and the <u>Adler Planetarium</u> as well as the <u>Art Institute</u>. The Lakefront Path wraps around Shedd Aquarium and passes Solider Field and <u>McCormick Place</u>. There are restrooms near <u>Soldier Field</u> and McCormick Place.

It is the southern portion of the Lakefront Path that allows for the best views of the lake. There is a small but beautiful park at <u>Promontory Point</u>. It is hard to imagine that this quiet place once bristled with a Nike missile battalion and a radar station during the Cold War. The University of Chicago was the place where the atom was split, a sustaining fission reaction was created, and having nuclear missiles at Promontory Park must have really brought home the New Frontier to the Hyde Park community.

The <u>59th Street Beach and Harbor</u> is a popular place for swimming and sunbathing, and the Chicago Park District facility here includes changing rooms and a lunch grill.

There is an overpass at 57th Street that allows access to <u>Hyde Park</u> and the <u>Museum of Science and Industry</u>. The Lakefront Path goes through <u>Jackson Park</u>, pushes past the marina and continues to the <u>South Shore Cultural Center</u>.

The curvings of Jackson Park show the hand of master landscape architect Frederick Law Olmstead. Olmstead, designer of New York's Central Park, and of Riverside, Illinois, is noted for his naturalistic approach. Jackson Park was first laid out by Olmstead's firm in 1869-71, along with the Midway Plaisance and

Promontory Point is a beautiful green space in Hyde Park.

South Park. This was to become the site of the 1892-3 World Columbian Exposition, a grand jamboree of culture and commercialism that excited the nation and trumpeted Chicago's entry into world-class city status. The Columbian Exposition drew 27 million visitors, and in England, the poet Alfred Lord Tennyson announced that the Chicago fair was "the Parliament of Man, the Federation of the World."

The great fair was especially surprising because it showed Chicago's vitality after the 1871 Chicago Fire, the shocking event in which 300 died and 90,000 were left immediately homeless in the October chill.

The Jackson Park Harbor is a beautiful sight. Boats slowly jostle in their slips. Gulls wing overhead. The trees and flowers here make a colorful and pleasant backdrop to it all.

The Grand Illinois Trail takes to city streets between the South Shore Cultural Center and Calumet Park. It is well marked. The streets are not very challenging, and there is only modest traffic. Better still, there are plenty of people who are accustomed to using the street route.

Take Coles Street south to 79th Street, then turn left toward the lake. Pick up Brandon Street and head south to 83rd Street. Take 83rd Street east and pick up Burley Street.

Head down Burley Street to 87th Street, then jog east about two blocks to Mackinaw Street. Take Mackinaw south.

At the end of Mackinaw Street is a heavy steel industrial bridge across the Calumet River. Keep your eyes open, and be alert to anything along the pavement that might harm your bike. The street may have glass or loose metal objects.

Pick up Ewing Street and head into Calumet Park. There is a great view from the lake of the power plant in Indiana. The park has a great beach, playing fields and a massive field house.

The Grand Illinois Trail connects with the Burnham Greenway at this point, heading south toward the Old Plank Road Trail and Joliet.

Additional Trails

Des Plaines River Trail

The Chicago metropolitan region has a number of trails that connect to the Grand Illinois Trail. The most significant secondary trail is the Des Plaines River Trail. The Des Plaines River Trail runs from the Wisconsin state line to Riverside Drive near Lincolnshire, Illinois for a distance of 29 miles. In Wisconsin, this very same trail route continues north all the way to Milwaukee using local roads and trails.

Lakefront Path

It is worth commenting on the Lakefront Path. While the Grand Illinois Trail route picks up the Lakefront Path at about its midsection and follows the trail south, the northern half of the Lakefront Path is a real treat. It continues north to Montrose Harbor, south of Evanston. This part of the Lakefront Path provides easy access to Lincoln Park (which

CHICAGO ROUTE

FROM ILLINOIS PRAIRIE PATH MAYWOOD ACCESS TO CALUMET PARK	FROM CALUMET PARK TO ILLINOIS PRAIRIE PATH MAYWOOD ACCESS
First Avenue north to Washington Street	Ewing Street north to Calumet River bridge crossing
Washington Street east to Keystone Street (Forest Park)	Mackinaw Street north to 87th Street
Keystone Street north to Augusta Boulevard	87th Street west to Burley Street
Augusta Boulevard east to Milwaukee Avenue	Burley Street north to 83rd Street
Milwaukee Avenue southeast to Chicago Avenue	83rd west to Brandon Street
Chicago Avenue east to Chicago Avenue Beach Access/Lakefront Path	Brandon Street north to 79th Street
Lakefront Path south to South Shore Cultural Center/Coles Street	79th Street west to Coles Street
Coles Street south to 79th Street	Coles Street north to South Shore Cultural Center/Lakefront Path
79th Street east to Brandon Street	Lakefront Path north to Chicago Avenue Beach Access
Brandon Street south to 83rd Street	Chicago Avenue Beach Access to Chicago Avenue
83rd Street east to Burley Street	Chicago Avenue west to Milwaukee Avenue
Burley Street south to 87th Street	Milwaukee Avenue northwest to Augusta Boulevard
87th Street east to Mackinaw Street	Augusta Boulevard west to Keystone Avenue
Mackinaw Street south to Calumet River bridge crossing	Keystone Avenue south to Hawthorne Street
Calumet River bridge east to Ewing Street	Hawthorne Street west to First Avenue
Ewing Street south to Calumet Park	First Avenue south to Illinois Prairie Path Maywood Access

contains lagoons, a conservatory and a zoo), to the Chicago Academy of Sciences and the Chicago Historical Society.

City Streets

Chicago has an extensive system of recommended city streets. Maps can be obtained through the Chicago Bicycle Federation and the City of Chicago.

Chicago POINTS OF INTEREST

Chicago Visitors Information Center
Chicago Cultural Center
163 E. Pearson Street at Michigan Avenue
(312) 744-2400

Chicago Convention and Tourism Bureau
McCormick Place
2301 S. Lake Shore Drive
(312) 567-8500

Adler Planetarium and Astronomy Museum
1300 S. Lake Shore Drive
The GIT runs right along the Adler; inside is a great collection of exhibits on space exploration, telescopes and navigation, and a fine Sky Show.

Art Institute of Chicago
Michigan Avenue at Adams Street
One of the world's great art collections, with a noteworthy collection of the French Impressionists. See the medieval armor, the architectural drawings, historic furnishings as well.

Chicago Academy of Sciences
Fullerton Parkway and Cannon Drive
At Lincoln Park, the museum features interactive environmental exhibits, including a butterfly haven and an early Chicago region habitat.

Chicago Architecture Foundation River Cruise
Lower level of Michigan Avenue Bridge and Wacker Drive
(312) 902-1500
Tour the city from a different perspective; river tour explores 53 architectural buildings and sites.

Chicago Athenaeum
307 N. Michigan Avenue
A unique museum focused on architecture and design, containing decorative arts, furniture and industrial objects.

Chicago Board of Trade
141 W. Jackson Boulevard
Visit the trading floors, view the action from the visitor gallery.

Chicago Cultural Center
78 E. Washington St.
Located along Michigan Avenue, the center has a busy schedule of performances and shows; interiors by Tiffany. Contains the Museum of Broadcast Communications.

Chicago Historical Society
Clark Street at North Avenue
If you haven't visited, you're in for a treat. The CHS has great and interesting exhibits, including a highly-regarded Lincoln collection.

Chicago Mercantile Exchange/International Monetary Market
30 S. Wacker Drive
Witness the hustle of the exchange from the guest gallery.

Daley Plaza
Washington and Dearborn Streets
See the famous Picasso; frequent open air performances.

DuSable Museum of African-American History
740 E. 56th Place
A significant collection focused on the black experience.

Field Museum of Natural History
1400 S. Lake Shore Drive
Just a great place for wandering in, and discovering new things about the world. Sue, the great Tyrannosaurus Rex, is waiting for you.

Garfield Park Conservatory
300 N. Central Park Avenue
In the Humboldt Park neighborhood, this conservatory features hundreds of unique plant varieties, across a range of environments and habitats. Visit the maze and the reconstruction of Monet's garden.

Glessner House Museum
1800 S. Prairie Avenue
A revolutionary stone structure by H. H. Richardson, a great mansion executed in the Romanesque style. Also at the site, the 1836 Clarke House, Chicago's oldest house.

Jane Addams' Hull House Museum
800 S. Halstead Street
At the University of Illinois at Chicago, tourists can explore this seminal laboratory of social work. Chicago's first settlement house, assisting immigrants.

Lincoln Park Zoo
2200 N. Cannon Drive
Over 2,000 animal species in a wonderful and inviting setting. Stop in at the
Farm in the Zoo. Also stop by the Lincoln Park Conservatory.

Mexican Fine Arts Center Museum
1852 W. 19th Street
The largest Mexican museum in the country, with collections of folk art and
contemporary Mexican art.

Michigan Avenue
Explore the Magnificent Mile, filled with interesting stores and boutiques.

Museum of Contemporary Art
220 E. Chicago Avenue
One of the city's newest and most intriguing museums, showing artwork across
a broad range of media: photography, sculpture, painting, video.

Museum of Science and Industry
57th Street and Lake Shore Drive
See the new train exhibit. Go through the coal mine and board the German
U-boat. Walk through the heart. There's something for everyone here.

Navy Pier
600 E. Grand Avenue
Navy Pier is 50 acres of parks, promenades, shops and attractions. The Pier
contains an IMAX theater, a four-masted schooner, a 15-story Ferris wheel and
an enclosed botanical garden, along with restaurants and other shops. Contains
the Chicago Children's Museum.

Oriental Institute Museum
University of Chicago
1155 E. 58th Street
Great and accessible collection of marvels from ancient days. Exhibits on
ancient Egypt and Persia.

Peace Museum
314 W. Institute Place
Dedicated to the promotion of peace, the museum explores the concept and
the challenge.

Polish Museum of America
984 N. Milwaukee Avenue
With so many Poles in Chicago, this is a major museum. Contains great
collections on the Polish immigrant experience: photos, folk art and
documents.

Pullman Historic District
11141 S. Cottage Grove Avenue
Visit the historic planned neighborhood built for Pullman Coach factory
workers.

Sears Tower Skydeck Observatory
233 S. Wacker Drive
Take an elevator to the 103rd floor and visit the clouds, in one of the world's
tallest buildings.

John G. Shedd Aquarium
1200 S. Lake Shore Drive
The Shedd is the world's largest indoor aquarium with more than 6,000 fishy
critters. See sharks, whales, dolphins, along with marine mammals.

David and Alfred Smart Museum of Art
University of Chicago
5550 S. Greenwood Avenue
A nice and intimate art collection; over 5,000 works ranging from ancient to
modern.

Spertus Museum of Judaica
618 S. Michigan Avenue
An award-winning museum that tells the grand story of Jewish history. Includes
the Zell Holocaust Memorial.

State Street
Between Wacker and Congress Streets
Prime Chicago shopping district, featuring historic stores such as Marshall
Field's and Carson Pirie Scott.

The Des Plaines River Trail

Lake County connects to the Grand Illinois Trail

The Lake County Forest Preserve District has admirably improved the Des Plaines River Trail, most recently by adding a four-mile section through Independence Grove. This new section allows the connection of the south and north sections of the Des Plaines River Trail—it links them together for the very first time.

The Des Plaines River Trail is 29 miles long and weaves a winding parallel to the Des Plaines River in Lake County. It begins at Russell Road in Wadsworth, Illinois near the Wisconsin state line and runs south to Riverside Drive near Lincolnshire.

An additional four miles are in planning to connect the trail to Lake-Cook Road at the county line.

The Des Plaines River Trail contains important elements of the Lake County Forest Preserve District. The trail is a major greenway in Lake County, protecting over 7,700 acres of land—a full 85% of the river's edge. The Des Plaines River Trail makes connections between 10 different forest preserves.

The north section of the Des Plaines River Trail runs from Russell Road to Independence Grove in Libertyville. This north section cuts through 972-acre Van Patten Woods Forest Preserve and the Wadsworth Prairie Forest Preserve outside of Wadsworth. Wadsworth Prairie is a 1,200-acre site and it is part of the Illinois Nature Preserve System. An extensive wetlands project is also along the north section.

The south section of the Des Plaines River Trail runs through Independence Grove. Independence Grove is a massive park resource, with a visitors center, restaurant, events plaza, internal trails and a 115-acre recreational lake. The south section runs through Old School Forest Preserve, MacArthur Woods and Half Day Forest Preserve next to Wright Woods Forest Preserve.

The Des Plaines River Trail will hook into the Grand Illinois Trail system by tying into the North Branch Trail. The North Branch Trail is configured to connect with the Chicago city routing of the Grand Illinois Trail.

Trail advocates see the possibility of tying the north end of the Des Plaines River Trail into the Grand Illinois Trail, by using a road route to extend the North Shore Path west to the Prairie Trail in McHenry County.

Lake County also contributes two more ancillary trails that are designed to eventually connect to the Grand Illinois Trail—the McClory Trail and the North Shore Path. The McClory Trail connects to the Green Bay Trail and runs near Lake Michigan. It will eventually be tied into the Chicago Lakefront Path.

Plans call for extending the North Shore Path, which roughly parallels Illinois Route 176, west into McHenry County where it will join the Prairie Trail. Trail developers call this the "Millennium Trail."

The Illinois Prairie Path

Maywood to Elgin

Rub two sticks together, what do you get? Nothing? What if you keep rubbing, even when you're tired and you don't see much result? What then?

Perhaps you can see a bit of blackening, some kind of charring. Or the smell of smoke. This is encouraging. So you continue.

After a time comes a glowing ember, just a warm-hot bit of wood. Catch that up in the right stuff, at the right time, and you get a much hotter ember. A happy ember that becomes fire, a brief tongue of flame and then a sustaining fire.

That's the story of the Illinois Prairie Path—the barest bit of an idea blown around, taken up and swirled together. From a simple but provocative idea to a major element of the landscape. Why not a path? Here and now?

It seemed to make sense. Convert an abandoned rail corridor into a linear park that could by used by everyone. The creation of the Illinois Prairie Path was America's first rails-to-trails conversion.

Today the Illinois Prairie Path is one of the most delightful features of DuPage County. It is a narrow band that wraps together many of the county's main communities. And in an era in which there has been accelerated development in DuPage County, the IPP remains one of the stable elements in the area. It admirably fulfills its task as a linear park and communities along the route find ways to add to it and embellish it. New purposes seem to keep getting found for it. Best of all, it has been a real leader in demonstrating the value of trails to a community. Starting with a great vision, a dedicated citizen's group has built a wonderful asset.

The timing was good. The Illinois Prairie Path took shape during the mid-1960s, during a time when people were becoming much more environmentally conscious. May Theilgaard Watts, a distinguished educator and author, and her friend Helen Turner, and their "committee of exploration" consisting of Jane Sindt, Lillian Lasch, Phoebe Ryerson and Elizabeth Holmes tackled trail development head on. They tirelessly spoke before hundreds of local clubs and civic organizations, delivering lectures on prairie plants, the importance of outdoor recreation and the possibilities of a prairie path. They went to countless tiresome governmental meetings. They organized public walks along the projected route, taking hundreds of people to tour nature.

While DuPage County and Wheaton officials dithered over the route, the committee of exploration developed grass roots support for

An express waits at the Chicago, Aurora & Elgin's Villa Avenue station in Villa Park, on an April day in 1956. (Photo courtesy of Richard Stark)

the Prairie Path. And they gained the support of a number of municipalities and local businesses. As urban planner William H. Whyte pointed out:

> *It is a rare right-of-way which does not have an incredibly complicated legal and political history behind it, and unsnarling questions of title and jurisdiction is difficult under the best of circumstances. It takes a hard core of screwballs to see this kind of project through.*

Fortunately there were "screwballs" enough in DuPage County to save the route. The committee of exploration became the Illinois Prairie Path Association and during its history the group has turned the old Chicago, Aurora & Elgin right-of-way from a rutted dirt path through a weed lot into one of the country's most admired recreation trails.

The Illinois Prairie Path Association's dedication to its mission is phenomenal. The IPP association has built fountains, information kiosks and rest stops. It has encouraged and organized countless thousands of man-hours of volunteer labor. It has acted as a voice of conscience to DuPage County officials. Two especially noteworthy examples of its leadership stand out and both involve bridges.

The route over the east branch of the DuPage River between Glen Ellyn and Lombard requires a bridge over the East Branch of the DuPage River. The IPP worked with the Illinois National Guard to build a footbridge. This was vandalized to bits. Bridge #2 lasted two years before being swept away in a flood. Hauled back, another flood soon came to unloose it again. The third bridge was a treat for a local arsonist. So was Bridge #4. Still determined, the Illinois Prairie Path Association hired a contractor to build an all-steel bridge in 1978. It holds fast today.

The other great bridge saga is Volunteer Bridge in Wheaton. This 373-foot span crosses the Chicago & Northwestern, two city streets and a small park! Eighty-nine IPP volunteers, along with welding and

Converted to new uses, the Villa Avenue station is now a main rest stop along the Illinois Prairie Path.

woodworking students, under the direction of Philip Hodge, a structural engineer and IPP vice president, built and set the bridge at a cost of only $25,000 in 1983. The original estimate had been a quarter million dollars!

Additions have increased trail rider options and trail use. The Chicago, Aurora & Elgin right-of-way in Kane County was finally purchased by the Illinois Department of Conservation in 1972 and in 1979 the department also bought the Cook County right-of-way. These essential parcels have since been augmented by the reconnection and surfacing of the Geneva Spur in 1996. And more development of connecting trails is projected along the East and West Branches of the DuPage River and Salt Creek.

All of the Illinois Prairie Path rests on the former right-of-way of the Chicago, Aurora & Elgin—the C. A. & E. This was an interurban commuter line that served the western suburbs from 1902 to 1957. Its origins lay in the early streetcar routes in the Fox River Valley, and the Fox River Trolley Museum on Illinois Route 31 in South Elgin retains streetcars and memories of those days. For a time the C. A. & E. was owned by financial titan Samuel Insull. The line competed with the Chicago & Northwestern railroad, which runs roughly parallel, for commuter business. The Chicago, Aurora & Elgin was called the Roarin' Elgin because of its clatter, and it was also known as the Third Rail since its electric power source came through an extra rail.

After World War II, the Congress Expressway project killed off the C. A. & E.—twice. First, the actual construction of the highway caused such a great diversion that the C. A. & E. was hopelessly rerouted. Then ridership dropped once the expressway was completed. This pretty much kayo'd the line, even though the Third Rail kept up operations until July 3, 1957.

During its heyday, the C. A. & E. operated commuter cars in and out of Chicago on an hourly basis during the week. These could reach up to 70 mph, shaking, shuddering, thundering and thumping along.

The Illinois Prairie Path

The sun was always in the eyes of the conductor, and this is why the C. A. & E. called itself the Sunset Lines. It is said that between 1944 and 1952 the line had 7.5 million passengers per year, each plunking down ten cents for a ride into the city or back home. The C. A. & E. also did some local freight business.

One rail historian has called the C. A. & E. "the single most progressive and innovative interurban railway operating in the history of the industry." Up until the early 1950s the line experienced growth in ridership, despite Chicago & Northwestern commuter competition and highway disruptions, but high operations cost, with no public subsidy, meant the end was inevitable.

Remnants and reminders of the Third Rail appear along the Illinois Prairie Path. The old commuter stations at Villa Avenue and Ardmore Avenue have found adaptive reuse as homes to the Villa Park Historical Society and the Villa Park Chamber of Commerce. The electric substations along the Elgin Branch, at Prince Road Crossing and Clintonville, still crowd trailside. A municipal building in Warrenville was a station. It is an amazing thing to think that today's Prairie Path—a well-developed trail with established trees and robust prairie gardens—was at one time a spare utility strip. The Founders and their successors have done their job well.

Following the Illinois Prairie Path

Trailhead access for the Illinois Prairie Path is at First Avenue in Maywood, Illinois, just three miles over the Cook County line. The Illinois Prairie Path begins right next to Duke of Oil service shop, about a quarter mile north of the Interstate 290/Congress Expressway, on the west side of First Avenue.

The Illinois Prairie Path Maywood access is directly opposite the Fourth District Circuit Court Building and the Cook County Sheriff's Police Department at Maybrook Square.

Don't park next to the Illinois Prairie Path here since you're likely to get a ticket. Park near the entrance to the trailhead area instead.

Riding west from First Avenue there is an immediate bend north in the trail, at 0.5 miles. This bend brings the trail route in line with the old Chicago, Aurora & Elgin commuter rail routing. The trail surface is an eight-foot asphalt strip.

At 1.7 miles out, you are in Bellwood, Illinois and a fairly industrial area. Bellwood, population 20,535, was incorporated in

1900. It has always been an industrial town, and a blacksmith opened shop here in the 1870s. There are storage facilities and truck van storage along the path. The Cement Mason's Union is just to the north, and so is Borg-Warner Transmission Systems. At this point, you reach Madison Street. There is no curb cut-out. This is a fast and busy four-lane with hustling traffic.

At 1.8 miles is the Bellwood Centennial Prairie, a nice assortment of purple coneflowers, grama grass, black-eyed susans and blazing star, dedicated by the Village of Bellwood and Borg-Warner in 2000. It is directly across from the large Chicago Contractor's Supply building and warehouse.

The Bellwood Water Department is at 2.2 miles, with Bellwood Avenue at 2.5 miles.

One of the busiest roads to cross on the Prairie Path is Mannheim Road, at 2.8 miles out. This is a tricky and difficult crossing. Cross Mannheim by taking the sidewalk north to the Washington St./ Illinois Route 56 and Mannheim Road intersection. There is a signal crossing here. Pass by Micky's Famous Italian Beef Sausages and Meatballs to get to Washington Street, punch the button, and cross into a strip retail block anchored by Firestone Tires.

Heading west, you arrive at Warren Avenue at 3.1 miles out. The Prairie Path is routed on Warren Avenue, a local road, for a short stretch. This passes by a small industrial center occupied by On-Time Printing & Finishing, VSA Stone Products, Hooray Valet dry cleaning, Peel & Stik Adhesive Products, Hillside Lumber and ATM Plastics. At 3.7 miles, Warren Avenue deadheads into Forrest Avenue. Turn right (north) on Forrest Avenue and you will find a friendly prairie path entrance only a short distance away. But to get to the IPP parkway, you will cross busy Butterfield Road. And you are now in Hillside, Illinois.

Four miles from the Maywood trail access is Memorial Park District's Eisenhower Park. This is a playground for everyone. There are ballfields, tennis courts, picnic areas and a large aquatic center. The park has water fountains and restroom facilities.

At 4.4 miles, the Illinois Prairie Path route takes a heavy-duty bridge over Wolf Road. This area continues to have a genuinely residential feel to it, a contrast to the more industrial Bellwood section. At 5.2 miles you cross Taft Avenue and you are in downtown Berkeley, Illinois. There is a small but tasteful municipal park, with flowerbeds, capped with a handsome central clock. There is no curb cut here so watch it.

Interstate 294 looms ahead at 5.6 miles from the Maywood IPP trailhead, with traffic rushing overhead on the massive overpass. You should note a small municipal road maintenance yard under the bridge. This part of the <u>Prairie Path</u>, from Maywood to Interstate 294 is the most recent addition to the route.

The trail surface shifts from asphalt to eight-foot limestone screenings at the Elmhurst village line. There are a lot of pros and cons to every trail surface, but everyone can appreciate the snickery-snick sound of limestone screenings under their tires. It is a restful sound. Along this entry to Elmhurst is a fine prairie planting. Heading west into Elmhurst is a nice, long descent. Take advantage of it. If you are on a bike, this is a good stretch to rest your legs, have some water and let the wheels do the work.

Elmhurst, population 42,762, incorporated 1882, is known for her historic elm trees. These trees were planted in 1868 by Jedidiah Lathrop and Seth Wadhams. The city was originally called Cottage Hill and was founded in 1845 by Gerry Bates. The city for years had two very distinct ethnic groups: German agriculturalists and settlers from New England. On the streets of Elmhurst you could hear German spoken freely up until World War I.

The Chicago Fire of 1871 did a lot for Elmhurst. It exposed city residents to the suburbs. The German Evangelical Synod of the Northwest established the core school that grew into present-day

The Prairie Path connects neighborhoods.

Elmhurst College. The college's <u>Old Main</u> (the *Hauptgebaude*) is on the National Register of Historic Places.

In the 1920s Elmhurst became the top city in DuPage County. Her population shot from 4,500 to 14,000. Among her residents was Carl Sandburg. Reinhold Neibuhr, the theologian, at one time also made Elmhurst his home. It was in the 1950s that Elmhurst really grew the most, adding new subdivisions and schools in the great postwar building boom.

At 6.3 miles out is the Poplar Avenue crossing. This portion continues to descend into Elmhurst, and there are established trees providing fine shade along the trail, and the IPP is outfitted here with antique-style lampposts all the way into downtown Elmhurst. Downtown Elmhurst features <u>Old Meadows Trace Park</u>, a park with drinking water, an old train depot and good opportunities for passive recreation.

It is interesting to see how many different people take to trails. This is especially the case with a neighborhood trail like the Illinois Prairie Path. Here you might run across a big trail constituency—small boys on bikes—and perhaps stroller-pushing young mothers. The Prairie Path gets a lot of use for physical fitness. You might find an older man on a bike, a woman taking her exercise very seriously and a family walking home from a neighborhood park. It is instructive to see all the rabbit runs along the way—narrow threads of pathways between the IPP and its next-door house lots. It is a popular trail.

At 7.2 miles the Prairie Path crosses the active tracks of the Illinois Central railroad. Exercise good judgment here. The IPP route takes a hard jog right and then goes up and over the railroad tracks. It is possible here to continue right (and north) toward <u>City Centre Wilder Park</u>.

<u>Pioneer Park</u> in Elmhurst is just on the other side of the IC tracks, a good neighborhood park for Little Leaguers. Just ahead, at 7.4 miles, is the <u>Oasis</u>, a rest area that has water and restrooms. Keep an eye open for the local hot dog vendor.

At 7.6 miles out, you will find the <u>Shooting Star Trail</u>, named after the beautiful, delicate pink and purplish prairie flower. They resemble shooting stars, petals spraying out like comet tails. This is a wonderfully large prairie planting.

The Ovaltine Factory in Villa Park, recently restored to residential use.

At 7.7 miles out you can get a first glimpse of the <u>Ovaltine Factory</u>'s towering smokestack. This is a major landmark on the Illinois Prairie Path. And here, too, at 7.7 miles, is the <u>Elmhurst Great Western Prairie</u>, planted and maintained by a special squad of the Elmhurst Park District. The prairie plantings begin to give you a feel for what Illinois must have been like to the first white settlers. And you realize that prairie really is a kind of unified ecosystem, despite its wild looks, its varying colors, and its weedy texture.

According to D. Farney in *Tallgrass Prairie*: "You can grow a prairie facsimile in five or six years. But some scientists think it could take 200 years to construct the intricate prairie ecosystem. Others think 500 years or more."

Many different prairie plants share the ability to snatch up water. Prairie grass roots burrow as much as eight feet into the ground. This fits them to Illinois' weather conditions. Most established prairies are about 20% prairie plant and 80% prairie grass.

There is a large bridge that rises over Salt Creek at about eight miles out. Just after this is an even larger span over Illinois Route 83 and all its traffic. Here you might pause to wonder: Why the constant hurry? Where does it all go?

Note: Use caution coming down from the Illinois Route 83 bridge. There is a cross street right at the end of the descent: be ready to stop. This is an entrance street into the still-new subdivision that was built on the Ovaltine factory site. The redevelopment took a shuttered factory and turned it into a high-end senior residential center.

The Ovaltine Factory is at 8.5 miles from the Maywood trail access. The factory cranked out the famous chocolate-flavored milk additive. The big "W" on the main factory building stands for Wander Company, the Swiss company that established the factory in 1917. It is a fun bit of history ("More Ovaltine, please!") and the Villa Park Historical Society, just across the street at 220 S. Villa Avenue, tells the story in detail. It also contains some Chicago, Aurora & Elgin materials. This is fitting, because the Society is in the old Villa Avenue C. A. & E. station.

The Villa Avenue station, you should know, was a premier stop on the C.A. & E. line. It was built to help promote residential development in Villa Park and it is on the National Register of Historic Places. It has mock Tudor features placed on a sturdy Craftsman-style building. During its heyday, a pharmacy also operated in the building. The Villa Avenue station was designed by Arthur U. Gerber and constructed in 1928. Here there is a nice trailhead with parking for 35 cars, restrooms and water.

The Great Western Trail can be reached from the Villa Avenue station by following Villa Avenue north for two blocks from this point. The Great Western Trail is a newer suburban trail opened in 1992 that runs all the way to St. Charles. Villa Park is its eastern trailhead.

Villa Park, population 22,075, incorporated 1915, is a true commuter rail community. It was farmland outside Chicago until the Aurora and Elgin was built. At that point, two profit-minded Chicago real estate developers came out, took a look, and took action.

Messrs. Ballard and Pottinger bought some land from a German farmer, platted house lots and built Ardmore School and a train depot as development inducements. They planted hundreds of poplar trees and said, "come live in the suburbs!" It worked. It was successful. The 1920s were great boom years for Villa Park.

At 8.8 miles you cross Summit Avenue in downtown Villa Park, and at 9.1 miles the cross street is Ardmore Avenue. Here you will find the famous Al's Smoke Shop, and just ahead is the C.A. & E.'s Ardmore Station at 10 W. Park Avenue. This now contains the <u>Villa Park Chamber of Commerce</u>. The <u>Ardmore Station</u> is another little architectural gem. It is a depot with a hipped horizontal Prairie style roof supported by river rock piers. It was built in 1910 and was designed by John S. Van Bergen in a robust manifestation of the Prairie style. Renovation of this National Register-listed station was led by Dick Diebold.

They named the streets in Villa Park after great universities, and at 9.5 miles out you cross Harvard Street. The Villa Park Rotary built the <u>Prairie Path Tot Lot</u> here, and there is a water fountain at this point.

At Addison Street you cross into Lombard.

Lombard, population 42,322, incorporated 1903, is known for its <u>Lilacia Park</u> and its annual Lilac Celebration. Lombard is among the older settlements in DuPage County, being located along an old stagecoach line between Chicago and St. Charles. Further early development occurred when the Galena and Chicago Union Railroad sited a depot in Lombard in 1851, making it a local stop.

The village was originally called Babcock's Grove and settler Sheldon Peck built the first house near Lombard Commons Park in 1837. The house is said to have later become a station on the Underground Railroad.

The temperance issue caused early political controversy, as the main two settling groups, Germans and New Englanders, held very different views on the value of drinking beer. The Chicago and Great Western Railroad went through the village in 1887. The village received its name from Josiah L. Lombard, a real estate man who successfully led the local effort to have the state charter the town. Growth was moderate until the 1920s when the population zoomed.

Points of interest in Lombard include the <u>Helen M. Plum Library</u> with Lilacia Park, laid out by noted landscape designer Jens Jensen. Interesting National Register sites include the <u>First Church of Lombard</u> at Maple and Main Streets, and the <u>DuPage Theater & DuPage Shoppes</u>, the theater is an ornate example of classic art-deco movie house extravagance along 101-109 S. Main Street.

Westmore Avenue is ahead, at 10.2 miles, and you will find a friendly water stop along the trail near the 7-11. There are plenty of street crossings in Lombard—Highland Avenue (10.4 miles), Lodge Lane (10.6 miles), Grace Street (11.0 miles) and a few others—it is tough to build up steam on a bike through this portion of the IPP. At the same time, this stretch has a high amount of local use. And it is useful—Lombard Commons is just two blocks north of the Illinois Prairie Path, off Grace Street, and this is a large village park with all the amenities.

More street crossings come up: Elizabeth Street, Brewster Avenue, Edson Avenue. At 12.2 miles there is an overpass on Finley Road/Illinois Route 53. And at 12.4 miles is a huge bridge over Interstate 355. The bridge cost the Illinois State Toll Highway Authority $1,000,000 to build in 1989, a sign of affection for the Illinois Prairie Path.

Exercise caution and good judgment coming off the Interstate 355 bridge. You descend to a narrow metal bridge over the East Branch of the DuPage River, with a bit of asphalt at the bridge approach. And you end up turning left and reaching a busy highway posted at 35 mph, which drivers often exceed. Turn left, then cross. At 13.5 a parallel railline can be seen—this is the Chicago & Northwestern. At 13.7 miles is an unusual bridge over Taylor Avenue. This is a cement viaduct that only allows one car through at a time. And Spicely Park with its prairie plants, benches and drinking fountain is just across Walnut Street to the south.

The Illinois Prairie Path reaches into downtown Glen Ellyn, with the path ending into a parking lot for the Metra commuter line.

Glen Ellyn, population 26,999, incorporated 1892, developed in an unusual fashion for a Chicago suburb—it began as a resort town. People from Chicago would travel out to Glen Ellyn to Prospect Park and to enjoy a spa with national repute, Lake Ellen Hotel. Originally the village was given the names "Newton Station" and "Danby," and then "Prospect Park." Glen Ellyn became "Glen Ellyn" in 1891, a name that referenced the town's glens and the favored Welsh spelling of the hotelkeeper's name.

The first settlers from New England were Deacon and Mary Churchill, who placed their cabin at the juncture of a pair of Indian trails called "The Corners." Stacy's Tavern, a stagecoach stop, was built in 1846 by Moses Stacy as an inn on the stagecoach route to St. Charles. It has long been a major historical site in the area, and is on the National Register of Historic Places. There is a small admission fee. Stacy's Tavern is at 557 Geneva Road at St. Charles Road. In 1911, Glen Ellyn was the recipient of a generous town-wide treeplanting by Dr. Frank Johnson.

The Glen Ellyn Prairie Path Park is at 14.2 miles from the Maywood trailhead, and it is outfitted with a water fountain and benches. Downtown Glen Ellyn has some noteworthy stores and eateries. The IPP is a ten-foot asphalt path, crossing Park Boulevard, Main Street and Prospect Avenue near the Glen Ellyn Library, and St. Petronille Grade School. The school has its own prairie planting, tended by the children.

Elmer J. Hoffman Park is named for a former county board member. It is adjacent to the IPP at 15.4 miles, and there is a fine, large prairie planting at 15.6 miles. At Hill Avenue (15.8 miles) keep your eyes open, cross the street with care, and take a jog to the right. You should see the Good News Publishers/Crossways Books building. You are now in Wheaton, Illinois. Continue along the edge of the commuter parking lot.

Wheaton, population 55,416, incorporated 1890, has been the county seat of DuPage County since 1867 when a classic "county seat war," was successfully waged against Naperville. Wheaton owes her birth to two very unique brothers, Warren and Jesse Wheaton, who platted town lots right alongside the Chicago and Galena Union Railroad (which later became the Chicago and Northwestern railroad) in 1849.

Wheaton is known for Wheaton College and for the college's most famous son, the evangelist Billy Graham. Wheaton College was originally the Illinois Institute, which opened in 1853. The school was reorganized by educationalist Jonathan Blanchard in 1865, who was a kind of professional college president, having hoisted the gavel at Knox College and Illinois College. A 1943 graduate, Billy Graham's organization contributed $13 million toward the building of the Billy Graham Center on the Wheaton College campus. Billy Graham memorabilia is kept for public display at the Billy Graham Center Museum at 500 E. College Avenue. Blanchard Hall on the college campus is on the National Register.

Other National Register sites include Adams Memorial Library at 102 E. Wesley Street, the DuPage County Courthouse at 200 Reber Street and Trinity Episcopal Church at 130 N. West Street.

The area is currently home to more than 50 Christian organizations, giving Wheaton much of its character and flavor. Wheaton is a center of Christian publishing, and was also home to the Charles Kerr Publishing Company, an early socialist press. But perhaps the key to attracting these organizations was a city whose political life was largely shaped by temperance advocate Warren Wheaton.

President Street (16.1 miles) is busy with downtown traffic. You can find a rewarding surprise a bit further along at Chase Street. Here the asphalt work has exposed a bit of the old Chicago, Aurora & Elgin rail. This is a nice artifact to find. Not everything in the county has been around for only ten or twelve years.

The Illinois Prairie Path route skirts the edges of parking lots in Wheaton, running on a narrow four-foot limestone path. West Street (17. 6 miles from Maywood) is a busy four-lane. Cross West Street into Founders Park.

Founders Park holds a granite boulder monument to the memory of May Theilgaard Watts. Ironically, the city of Wheaton posed some of the more difficult challenges to the development of the Illinois Prairie Path, first blocking the route because city officials feared a county expressway would be placed on the old C. A. & E. routing, and then they blocked the path because of a simple desire for more downtown parking.

Founders Park happens to be laid out at the very spot the old C. A. & E. commuter cars turned off to enter their main railyard and repair shop. The railyards now are ground level for a 20-floor apartment complex. The Prairie Path route here is on a sidewalk that mirrors the original C. A. & E. turn into the railyards. Continue along Liberty Drive past the apartment building to Carlton Avenue.

At 18.1 miles is the great junction point of the Illinois Prairie Path at Volunteer Park. From here, the Illinois Prairie Path runs southwest toward Aurora, reaching the City of Light some 13 miles away. Another branch runs northwest toward Elgin, Illinois, about 14 miles away.

The IPP Junction Point is at the intersection of Liberty Drive and Carlton Avenue in Wheaton. It has a useful information kiosk, a water fountain and a portapotty. A landmark here is the *Rails to*

The Old and the New. Here at Volunteers Park in Wheaton is a sculpture made from the iron of old interurban equipment. In the background are high-rise apartments directly on the site of the former Chicago, Aurora & Elgin yards.

Trails sculpture by Erika Marija Bajuk. The sculpture commemorates the old C. A. & E. even as it points to the route's new trail use. Much of the sculpture (except the wheel) comes from old C. A. & E. parts.

The Aurora Branch has some interesting aspects, especially the Batavia spur around Fermilab.

The Grand Illinois Trail route requires taking the Elgin branch that connects to the <u>Fox River Trail</u> just south of downtown Elgin. The route then picks up the Prairie Trail in Algonquin at the McHenry county line.

The Elgin Branch heads up and over an old iron truss bridge built in 1906 over the former Chicago and Northwestern railroad and extended north by three new bridge sections built by IPP volunteers in 1983, a major piece of trail engineering. The <u>Volunteer Bridge</u> carries the Elgin Branch and connects to the Fox River Trail just outside of Elgin.

The trail surface here becomes eight-foot limestone screenings. There are steep drop-offs on either side of the trail. You enjoy a nice downhill from here to Lincoln Avenue at 18.9 miles, and there is a neighborhood tot lot with water here.

This part of the Illinois Prairie Path contains a lot fewer road crossings than the IPP Main Stem. And during the C. A. & E.'s heyday, there were fewer stops. The commuter trains could open up and reach top speeds along such stretches, reaching 50 mph. It is interesting to come across old remnant elements of the C. A.

& E. system—the restored stations in Villa Park, the crumbling Prince Crossing station and the Clintonville station.

Lincoln Marsh, complete with cattails and frogs and a nature trail, is at nineteen miles from Maywood. On this section there is a slight rising grade, which continues to Jewel Road (19.5). Pleasant Hill Road (19.9 miles) appears. About 21 miles from Maywood is Geneva Road/County Farm Road, and the "Prairie Trail Center" is the name of the big retail area here.

There is plenty of traffic. Geneva Road/County Farm Road takes attention to cross. You come out next to a double four-lane intersection. Use the crosswalks here to get over to the small trailhead at the northwest corner. Here there are map boards and parking for 12 cars. This is the junction point for the IPP spur to Geneva, Illinois. The trailhead also accesses Timber Ridge Trail and Kline Creek Farm. Kline Creek Farm is a living history museum that recreates life on an old-time Illinois farm, complete with exhibits and events. The main trail to Elgin starts at the very end of the parking lot.

Timber Ridge is at 21.4 miles and there is a wood bridge with a fine view of a prairie marsh and creek. A concrete bridge is at 22.7 miles, with fine park views and a nearby bench.

Prince Crossing Road is at 23.2 miles. Be very careful crossing the road here—hikers and bikers have been struck by cars hurtling hell-for-leather over the hilltop just south of the trail crossing. It is recommended that you accept the road engineer's advice and take the 11-foot wide asphalt path along the road north to the new crossing point. This is also the crossing for the Great Western Trail. These two large trail systems, the IPP and the Great Western, also intersect about a half-mile ahead. So you could stay on the Great Western until you return to the IPP Elgin Branch.

Continue west. After crossing the road, double back to the IPP trail and take a closer look at the C.A. & E. Prince Road Crossing electric substation. This two-story brick structure served as a power source and as a commuter stop. It is difficult to imagine what this could ever be reasonably adapted to. But maybe there is a function in simply having ruins to remind us of other times, other ways of living and that things have ends as well as beginnings.

There is a road crossing at Illinois Route 64/North Avenue at 24.3 miles. Just past this is a large road overpass, carrying Illinois Route 59 over the IPP. At 25.2 miles the path splits in two, and a path to the left heads down toward Illinois Route 59 at road grade. By staying right, you take the huge concrete overpass over Illinois Route 59. And from here you should be seeing the broad green panoramic of St. Andrew's Golf Course.

Be ready for an immediate stop coming off the bridge. Diversey Parkway is close to the bridge ramparts. There are some fine black walnut trees across the street; head for these and you will be on the IPP Elgin Branch.

At 26.7 miles you will get your first sight of Illinois cornfields. And Smith Road is at 26.8 miles. It is a pretty section of trail.

Warning signs along the trail tell bike riders to dismount and walk their bikes at 27.9 miles out. Do this! It is a tough downhill, impossible to negotiate even for talented mountain bikers, with sliding stones and railroad ties and a sharp curving at the end of the drop. Walk the bike and stay on the railroad tie steps.

At the very bottom is E. J. & E. railroad. And across the way are a few rabbit-run paths. These only lead to local backyards. The IPP Elgin Branch runs along the far right once you have crossed the railroad tracks. This should give you the big view of Pratt's Wayne Woods.

Pratt's Wayne Woods is the largest forest preserve in DuPage County, occupying more than 3,900 acres of wetlands, woods, marshes, savanna and meadows. It offers equestrian trails and hiking trails, fishing and picnicking.

Army Trail Road and the Army Trail Road trailhead are ahead, at 28.3 miles. Here there is parking for about 12 cars, a portapotty and refreshing water. One neat thing here is the water fountain you have to pump—it makes getting water a fun thing.

Crossing Powis Road (28.4 miles), you travel into Pratt's Wayne Woods Forest Preserve at 29.2 miles.

At 30.4 miles is the busy crossing for Dunham Road. Don't be surprised to see horses around here. This is a pretty equestrian area. Bicyclists should avoid sharp and sudden moves, and give horseback riders comfortable berth. Horses don't like getting startled.

The Canadian National Railroad is at 30.7 miles, and the IPP Elgin Branch takes a wood-decked bridge over it. From this point you can see a large equestrian facility and a large concrete pipe storage site.

The path here is asphalt, and it returns to limestone screenings while you are passing through Bluff City Sand & Gravel. There is a busy and fast road crossing at Illinois Route 25 at 32.2 miles, and just a half-mile ahead is the C.A. & E.'s Clintonville station.

The Clintonville station is now headquarters for the Valley Model Railroad Association. It has been kept up and an original C.A. & E. flagstand has been placed in front of the station. The flagstand was used to signal train operators to stop at the station and pick up passengers.

Past this, the route passes through some large commercial parcels at this point, and a truck crossing on the trail.

Raymond Street is at 33.5 miles, and just ahead, at 33.7 miles, is South Elgin and the connection with the Fox River Trail. This important connection point could be spruced up. This would make a great spot for some sculpture or massive trailmarker.

You should be able to see the dressed-stone bridge of the Fox River Trail to the left (west). Follow through the bridge and you will be on your way south, through South Elgin, St. Charles, Geneva, Batavia, Aurora and down to Oswego. It is not hard to hope to see the Fox River Trail continued all the way south to its junction with the Illinois River at Ottawa.

But taking the Fox River Trail north takes you through Elgin and toward the McHenry County communities of Algonquin and Crystal Lake. The Fox River Trail takes a new name, the Prairie Trail, once it crosses from Kane County into McHenry County. The Prairie Trail actually continues across the Illinois state line into Genoa City, Wisconsin. The Grand Illinois Trail uses this northern portion of the Prairie Trail, running to Richmond, Illinois and then turning west on other trails to Galena.

Birth of the Illinois Prairie Path

Converting the old Chicago, Aurora & Elgin interurban line took a lot of work on the part of many community-minded people in Chicago's western suburbs. Perhaps the most important in the effort was May Theilgaard Watts, a profound teacher, writer and instructor at the Morton Arboretum. Watt's *Letter to the Editor* made an eloquent case for the Illinois Prairie Path. It is the document that sparked the whole rails-to-trails movement in America.

Letter to the Editor
Chicago Tribune
September 1963
May Watts

Dear Editor:

We are human beings. We are able to walk upright on two feet. We need a footpath. Right now there is a chance for Chicago and its suburbs to have a footpath, a long one.

The right of way of the Aurora electric road lies waiting. If we have courage and foresight, such as made possible the Long trail in Vermont and the Appalachian trail from Maine to Georgia, and the network of the public footpaths in Britain, then we can create from this strip a proud resource.

Look ahead some years into the future. Imagine yourself going for a walk on an autumn day. Choose some part of the famed Illinois footpath. Where the highway crosses it, you enter over a stile. . . The grass is cut and garden flowers bloom in great beds. This part you may learn is maintained by the Chicago Horticultural Society. Beyond the garden you enter a forest again, maintained by the Morton Arboretum. At its edge begins a long stretch of water with mud banks, maintained for water birds and waders, by the Ornithological society. You notice an abundance of red-fruited shrubs. The birds have the Audubon societies to thank for those. You rest on one of the stout benches provided by the Prairie club, beside a thicket of wild crab trees planted by the Garden Club of Illinois.

Then you walk thru prairie again. Four Boy Scouts pass. They are hiking the entire length of the trail. This fulfills a requirement for some merit badge. A troop of Scouts is planting acorns in a grove of cottonwood trees. Most of the time you find yourself in prairie or woodland of native Illinois plants. These stretches of the trail need little or no upkeep. You come to one stretch, a long stretch, where nothing has been done. But university students are identifying and listing plants. The University of Chicago ecology department is in charge of this strip. They are watching to see what time and nature will do. . .

That is all in the future, the possible future. Right now the right of way lies waiting, and many hands are itching for it. Many bulldozers are drooling.

May Watts

Fox River Trail

South Elgin to Algonquin

The Fox River springs from its Wisconsin headwaters in Menomonee Falls, Wisconsin south to join the Illinois River at Ottawa. For such a shallow river, the Fox has been important to Illinois. The Fox River served as a major transportation route for the early French voyageurs in the 1670s. And it quickly became an important source of power for early industry.

It is a twisting and shallow river and there is plenty of sand and gravel, and the Fox River has a slow current as well. You notice when the river is high and you notice when it is low. Dams across the river keep the local water level high enough for recreation craft and decent fishing and they help regulate the river's flow.

Fox River communities seem to enjoy being near Chicago and being a part of the western suburbs. But they have a distinct identity. The towns are older. There is a lot of architectural variety. Famous people have worked and walked here. The streets acknowledge the river.

Hiking and biking in the Fox River region means diversity. There are forest preserves and nature preserves and city parks lining the river.

The Fox River Trail was first developed in 1988 and much of it runs along the former route of the Chicago & Northwestern railroad.

The Grand Illinois Trail makes contact with the Fox River Trail at a triangular clearing in the woods, just between Elgin and South Elgin. It

Fishing opportunities at the South Elgin Fox River spillway.

is a plain place. By rights, some kind of monument should now be here or perhaps a piece of public art. Nearby is trailhead parking for about ten cars, right along Raymond Road in South Elgin.

This meeting-ground is at the western end of the Illinois Prairie Path's Elgin Branch. It connects at about the midsection of the Fox River Trail. From this meeting spot, take the Fox River Trail north (hard right when coming off the IPP). You immediately cross Poplar Creek.

Elgin has a population of 94,487, and it was first settled in 1835 and incorporated in 1855. Elgin is a grand old town in a region filled with newer suburbs. Elgin's first settlers were the brothers James and Hezekiah Gifford, who arrived here in 1835 in the aftermath of the Black Hawk War. James' wife didn't believe him when he said he wanted to build a city. The Gifford boys got busy, laid out a roadway to Belvidere, and it happened—the hustle and bustle of stagecoaches, stores and shops and hotels. Elgin was on the route to Galena, passing the Gifford's sawmill and gristmill. The Giffords passed on to Elgin some of their entrepreneurial hustle, and the town grew with the Chicago & Galena Railroad.

Elgin always feels Chicago's presence. The Elgin National Watch Company was formed by four investors, the "Four Immortals," one of which was an ex-mayor of Chicago, the estimable Mr. Benjamin Raymond. The company was formed in 1867 by men associated with the American Watch Company in Waltham, Massachusetts.

The Grand Illinois Trail passes near the former site of the watch factory. At one time, the Elgin company employed thousands, and by the 1920's was making over a million watch movements each year. It

Whipping up the Fox River Trail. This is near its meeting point with the Illinois Prairie Path in South Elgin.

took the advent of the Timex, as well as the concerted efforts of Swiss watchmakers, to cause the demise of Elgin in 1965.

The Elgin National Watch Observatory at the corner of Watch and Raymond Streets, built in 1910, is on the National Register of Historic Places. The observatory was used to synchronize watches by calculating the duration of the earth's rotation in reference to fixed stars. The observatory was thus a kind of "master clock."

Oddball inventor Gail Borden took up headquarters in Elgin, and made the town an important dairy center. Borden had knocked around in Texas, where he was surveyor of the City of Galveston and a fighter in the Texas War of Independence. He was a teacher and publisher before becoming an inventor. His big success, of course, was with condensed milk. And the Eagle Brand of condensed milk can still be found in grocery stores today. His lesser-known inventions include the lazy susan (or so he claimed), the meat biscuit (was Borden the grandfather of Spam?) and a queer contraption, the "terraqueous prairie schooner," a kind of amphibian cart. The Elgin Milk Condensing Company was along Brook and Water Street.

Currently, the Grand Victoria Casino is a major pull, drawing thousands to the city. And it provides great tax revenues for the community. The Grand Victoria has a superb rest area just off the trail. It has benches and water and restrooms. It's even equipped with an air pump.

Following the Fox River Trail

From the Grand Victoria Casino heading north through Elgin riders pass a great wildflower and prairie planting, with different, brightly-colored, delicate flowers.

In Elgin, the Prairie Rock Brewery, at 127 S. Grove Avenue, is an attractive stop. Gasthaus zur Linde offers German food, at 15 N. Grove Street, Elgin. Elgin is home to the annual Four Bridges International Bike Race. At Kimble Street is the great Trygve Rovelstad sculpture group, "The Pioneers." This has more than an echo of Lorado Taft to it—Rovelstad studied under the great master. The statue was conceived in 1929, but economic circumstances changed. There was a Depression, there was a war, and other things along the way, and it was not until the year 2001 that the great artwork was dedicated. The sculpture honors Elgin's founders and hints at the hardships they endured and the strength of their vision.

A pleasant trip along the Fox River Trail.

At the City of Elgin's Slade Avenue facility, turn to the left and follow the roadway along the Fox River. Here you should see artistic waste treatment reservoirs. More important is a great water fountain right on the trail. It is good asphalt here—don't be surprised to find rollerbladers—and there are also prairie plantings.

There is a small trailhead about 1.5 miles north of Slade Avenue. There is space for about six cars.

Just after this is <u>Trout Park</u>, a well-established riverside park. Trout Park has been around since the 1920s. There are restrooms and water, picnic shelters and resting spots. It is immediately south of the Interstate 90 bridge. It is possible to take a pedestrian bridge across the Fox River to reach <u>Voyageur Landing Forest Preserve</u> and <u>Tyler Creek Forest Preserve</u>. Schmidt's Canoe Service is at Voyageur Landing.

Elgin has a number of noteworthy structures that are listed on the National Register of Historic Places. These include:

- <u>Elgin Historic District</u>, the city region bounded by Villa, Center, Park and N. Liberty, Channing Streets.

- <u>Elgin National Watch Observatory</u> (1910)at 312 Watch Street.

- <u>Fire Barn 5</u> (1903) a classic turn of the century firehouse at 533 St. Charles Road.

- The <u>First Universalist Church</u> on 55 Villa Street.

- <u>Gifford-Davidson House</u> at 363-365 Prairie Street.

- <u>Ora Pelton House</u> at 214 S. State Street.

- <u>Teeple Barn</u> located northwest of Elgin on Randall Road.

East Dundee, population 2,955, was incorporated 1887; West Dundee, Illinois, with a population of 5,428, was incorporated 1887. The Dundee area, East and West Dundee, was settled in the 1830s, and they have always had a combined history and occasional talk of municipal union. West Dundee was settled by Scots and English settlers, who named the town after Dundee, Scotland. It began with typical mill operations along the Fox River. Allan Pinkerton, private eye, began his famous detective work here when he spotted counterfeiters on local Bogus Island. He later formed the U.S. Secret Service agency and his Pinkerton's Detective Agency. The "baseball evangelist" Billy Sunday lived out this way at the turn-of-the-century, taking vacations away from the crowds, the spotlights, the tents and the sawdust trails on a farm owned by his wife's family.

As you arrive in East Dundee, the Fox River Trail runs right behind world-famous <u>Haegar Pottery</u>. Stop here and look into their retail outlet store. This is a neat place to shop. Haegar makes all kinds of things for all kinds of uses, and it is a cornucopia of cornucopias. And there is even a special little pottery museum built into the store that includes busts of the company founder and Carl Sandburg, the onetime Eminence of Elmhurst.

Just a few blocks north along the trail is <u>Duran's by Brian</u>, a sit-down restaurant. Just beyond this is River Street, where you need a bit of caution to cross. A special landmark here is the Dundee Dairy Queen.

East Dundee features a redeveloping commercial area, with retailers revitalizing attractive Victorian buildings, with shops like Kava Kava coffee and Artful Objects. <u>The Bicycle Garage</u> is here as well.

The <u>Dundee Township Tourist Center</u>, at 319 N. River Street, is a nicely converted train station, and it now guides area visitors. This is worth stopping into: it contains a fantastic assortment of area literature and printed items, along with restrooms and a water fountain. The Depot sits in a nice park setting and there is water, parking, restrooms and a wide selection of useful brochures. The <u>Dundee Township Historic District</u>, on the National Register, is on both sides of the Fox River. Just across the river in West Dundee is Emmett's Tavern & Brewing Company, at 128 W. Main Street.

<u>Otto Engineering</u>, makers of switches, is along the way north. The company campus is a handsome set of brick buildings on both sides of the Fox River. The company lets the public use some of its grounds, and you can find plenty of people fishing along the riverbanks.

Carpentersville, Illinois, population 30,586, first incorporated 1887, was settled in the 1830s by a young dynamo of business, Angelo Carpenter. Carpenter knew the Fox River area would develop, and he began a number of businesses. He platted the town in 1851, and set to work building a sawmill (to provide lumber for all the new housing) and a gristmill (for trade with farmers in the area). He did well, and soon enough added a grocery store and a woolen mill. He later built Illinois Iron and Bolt Company. Angelo was a philanthropist who liked to see immediate results, and Angelo was known for dispensing town lots and houses to the poor. He contributed parks and a community hall to Carpentersville, and it's just right after all this that the town bears his name.

<u>Library Hall</u>, at 21 N. Washington Street, is on the National Register.

At the Kane County/McHenry County line, the Fox River Trail formally ends. But the route continues, now renamed the Prairie Trail in McHenry County.

Additional Trails

Fox River Trail (south)

In fact, the whole Fox River Trail is worth riding. The Grand Illinois Trail may only use the northern portion of it, but the entire 42-mile route is among the best recreational trails in Illinois. The Fox River Trolley Museum, along Illinois Route 31 in South Elgin, is well worth a visit. Here you can see what interurban trolleys looked like, the kind that regularly carried passengers through the Fox River valley.

The Fox River Trail sticks to the river, running on the west side of the river from Oswego to South Elgin. At South Elgin, a bridge carries the trail across to the east side. The Fox River Trail goes through Aurora, Batavia, Geneva, St. Charles, Valley View, Elgin, East Dundee and Carpentersville. It gives a very full view of the Fox Valley region, and there are numerous trailheads:

Fabyan Forest Preserve
Shoemaker Nature Preserve
Batavia Depot Museum
South Elgin Railroad Museum

The Fox River Trail connects to the Illinois Prairie Path at South Elgin (this is the Elgin Branch of the IPP, part of the Grand Illinois Trail), and at Batavia and Aurora (these are the Batavia spur of the Aurora Branch, and the Aurora Branch itself).

The Great Western Trail (west section)

This trail runs from St. Charles to Sycamore, near DeKalb, running through the towns of Wasco, Lily Lake and Virgil along the way. A popular Fox Valley trailhead is at Leroy Oakes Forest Preserve, just off Randall Road in St. Charles. The west section of the Great Western Trail is 18 miles long. The eastern section of the Great Western Trail runs from Villa Park to West Chicago.

The Virgil L. Gilman Trail

This is a 9.7-mile long trail running from Waubonsee Community College outside of Sugar Grove, across Copley Park and the Fox River, and through Aurora, to Hill Avenue/Business Route 30.

The train museum in South Elgin has a surviving interurban car of just the kind that used to run through the Fox River valley each day.

Fox River Trail

The Prairie Trail

Through McHenry County to Richmond, Illinois

This trail is a dynamic trail and it offers something for everyone. There are great natural features, long straight-aways for racers, level and hilly stretches, parkways and parks.

The McHenry County Conservation District built the Prairie Trail in 1989. They are still adding to it. For most of the route the Prairie Trail is a simply eight-foot asphalt strip, laid out along an old Chicago and Northwestern railroad route to Milwaukee.

Following the Prairie Trail

Start your ride in Algonquin at the Prairie Bike Shop. This is a good trail access point and just near Illinois Route 31 that runs along the west side of the Fox River.

At 0.3 miles is a small bridge over a creek in the woods, but a fun arching bridge is over Illinois Route 62/Algonquin Road. This has a slight hump to it and it's just fun to cross it. There is a fine trailhead access to the Prairie Trail at 0.7 miles from the bike shop—this is the Algonquin Road trailhead and it has parking and picnic and restroom facilities.

The Prairie Trail winds through a sand quarry operated by Material Services Corporation for the next two miles. Huge billows of big bluestem line the trail and nod their heads to and fro in the breeze. This grass takes its name from the color of their tips; it's a deep purplish blue. Big bluestem is the official state prairie grass, and it can grow up to eight feet tall. An access trail to a neighborhood park is at 1.4 miles.

Larsen Prairie, about twenty acres in size, is at 2.2 miles out. Larsen Prairie has a central marshy area filled with cattails and diverse prairie plants surround it. The prairie grows along slight slopes, and you can get a really fine view of the dense, luxuriant growth. A bright yellow goldfinch flickered here across the trail and landed in the branches of a tree. Underneath the tree, you could tell deer had nestled in the grass below the night before.

An unusual belt conveyor—used for pulling up sand from the sand pit to the sorting tower—is at 2.5 miles out, draped with a

Wonderful old pines line the trail at Crystal Lake's Veterans Park. . . but it's a steep hill going down, and even steeper going up!

sign congratulating the McHenry County Conservation District. The trail ducks into a nicely shaded route, with scrub elm trees making a pleasant sort of tunnel for the trail. At 3.3 miles there is a sharp turn to the left (west) and you are out in the open, with the trail running along an edge of the quarry. The quarry is getting re-vegetated. Weed species that thrive in rocky, sandy soil are first to make an appearance. It will take some time, but more plant varieties will grow here as soil is built up.

Lake in the Hills Airport is just across the road from the quarry. The driveway for L & V Distributors, purveyors of Old Style, cuts the trail at four miles from Algonquin. Just ahead the trail crosses James R. Rakow Road, a busy four-lane.

Crystal Lake Ski and Bike, a trailside bike shop, is at 4.4 miles. It is just up ahead that you need to make a double road-cross, first crossing Virginia Road and then Pyott Road/Main Street.

Berkshire Drive is at 4.6 miles, and just ahead is a quaint wood bridge walkthrough along the path—part of the imaginative and beautiful Crystal Lake Greenway Corridor and the Diverse City Prairie Access. This area is a successful community beautification

Great for Rollerblading! The Prairie Trail runs through urban and natural areas in McHenry County.

project, showing support of local schools, businesses and government. Here Crystal Lake School District 47 worked with the McHenry County Conservation District to plant 11,300 prairie grass clumps, 180 trees and 1,175 shrubs. The Diverse City Prairie Access really lets you get close to many different kinds of prairie plants, and the show helps develop your appreciation for this kind of environment.

Follow the trail under the Illinois Route 14/Illinois Route 12 intersection. This is just over five miles from your start. The underpass here is one of the most impressive underpasses that can be built. It is gated and illuminated and nicely wide. At 5.3 miles, the Prairie Trail turns to an eight-foot asphalt strip. Just ahead is a busy entrance to a strip mall—with drivers quickly turning in and out of the lot. Keep alert here.

The Canadian Pacific railroad still operates on the tracks at this point, and you can see heaps of ballast and cast-off rails next to the trail.

Main Street and Crystal Lake Avenue intersect just south of Crystal Lake's central business district at 6.3 miles. Across the way are branches of Columbia College and Webster University. This is another double street crossing, and it is best to stop to push the crosswalk buttons here. First, cross Crystal Lake Avenue, then Main Street. This is near downtown Crystal Lake. The Prairie Trail is routed on residential streets around the downtown area.

Take Crystal Lake Avenue east, crossing railroad tracks as you go, and then go north on East Street. This is at 6.7 miles out. East

Street makes a lazy left-hand turn and then crosses west across railroad tracks. Just after the tracks get on Glenn Street and head north for two blocks, up to Terra Cotta Avenue, at 7.2 miles. Terra Cotta Avenue is a busy road. Dismount and wait for your chance to cross it.

Cross over, and just to the right is Lorraine Street, which runs up into a newer residential area. At the top of Lorraine Street is a nice surprise—the Veterans Acres Park trailhead. Here there is only parking. The Prairie Trail continues on the east side of the parking lot.

The route through Veterans Acres Park is a major highlight of the Prairie Trail. There is a strong hint of Minnesota here—absolutely towering pines and tall, thriving white birches. There is even a whiff of pine in the air. This is a wonderful forest to ride a bike through. It is kind of like biking through a scout camp.

At 7.7 miles there is a significant descent. The trail dives downward through long rows of pines. If you are on a bicycle this is a place for great caution. The trail can be a wet and slippery matt of pine needles and leaves, and sunrays do not always penetrate the shade to dry the trail.

Exercise caution and your handbrakes on any descent.

Huge power towers cut through the woods at midsection. There is a steep uphill alongside them at 7.9 miles. These power lines look like great fences holding back the green pines. At a half mile ahead is another long descent, the payback for the climb, and this takes you dropping and curving through the woods. The forest ends abruptly after another mile.

The Hillside Road Access is at nine miles from the Algonquin trailhead. Hillside has parking for 40 cars and water from a water pump here, along with basic information. The local bike club, the McHenry County Bike Club, has helped to make this a better place for the public. Continuing on, you cross Hillside Road, cross the railroad tracks and then take a hard left and head north. The trail here goes alongside some elevated railroad tracks and at 9.7 miles is the Pleasant Hill Road crossing. This is a four-way stop. But take care here—cars coming through the railroad bridge just may not see you.

Ten miles out from Algonquin, you cross rail lines that are active only during the work week. Across the street is Nunda Township Offices & Town Hall. The Edgewater Road crossing is a half-mile ahead and here you should see the new Cobbleston Woods subdivision.

The route crosses Edgewater Road, goes back over the railroad tracks, and picks up again on the west side of the rails. There is an enormous sod farm here, lying flat against the valley—acres of brilliant green and bursting with life.

For the next three miles this part of the Prairie Trail is a long asphalt-paved straightaway. This stretch of the Prairie Trail is made to order for bicycle racers in training and for rollerbladers.

At 13.3 miles is Bull Valley Road, a busy two-lane. At 14.6 miles is Lillian Street. A half-mile ahead you turn off the path at a small apartment building, Westside Crest, and the route follows city streets through McHenry, Illinois. It is well striped and you cannot miss it. This is a residential street with a bit of Mexican music in the air.

McHenry, Illinois, population 21,501, was first incorporated in 1855. Over the years McHenry has seen the summer tourist trade, taken part in the dairy industry and has been home to a number of small industries.

Plans are in the works to find a convenient spur from the Grand Illinois Trail to Moraine Hills State Park. This is a sprawling 1,690

Here's a great way to baby-sit! Take the kids on a trail! This group loves rollerblading on the Prairie Trail north of McHenry.

acre state park just about three miles southeast of McHenry on the west side of the Fox River. Lake Defiance was formed by the melting of a massive glacier ice block and it is slowly but surely filling in with peat. The park is a study of glacier effects. Leatherleaf Bog shows kettle moraine features and was formed by the melting of another ice block. Pike Marsh has interesting marsh wetlands and here you find plants such as goldenrod, lobelia, cattails and bulrushes, as well as pitcher plants that specialize in attracting and eating live insects! Moraine Hills State Park has internal hiking paths, drinking water, restrooms, food concessions and boat rentals.

In McHenry, pass by Crestwood and cross Crystal Lake Road. At 15.5 miles is Whispering Oaks Park. Whispering Oaks is good place to take a break and the park is next to "Fort McHenry," a children's playground. There are convenient restrooms and a water fountain.

On its way through McHenry, the Prairie Trail continues through Whispering Oaks Park and crosses busy Illinois Route 120 just across from the IHOP. The route turns right onto a striped city sidewalk/trail for about a block, and then it turns left. A sign here announces Brookside Trail Park—it is actually the Prairie Trail and the slight brook here is Boone Creek. This is a small wooded area and you cross a long wood bridge before reaching Orleans Street. Here you cross and follow the trail.

Peterson Park and Beach is about 17 miles from Algonquin, and here is a large and beautiful lake. All the traditional municipal park features are here. And there is a large, sandy beach, possibly a good place for a quick swim.

McCullon Lake Road is at 17.3 miles. Cross this and continue north and two miles later is Ringwood, Illinois. You first see Ringwood from Barnard Mill Road, and there is a Rohm and Haas manufacturing facility next to the trail.

From here to Richmond—and further beyond to Wisconsin—the Prairie Trail moves from an asphalt surface to a limestone and gravel mix. There are pros and cons to every trail surface and it seems appropriate to have gravel through Glacial Park.

There are road crossings at 19.6 miles and 20 miles. You can spot dairy cows, brown Herefords grazing next to fine red barns.

A developing oak savannah along the Prairie Trail.

The route is clear for two miles. There is a broad valley view, the kind of vista that encourages you to sit and think about the first settlement of the area. What did the trappers, traders, settlers and farmers think when they first came here, their future stretching ahead of them and the state still so young? How was the land divided and traded? What kinds of things were grown here and what grew best? When were the toughest winters and the warmest summers?

There are a lot of handles to the Grand Illinois Trail, a lot of ways to appreciate the sights and scenes that you come across. The Prairie Trail seems to underscore all this in such a short distance.

There is a road crossing and a trailhead with parking at 21.9 miles. And a long wooden bridge hidden in the woods is at 22.8 miles.

Richmond, Illinois is only a half-mile ahead. There are several road crossings, and the Prairie Trail passes directly in front of Richmond-Burton Community High School, Home of the Rockets.

The trail crosses Illinois Route 12 at 24 miles, and here you should see the "neo-Gothic" roof of Castle Gardens Nursery. The Prairie Trail continues through Richmond and there are several more modest road and driveway crossings. Downtown Richmond is at 26.4 miles. Richmond, with a population of 1,091, was incorporated in 1865; the town boasts of an attractive downtown with many antique and specialty stores. It makes a fine final destination point for the Prairie Trail: finish your ride with fresh ice cream!

If you stay on the trail, the Wisconsin state line and Genoa City, Wisconsin are just two miles ahead. If you go there you will find an abrupt end to a magnificent trail. A simple sign declares the end of the trail, and so it does. And a little neighborhood gravel path takes you into a Genoa City neighborhood.

From Richmond, the Grand Illinois Trail route makes a sharp turn west, using county roads and trails to pass through McHenry and Boone counties on the way to Rockford. The McHenry County Conservation District is developing a two-mile off-road spur from the Prairie Trail to the new Hebron Trail.

Additional Trails

The Huntley, Union, and Marengo (HUM) Trail

The HUM Trail on the south side of McHenry County is slated to open soon. This will be a 15-mile trail adjacent to an active rail line. The route will run through Huntley, Union and Marengo on its way to the county line.

The county is also developing plans for extending the Long Prairie Trail from the Boone County/McHenry County line to Harvard, Illinois.

Trails rank high among desired residential amenities according to experts.

Forests of Illinois

Evidence shows that the whole state of Illinois was covered in spruce and pine. But that was 14,000 years ago, before the last glacier and before a great climatic change that caused prairie to grow and take root across the Illinois country.

While much of southern Illinois remained well-treed, the forests in northern Illinois grew up mainly along rivers and creeks. Trees also survived on hillier ground. Stout, prairie-fire resistant oaks managed to grow together in impressive groves out on the open prairie. Wooded areas were also found along the east side of streams, since the run of water might block prairie-fires.

Typically there is a progression in the growth of a forest, called natural succession. Over time, quick growing scrub trees eventually lead to the hardwood trees found in established, undisturbed woodlands.

The Grand Illinois Trail sweeps its routes through some important forest resources.

- Along the I & M Canal trail, you can find all the trees that grow best in wet, watery conditions. Here there are cottonwoods, willows, sumacs and elms. There are also fine, established hardwood forests at Gebhard Woods in Morris and Channahon State Park in Channahon.

- In the Starved Rock region, there is a well-established oak and hickory forest. These trees do well on hillsides. The varieties of oak trees are many: black oak, red oak, white oak, Hill's oak and burr oak. Soil and water conditions have also made possible a wide variety of fern species at Starved Rock.

- Mississippi Palisades State Park gives another twist to trees. Here, the cooler climate and poorer soil is more conducive to pines and birches. The park features river birch, yellow birch, paper birch and white birch. And plenty of white pine,

- Glacier Park in Crystal Lake offers a wide range of tree types. Here there are old pine stands and birch trees. The many environments here let you see bottomland trees such as willows, cottonwoods and elms, as well as upland hardwoods like sugar maple, hickory and oak.

101 Things to See on The Grand Illinois Trail

Bicyclists
Runners
People walking dogs
Ice cream stands
Lovers
Boys on bikes
Fishermen
Dragonflies
Ice skaters and hockey players
Babysitters with little kids
Families enjoying the fresh air
Women picking decorative weeds and flowers
Horseback riders
Rollerbladers
Bird watchers and binoculars
Dainty ferns
Mountain bikers
Tots in strollers
Seniors walking for their health
Mulberry trees
Boy Scouts
Old friends
Soccer players
Dreamers
Snowmobilers
Cross-country skiers
Bodybuilders getting some aerobic exercise
History buffs
The Illinois River
Little Leaguers
Kids on their way to school
Folks headed to work
Limestone screenings
Big Bluestem
Poison ivy

Railroad spikes
Muskrats
Aqueducts
Bluebirds
Sunflowers
Robins
Historic Indian mounds
Stout Civilian Conservation Corps shelters
Monarch butterflies
Daisies
Haegar Pottery
Big cottonwood trees
Oak leaves underfoot
Prairie grasses
The Museum of Science and Industry
Old stonework
Painted turtles basking in the sun
Bald eagles scanning for field mice
Cup plants
Deer at the edges of cornfields
Red-tailed hawks
The Ovaltine Factory
Sunsets
Antique steel-beam bridges rusting scenically
Squirrels on the make
Skunks
Navy Pier
The Mississippi River
Fireflies marking the summer night
Corn snakes
Weeping willows
Prickly pear cactus
Frank Lloyd Wright houses
Kids swimming

Competitive walkers
Teen girls in deep rapt conversation
Bicycle racers in bright lycra outfits
Kayakers and splashes
People headed to the local convenient store
Gardeners
Dandelions
The Fox River
Local schools
Sailboats
Classic Schwinn Varsity 10-speeds
Picnickers
Shuttered factories
Milkweed
Weather-beaten cemeteries
Coffee shops
The Rock River
Dads hauling Burleys
Wild strawberries
Grazing cattle, eating and philosophizing
Ice fishermen
Wooden trestle bridges
Public sculpture
Curious horses
Speedboats
Lincoln and Douglas in debate
Awesome possums
Ancient dolomite layers
Girl Scouts earning badges
Dresden Nuclear Power Plant
Lazy carp
Split Rock on the I & M Canal

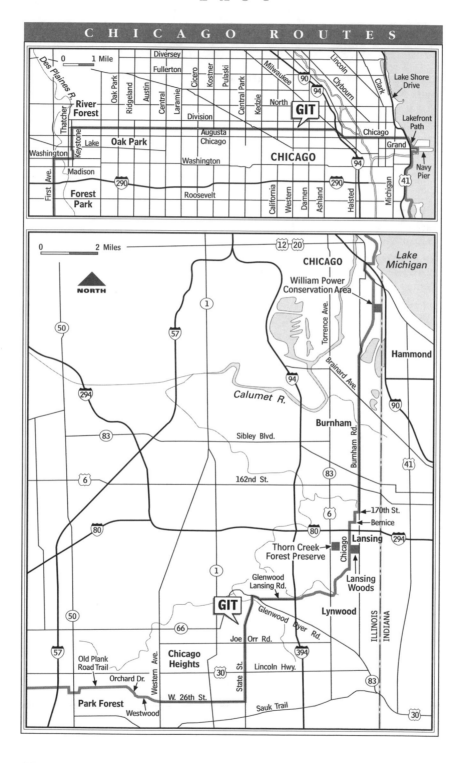

CHICAGO ROUTES

Chicago Routes

The Burnham Greenway

From Calumet Park to the Old Plank Road Trail

The Burnham Greenway takes its name from Daniel H. Burnham, the famous Chicago architect and city planner. As an architect, his partnership with John W. Root resulted in splendid buildings shooting up around Chicago after the 1871 Chicago Fire. As a city designer, Daniel H. Burnham's 1909 plan for Chicago was based on the simple idea of providing park access for everyone. Parks then, and now, are important social resources. The Burnham Greenway is perfectly named: it is a lace of green connecting important park resources on Chicago's south side.

It is a new and rapidly improving trail. Expect more to happen in this area. Like the great Burnham, this route calls for "no little plans," and this portion of the Grand Illinois Trail presently requires a bit more planning and opportunities for execution. The perfect GIT route through this part of Chicago is still in the making and the following descriptions should be useful tools for following the GIT through its present trail route.

This portion of the Grand Illinois Trail is really a local trail system, good for non-motorized transportation through the south side. The Burnham Greenway allows for the connection between the Old Plank Road Trail and the Chicago Lakefront Path. The use of a Commonwealth Edison utility corridor allows the use of existing and new parklands. The Lake Calumet area will continue to add recreational amenities to the area as old industrial sites are cleaned up.

This part of Chicago grew rapidly, robustly with the growth of Calumet Harbor and its steel industries. It was the first Marshall Field, one of the wealthiest Americans of his day and a board member of U.S. Steel who took a look at the map, saw Gary, Indiana, and said "build it here," disagreeing with Andrew Carnegie who wanted to expand the steel plants in Pennsylvania.

This is an historically blue-collar ethnic area, home to a rich mix of Czechs, Slavs, Italians and Mexicans. After World War I, blacks from the south also made the area home. This was the place for heavy industry such as Wisconsin Steel and Inland Steel and a number of other steel and iron plants. They benefited from the access to water, coal and good transportation. But it was devastated in the 1980s by the collapse of the American steel industry—its transformation to smaller, more productive mini-mills and its market loss to imported steel. Steel jobs left and did not return.

Near the Burnham Greenway, St. Francis de Sales Church and High School on Chicago's south side is a local landmark.

Chemical plants and refineries have also been important to Calumet Harbor. During the 1960s, some 700 ships would dock at the harbor. While there was talk of Calumet Harbor becoming a major world port, changes in transportation worked in the other direction and freight declined.

Industry left heavy marks on this area. Look at a map and you'll find that Calumet Harbor is square. Curiously, the lake at William Powers Conservation Area has a perfectly straight shoreline, running exactly along the Illinois-Indiana state line. No coincidence there! Heavy rail lines cross through this part of Illinois, carrying basic commodities around the city region and into the city.

But oddly enough, this heavy hand of industry spared some very unique areas. Because this part of the state has been historically marshy—the old Sauk Trail followed a high morainal ridge through this area and so does U.S. Route 30—not all the land could be developed. These parts and parcels of land sometimes even contain virgin prairie, with land untouched by any settler's plow or developer's concoction.

The Burnham Greenway will connect Eggers Woods, the William Powers Conservation Area, Powderhorn Lake Prairie, Burnham Prairie, Calumet City Prairie, Wentworth Prairie, Sandridge Nature Preserve and the Thornton High School Prairie. Nearby are the 130th Street Marsh and the Dolton Avenue Prairie.

It is these ecosystems that make the area interesting. So close to Chicago and yet so pristine.

This portion of the Grand Illinois Trail has received considerable funding for trail development. It needs yet more. Plans have been in the works to extend the Old Plank Road Trail further toward the Burnham Greenway through Chicago Heights and there are plans for other portions of this general route. The more of this portion of the Grand Illinois Trail that becomes off-road trail, the better. This is a dense transportation grid.

It is true that parts of this area have been unsavory places and bodies have been found in curious places. There are plenty of perceptions of danger. But the routing of the Burnham Greenway relies on very visible streets and highly public areas, and there really should be no problem touring through this part of the city. But remember: this section of the Grand Illinois Trail is an area with plenty of regular traffic.

Following the Burnham Greenway

The Burnham Greenway begins at Calumet Park in Chicago. From the Calumet Park Fieldhouse, take 100th Avenue out of Calumet Park (the road is at the south end of the park), and head west to Ewing Avenue.

Take Ewing Avenue south and go under the thund'rous Chicago skyway. Take a snapshot of the tank that crowns the veterans memorial park here. The Burnham Greenway is immediately south of the skyway, and it runs in a narrow strip alongside Indiana Avenue/Chicago Skyway for about six blocks east to Avenue D. The very start of the Burnham Greenway is close to the Avenue D and 104th Street intersection. The 10-foot asphalt trail runs through an old railroad corridor directly south through backyards and barbecues into Eggers Woods Forest Preserves and the William Powers Conservation Area.

The 580-acre William Powers Conservation Area used to be called the Wolf Lake Conservation Area but the name was changed in 1965 to honor a state legislator. The park area includes 419-acre Wolf Lake. The lake has bass, pike, bluegill, crappie and perch, and boats are allowed. There is a main picnic area here, and the park has restrooms and water facilities.

The Burnham Greenway presently ends at the south end of William Powers Conservation Area near 130th Street. From this point on, the Grand Illinois Trail route relies on local roads to get south to Lansing and the Lansing Woods.

Take Avenue O/Burnham Avenue south for five miles to 170th Street. Believe it or not, it is possible to get under Interstate 80/94.

Head west on 170th Street for four blocks to Chicago Avenue. Take Chicago Avenue south for four blocks to Bernice Street. Turn right (west) on Bernice and head to Railroad Avenue. This is not too far away.

Railroad Avenue scoots under the Kingery, also known as Interstate 80/94. Here you will find a playground and immediately pick up Chicago Avenue, heading south past a skateboard park and the offices of the Lan-Oak Park District. You are now in Lansing.

Lansing, Illinois, population 28,332, was incorporated in 1893, and the city enjoys close transportation links to Chicago. While everything around you looks pretty new, Lansing is actually a town site dating back to the 1830s.

Take Chicago Avenue south through residential Lansing to 186th Street, this is a distance of about 1.5 miles. At 186th turn left and head four blocks to Lansing Woods.

<u>Lansing Woods</u> is a beautiful park and part of a large and rambling forest preserve, <u>Thorn Creek</u>, that spreads across Lansing, Glenwood and Chicago Heights. Continue through the park's parking lot to the very west end: here you can pick up the Thorn Creek Trail. There is trailhead parking at Lansing Woods.

The <u>Thorn Creek Trail</u> is a nicely looping trail, a ten-foot asphalt trail, through the forest preserve. It is a busy trail, with runners and bikers. And it is a nice park filled with families, softball players, soccer players and folks throwing Frisbees.

On the Thorn Creek paths, head south to the Torrence Avenue crossing and then head west for about 1.2 miles to the Cottage Grove Avenue crossing.

At this point, jump off onto Glenwood-Lansing Road/Main Street heading next to State Street. Go south on State Street for about 3.5 miles to reach 26th Street/Norwood. Once on Norwood, travel west to Westwood; this is a distance of 3.2 miles. You are in Chicago Heights.

Chicago Heights, Illinois, population 32,776, incorporated 1892, is a kind of transportation crossroads. Here is where U.S. Route 30 runs, along with Interstate 80. This is the birthplace of Inland Steel. Chicago Heights has been a railroad center, and a number of lines have run through the city: the Chicago and Eastern Illinois, the Elgin Joliet Eastern, the Illinois Central and the Chicago Heights Terminal Transfer.

Chicago Heights first began growing because of the California Gold Rush, when so many men and horses, wagons and provisions came rolling through town. These Easterners were sprinting to the gold fields and Chicago Heights was a good stop on the way, a good place to pick up provisions. Around the same time, the failed 1848 liberal revolution brought many Germans to Chicago Heights.

As the railroads were developed the area became more settled and eventually Scots, Irish, Greeks, Poles, Slaves, Balts, Mexicans and other groups became established here.

On the Grand Illinois Trail route, take Westwood Drive northwest to Orchard Drive. Travel north and you come to the Old Plank Road Trail. (The Old Plank Road Trail currently ends at Western Avenue, with plans to push it through to the Thorn Creek South Forest Preserve near downtown Chicago Heights.)

The total distance from Calumet Park on Lake Michigan to the Old Plank Road Trail is 23.6 miles.

Constant work is being done to develop a completely off-road trail through this congested area. The Burnham Greenway is currently in two large sections and the missing link is a high priority. But there are other projects that have been drafted, and a recent proposal listed the elements needed to finish the Burnham Greenway and bring it south to the Old Plank Road Trail.

The Grand Illinois Trail in Chicago's Southland will connect the Chicago Lakefront to the Old Plank Road Trail, which extends into Will County. Currently, the trail consists of two completed segments of the Burnham Greenway from Chicago into Lansing and the Thorn Creek South trail, supplemented by on-road routes. Four high priority gaps requiring two major bridges remain to replace relatively high-trafficked sections of the on-road routes. Per a recent planning document, these are:

- 3.29-mile gap in the Burnham Greenway from the William Powers State Conservation Area south, connecting to existing trails and the communities of Burnham and Calument City,

- the Lan-Oak trail connecting the Lansing Trail at Wentworth Avenue to the Thorn Creek South Trail.

- A 1.5 mile segment of the Thorn Creek Connector Trail between the Thorn Creek South Trail and Main Street in Glenwood

- A 2.7-mile segment of the Thorn Creek Connector Trail through the City of Chicago Heights from north of Joe Orr Road to 26th Street.

The Forest Preserve District of Cook County has long desired to join the Thorn Creek North and Thorn Creek South trails. This may be done by using an old railroad corridor. If and when this happens, the route is clear for extending an off-road trail from the Old Plank Road Trail up to Lansing Woods.

Additional Trail

The Village of Lansing has purchased the old Penn Central rail corridor, with plans to develop a trail through Lansing. This will run on a diagonal through town that will connect to the Grand Illinois Trail route near Bernice Avenue and run south to the Indiana state line. This connects to existing Indiana trails and may become a main route through Lansing for the Grand Illinois Trail.

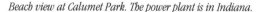
Beach view at Calumet Park. The power plant is in Indiana.

CALUMET PARK/OLD PLANK ROAD

FROM CALUMET PARK TO THE OLD PLANK ROAD TRAIL

Take 100th Avenue (at the south of Calumet
Park) west to Ewing Avenue

Ewing Avenue south to Indiana Avenue
adjacent to Chicago Skyway

Indiana Avenue east to Avenue D/Burnham
Greenway trail access

Burnham Greenway south to William Powers
Conservation Area

William Powers Conservation Area roads to
Avenue O/Burnham Avenue

Avenue O/Burnham Avenue south to 170th
Street

170th Street west to Chicago Avenue

Chicago Avenue south to Bernice Avenue

Bernice Avenue west to Railroad Avenue

Railroad Avenue southeast to Chicago
Avenue

Chicago Avenue south to 186th Street

186th Street to Lansing Woods

Lansing Woods/Thorn Creek North west to
Cottage Grove Avenue crossing

Here take Glenwood-Lansing Road/Main
Street west to State Street

State Street south to 26th Street/Norwood

26th Street/Norwood west to Westwood Drive

Westwood Drive west to Orchard Street

Orchard Street north to the Old Plank Road
Trail

FROM THE OLD PLANK ROAD TRAIL TO CALUMET PARK

Orchard Street south to Westwood Drive

Westwood Drive east to 26th Street/Norwood

26th Street/Norwood east to State Street

State Street north to Glenwood-Lansing
Road/Main Street

Glenwood-Lansing Road/Main Street east to
Thorn Creek North trails

Thorn Creek North/Lansing Woods northeast
to 186th Street

186th Street east to Chicago Avenue

Chicago Avenue north to Railroad Avenue

Railroad Avenue northwest to Bernice Street

Bernice Street west to Chicago Avenue

Chicago Avenue north to 170th Street

170th Street west to Avenue O/Burnham
Avenue

Avenue O/Burnham Avenue north to William
Powers Conservation Area

William Powers Conservation Area Burnham
Greenway access north to Indiana Avenue

Indiana Avenue northwest to Ewing Avenue

Ewing Avenue north to 100th Avenue

100th Avenue east to Calumet Park

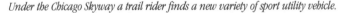

Under the Chicago Skyway a trail rider finds a new variety of sport utility vehicle.

Old Plank Road Trail

From Joliet to Chicago Heights

The Old Plank Road Trail makes for a sweet ride in the summer. The path is perfect: clear asphalt ready to accommodate hikers, bikers, runners and walkers. The Old Plank Road Trail runs for just under 20 miles, connecting the towns of Joliet, New Lenox, Frankfort, Matteson, Park Forest and Chicago Heights.

The route parallels the old Sauk Trail. Native Sauk and Fox tribes took this route on their way to Vincennes, Indiana to collect regular government annuities, paid out for their lands. And even before then, the route along Hickory Creek was popular for basic travel around the marshy regions south of Chicago.

It was such a good route around Chicago that a company was formed, the Oswego and Indiana Plank Road, and a plank road was proposed and chartered in 1849. It is this proposal that gives the trail its name and is the real origin of the route. But the plank road was never built. Rail had proved its transportation superiority to plank roads and even canals.

And getting around the Chicago area was important to Carl Fisher, Detroit automaker and promoter of U.S. Route 30, the Lincoln Highway. The Lincoln Highway is the nation's first transcontinental road, running 3,389 miles from Times Square in New York to Lincoln Park in San Francisco. Fisher's promotional tactics (he was also founder of the Indianapolis Speedway, the Indy 500) helped boost the auto industry: how can you have cars with no roads? U.S. 30 was made a National Scenic Byway in 2000, and in Illinois it weaves from Chicago Heights to Joliet to Aurora to Geneva to DeKalb and to Fulton.

Riders flying down the Frankfurt bridge on a summer day.

The New York Central, later the Penn Central, used part of this major transportation corridor to circumvent the busy Chicago rail gateway. Grain from the Midwest could be shipped east, and manufactured consumer goods returned west. The route was abandoned as a rail line in 1976.

The Old Plank Road Trail was born in 1988. It was then that communities along the route selected representatives to form a trail committee. The Illinois Department of Conservation made special grants for the project totaling $2.2 million, the money coming from ISTEA federal transportation enhancement funds. At a cost of $2.5 million, the trail was opened in 1996.

All told, the Old Plank Road Trail is a trail to warm the heart. It's here that busy people come to relax. It's here that long distance runners and lycra'd rollerbladers work out. Friends take long walks, some chatting, and some walking dogs. And there are prairies and parks all along the way.

There are plans to extend the Old Plank Road Trail from Western Avenue in Park Forest to Thorn Creek in Chicago Heights. This trail extension will eventually create a total off-road trail from Joliet to the Chicago lakefront, since this links into the Burnham Greenway system.

The American Discovery Trail uses the Old Plank Road Trail as it crosses the top part of Illinois. The ADT crosses Joliet, and then takes the I & M Canal Trail, Kaskaskia Alliance Trail and Hennepin Canal Trail to cross the state.

The Old Plank Road Trail is paved with asphalt, ten feet wide for its 19.9 mile length. It is well maintained. The Old Plank Road Trail runs straight and clean from Joliet to Chicago Heights.

Following the Old Plank Road Trail

Start at Ingalls Park in Joliet. Ingalls Park is a small neighborhood park alongside Park Road, just off the south side of U.S. 30, east of Pilcher Park on Joliet's east side. This is a popular trailhead for a popular trail, and there are plenty of walkers and cyclists. The trailhead has a portable toilet and parking for about a dozen cars.

Just under a mile out, the Old Plank Road Trail crosses busy Washington Street. At 1.5 miles, you can see the playing fields of Providence High School, Home of the Celtics.

A major bridge, at 2.2 miles out, takes the trail over Interstate 80, at New Lenox. And about 2.5 miles from the Joliet Park Road trailhead is the New Lenox Village Hall. Here there is an admirable monument, dedicated by the New Lenox Service Club, honoring those who died in World War II. Haven Avenue crosses the trail here.

New Lenox, Illinois, population 17,771, incorporated 1946, looks like a completely new town, but it has much older roots. Today it is a residential suburb, but at one time it was one of the earliest Will County settlements, called Hickory Hills, with two fur traders building their cabin here in 1829. George Gaylord of Lockport laid it out as a town in 1858. New Lenox grew along with the Chicago and Rock Island Railroad, and, later, with U.S. 30.

At 3.6 miles, the Lions Den Athletic Field appears, at Cedar Road. The New Lenox Library and a Metra stop are here near the trail.

Just over four miles from Park Road is Martino Junior School, at Lake Street.

At 7.5 miles is the Hickory Creek Bikeway trailhead. This is a very large park and natural lands area, with a bridge that crosses over U.S. Rt. 30 to trailhead amenities. There is parking for 70 cars, water, a picnic shelter and a rambling playground. This is a good spot to get water and to drink water, to rest a bit and watch parents and children at play. On a casual Saturday, you might see a T-38 airplane practice stunt dives, plummeting down in loop-the-loops, slowly rising and twisting up, and then plummeting down again.

At about seven miles from Ingalls Park is Eisner Road in Frankfort. Here is Pleasant Hill Cemetery, and also the Michele Bingham Memorial Park. The park contains soccer fields, a baseball field, parking and portable toilets.

Frankfort, Illinois, population 10,391, incorporated 1879, is named after the German city, Frankfurt-Am-Main, since the town was first settled by German farmers and was a market town. Its downtown area is a popular stopping point on the Old Plank Road Trail, with plenty of amenities for people using the trail.

Downtown Frankfort is 11.5 miles from the Park Road trailhead. It's a great trip into town. A beautiful A-frame bridge over Illinois Route 45 brings you in, and the village has really incorporated the trail. It is a bike-friendly community. Just south of the bridge is Frankfort Main Park, with playground equipment, playing

The Old Plank Road Trail runs directly through Frankfurt and leads to a nice park and downtown shopping.

fields and restroom facilities. The Burton Breidert Village Green is a pleasant rest area, a fine park lining the trailway with a picturesque grain elevator. You will feel like a pro racer entering the green: the iron gate proclaiming the Old Plank Road Trail. The village green has pizza and other food opportunities, gift shops, a doll shop and parking for plenty of cars. There are restroom, water and phone facilities at the Trolley Barn.

Just beyond this is <u>Prairie Park</u>. Here, an interior trail wraps around a small fishing pond, and a dock and boardwalk extends over the water. The <u>Indian Boundary Park</u> is just up the way, with the classic combination of playgrounds and playing fields.

A spur off the trail at 13 miles leads north to the local library; this is at Pfeiffer Road. Another spur here travels south to Commissioner's Park, which features the impressive Fort Frankfort playground.

You will enter a region of high-voltage, high-tension wires and towers rambling all over. Here the Old Plank Road Trail passes by the Dewey Helmick Nature Preserve. It is a nicely maintained 12-acre prairie—a great spot of nature, and a good place for basic birdwatching.

About 15 miles from Ingalls Park is the Harlem Avenue mini-trailhead, with space for 15 cars. Some little bluestem grass could be found blowing in the breeze under the howling overpass of Interstate 57 in Matteson.

At 18 miles is the trail depot gazebo at Cicero Avenue. Here you find yourself deep in the middle of 21st century commercial development. Cars whiz by. The trail goes between Target and Sam's Club, and here the narrow strip is a visual treat amongst the great asphalt seas, containing great diversity of plant life. The gazebo is a fine resting point, and you can keep in touch with local trail activities and events by reading its bulletin board.

Another mile takes you to Governor's Trail Park, a local 20-acre park containing plenty of playing grounds and restroom facilities.

Twenty miles from Park Road is a little red caboose proudly placed next to the trail. This is Caboose Park, featuring Illinois Central caboose #9951. The caboose honors Joseph T. Feehery, Matteson village president for 24 years. This is a good departure point for spinning or walking through downtown Matteson.

Matteson, Illinois, population 12,928, incorporated 1889, was originally founded in 1855 and named after an Illinois Governor.

Park Forest, Illinois, population 23,462, incorporated 1949, was one of the first large-scale planned communities built right after World War II to accommodate returning veterans and their families. Some may recall it because William H. Whyte's *Organization Man* was a best-selling 1950s study of community residents.

Logan Park, a fine large park with seasonal restrooms and water, is about 22 miles from Park Road. The Old Plank Road Trail ends just ahead, at Western Avenue in Chicago Heights. Just across the street is <u>Dominic J. Sesto Park</u>, a basketball playground (which also has water).

You can access downtown Park Forest simply by heading south of Logan Park on Orchard Street. Downtown has a large park, with an aquatic center. There are art galleries and shops, along with the Park Forest Library and community center.

To access the Burnham Greenway trail system turn off on Orchard Drive and head south. Orchard Drive crosses the Old Plank Road just past Logan Park in Matteson. A road route has been selected that takes the Grand Illinois Trail through Chicago Heights and Glenwood to the Thorn Creek Forest Preserve trails and then leads north to Calumet Park and the Chicago Lakefront Path. Check the Burnham Greenway section of this book for routing.

A Metra stop is between Park Forest and Matteson, which would allow rail access to downtown Chicago. This is just west of Logan Park.

The present end of the Old Plank Road Trail is at Western Avenue on the edge of Chicago Heights. There are plans to extend the Old Plank Road Trail further east along the old New York Central railbed to Campbell Avenue and the Thorn Creek Forest Preserve.

Additional Trails

There are a number of spurs that run off the Old Plank Road Trail. These trail spurs take you into Hickory Creek Junction and Hickory Creek Bikeway-East Branch. A new link will shortly be completed to connect with the Tinley Creek Trail.

Local spurs in Frankfort and New Lenox connect neighborhoods to the trail.

Why the "Old Plank Road" Trail?

. . . because it is built along a corridor that was originally supposed to be a road really built of wood planks. Early roads through the area were a disaster. You couldn't get through. They were often muddy and rutted because of poor water drainage and large marshy areas. It was hard to be a settler and a farmer because you couldn't get your produce to market.

Plank roads offered a solution. Heavy oak planks were nailed on top of log stringers placed parallel to the ground and set on the roadbed. With plank roads, a horse and carriage could travel along at a pretty fast clip—nine miles per hour or so. This was a real marvel and worth the nickel toll you would have to pay to the toll keeper every so often along the way. Even so, railroads were better at carrying passengers and freight, and the era of the plank road was pretty much ended by 1860.

Downtown Frankfort opens a wide gate to Grand Illinois Trail visitors.

Eastern Section Resources

EMERGENCY

ILLINOIS STATE POLICE, DISTRICT 5
(Lockport)
(815) 726-6291 for Will and
Grundy counties.

ILLINOIS STATE POLICE, DISTRICT 3
(Des Plaines)
(847) 294-4400 for Cook
County.

ILLINOIS STATE POLICE, CHICAGO
DISTRICT
(630) 294-4400

LOCAL TOURISM CONTACTS

CHICAGO AREA

CHICAGO VISITORS INFORMATION
CENTER
78 E. Washington Street
Chicago, Illinois 60602
(312) 744-2400

CHICAGO OFFICE OF TOURISM
(877) 244-2246
www.877chicago.com

CHICAGO CONVENTION AND TOURISM
BUREAU
McCormick Place
2301 S. Lake Shore Drive
Chicago, Illinois 60616
(312) 567-8500
www.choosechicago.com

OAK PARK AREA CONVENTION AND
VISITORS BUREAU
158 N. Forest Avenue
Oak Park, Illinois 60301
(708) 848-1500
(888) 625-7275
www.visitoakpark.com

WESTRN SUBURBS

ELGIN AREA CONVENTION AND
VISITORS BUREAU
77 Riverside Drive
Elgin, Illinois 60120-6425
(847) 695-7668
(800) 217-5362
www.enjoyelgin.com

DUPAGE COUNTY CONVENTION AND
VISITORS BUREAU
915 Harger Road, Ste. 240
Oak Brook, Illinois 60532
(630) 575-8070
(800) 232-0502
www.dupagecvb.com

RICHMOND CHAMBER OF COMMERCE
Post Office Box 475
Richmond, Illinois 60071
(815) 678-7742

ILLINOIS TOURISM BUREAU
(800) 2-CONNECT

BED & BREAKFASTS

CHICAGO AREA

Chicago
GOLD COAST GUEST HOUSE B & B
113 W. Elm Street
(312) 337-0362
www.bbchicago.com

WHEELER MANSION
2020 S. Calumet Avenue
(312) 945-2020
www.wheelermansion.com

WOODED ISLE SUITES
5750 S. Stony Island Avenue
(800) 290-6844
www.woodedisle.com

YOUTH HOSTEL CHICAGO
INTERNATIONAL
6318 N. Winthrop
(773) 262-1011

HOSTELING INTERNATIONAL
24 E. Congress Parkway
(312) 360-0300

Oak Park
BR GUEST HOUSE
1044 N. Humphrey Avenue
(708) 383-9977
www.brguesthouse.com

LONGWELL HALL B & B
301 N. Scoville Avenue
www.oakparknet.com
(708) 386-5043

UNDER THE GINGKO TREE B & B
300 N. Kenilworth Avenue
(708) 524-2327

WRIGHT'S CHENEY HOUSE B & B
520 N. East Avenue
(708) 524-2067
www.oakparknet.com

WESTERN SUBURBS

Wheaton
THE WHEATON INN
301 W. Roosevelt Road
www.wheatoninn.com
(800) 447-4667
(630) 690-2600

Algonquin
VICTORIAN ROSE GARDEN BED &
BREAKFAST
314 Washington Street
(847) 854-9667
www.sleepandeat.com

West Dundee
IRONHEDGE INN B & B
305 Oregon Avenue
www.ironhedge.net
(847) 426-7777

HOTELS & MOTELS

Elgin

MISSION BAY MULTISPORT
1110 South Street
(847) 888-2240

BAYMONT INN/ELGIN
500 Tollgate Road (I-90 &
Rt. 31)
(847) 931-4800
www.baymont.net/elgin

COLONIAL LODGE MOTEL/ELGIN
788 Villa Street
(847) 742-2790

CROWNE PLAZA HOTEL/ELGIN
495 Airport Road (I-90 &
Rt. 31)
(847) 488-9000
www.crowneplaza.com

DAYS INN/ELGIN
1585 Dundee Avenue (I-90 &
Rt. 25)
(847) 695-2100

HAMPTON INN/ELGIN
405 Airport Road (I-90 & Rt. 31)
(847) 931-1940
www.hamptoninn.com

RAMADA INN/ELGIN
345 W. River Road (I-90 &
Rt. 25)
(847) 695-5000

SUPER 8 MOTEL/ELGIN
435 Airport Road (I-90 & Rt. 31)
(847) 697-8828

West Dundee

TOWNEPLACE SUITES BY MARRIOTT
COURTYARD BY MARRIOTT
2185 Marriott Drive (I-90 &
Rt. 31)
(847) 608-6320

CAMPING

BUFFALO PARK
Illinois Route 31 at Kane County
Line
Algonquin, Illinois
(847) 658-1188
www.co.kane.il.us/forest/camping.
htm

PAUL WOLFF CAMPGROUND
38 W. 235 Big Timber Road
(847) 695-8410
www.co.kane.il.us/forest

CAMP TU-ENDIE-WEI
6N921 Illinois Route 25
(847) 742-2169
www.geocities.com/tuendiewei

BLACKWELL FOREST PRESERVE FAMILY
CAMPGROUND
Butterfield Road, West of
Winfield Road
Glen Ellyn
(630) 933-7248
www.dupageforest.com

BIKE STORES/ REPAIR CENTERS

CHICAGO AREA

Chicago

ART'S CYCLE
1636 E. 55th Street
(773) 363-7524

KOZY'S
601 S. LaSalle Street
(312) 360-0020

MISSION BAY
738 W. Randolph Street
(312) 466-9111

RAPID TRANSIT CYCLE SHOP
1900 W. North Avenue
(773) 227-2288

RECYCLE BICYCLE SHOP
1465 S. Michigan Avenue
(312) 987-1080

VILLAGE CYCLE CENTER
1337 N. Wells Street
(312) 751-2488

WHEELS & THINGS
5210 S. Harper
(773) 493-1781

WESTERN SUBURBS

OAK PARK CYCLERY
1113 Chicago Avenue
Oak Park, Illinois 60302
(708) 524-2453

LICKTON CYCLE
310 Lake Street
Oak Park, Illinois 60302
(708) 383-2130

BARNARD'S SCHWINN
6109 W. North Avenue
Oak Park, Illinois 60302
(708) 524-2660

THE BICYCLE GARAGE
11 Jackson Street
East Dundee, Illinois 60118
(847) 428-2600

MISSION BAY
1110 South Street
Elgin, Illinois 60123
(847) 888-3340

STEMPLE'S CYCLE CENTER
494 Spring Road
Elmhurst, Illinois 60126
(630) 834-1012

GLEN ELLYN CYCLERY
460 Roosevelt Road
Glen Ellyn. Illinois 60137
(630) 858-6400

J & R CYCLE & SKI
716 S. Main Street
Lombard, Illinois 60148
(630) 620-1606

KOSLOW CYCLE, INC.
21 W 415 North Avenue
Lombard, Illinois 60148
(630) 629-4773

MIDWEST CYCLERY
117 E. Front Street
Wheaton, Illinois 60187
(630) 668-2424

SPOKES
223 Rich Lake Square
Wheaton, Illinois 60187
(630) 690-2050

VILLAGE PEDALER
300 N. La Fox Street
South Elgin, Illinois 60177
(847) 741-5938

PRAIRIE TRAIL BIKE SHOP
315 Railroad Street
Algonquin, Illinois 60102
(847) 658-1154

WALLY'S BIKE HAVEN
2908 W. Illinois Route 120
McHenry, Illinois 60050
(815) 385-4642

Fun and fresh air on a family outing on the Fox River Trail.

More
Trail
Options

Hiking the Trail

Hiking sometimes gets overlooked as a sport, even though walking and hiking are among the most popular recreational activities.

The best thing about walking is that it opens up the possibility of meeting with pleasant surprises. You can discover a bluebird along the edge of a field. You can watch tadpoles wiggle along a stream. A hike is a walk with a purpose, either to observe nature or merely to get to a destination. Leisurely hikes give you the opportunity to stop along the way, to unravel prairie grasses, to watch carp lazily swim, to marvel at the way leaves shake in the wind. To stare back at the great blue heron that's been suspiciously eyeing you from atop his tree.

Why hike? Because it's the first step toward appreciating nature. Hiking gives you time to think, a chance to engage in a good conversation with a friend. It's healthy, too. You get a sense of freedom: you can range anywhere on foot, across roads, down paths, and through fields and woods. And you can let your feet take you anywhere: close to unusual mushrooms, up to ancient oaks, down into grassy hillsides.

There are also specialty hikes. Tree hikes involve identifying tree types. Night hikes and astronomy hikes let you see the constellations or meteor showers in the open air. Photographic hikes involve taking pictures; picnic hikes call for paper bags and sandwiches.

The Grand Illinois Trail offers a number of good sections for hiking and for nature sightseeing. These points include:

- Hennepin Canal: from the Visitors Center outside of Sheffield to the Lock 21 day use area at Wyanet. This is about 5.5 miles. The Hennepin Canal also offers a good hike between Geneseo and Colona, a distance of about 13.7 miles.

- The I & M Canal has many opportunities for hiking. The span from La Salle to Utica is 4.5 miles, and from Utica to Ottawa is just over 10 miles. The canal towpath from Gebhard Woods in Morris to Channahon State Park is 15.1 miles. This route takes you next to the Illinois River and its Lock and Dam at Dresden.

- Of course, the Illinois Prairie Path, the Old Plank Road Trail and the Fox River Trail offer more in-town hiking opportunities.

- Finally, both the Long Prairie Trail and the Jane Addams Trails are fine for hikes. The Long Prairie Trail is 11.5 miles long and the Jane Addams Trail is 12.4 miles long.

Bird Watching

ALONG THE GRAND ILLINOIS TRAIL

Important flyways exist along the Grand Illinois Trail, and the trail provides access to some good points and places for serious bird watching.

Glacier Park in McHenry County, Crystal Lake

Glacier Park is a 2,800-acre park containing a variety of natural habitats: established woods, grasslands, marsh and wetlands. So Glacier Park contains a wide range of bird species. Some of the most rare include the Long-billed Dowitcher, the Carolina Wren, the Horned Grebe, the American Bittern, the Cattle Egret, the Yellow-crowned Night-Heron and the Greater Scaup.

More uncommonly found types include the Virginia Rail, the Osprey, the Red-shouldered Hawk, the Peregrine Falcon, the Gray Partridge, Forster's Terns, Acadian Flycatchers, White-eyed Vireos, Western Meadowlarks, Henslow's Sparrow, the Snow Bunting and the Lapland Longspur.

A McHenry County field check list can be obtained through the McHenry County Conservation District.

Midewin National Tallgrass Prairie, Goose Lake Prairie and Heidecke Lake Fish and Wildlife Area: the "Prairie Parklands"

This area, 239 square miles in size, holds plenty of migratory waterfowl and grassland species. The terrain runs from wetlands, streams and prairies. Some of the rare birds spotted in the Prairie Parklands include the Cinnamon Teal, the Oldsquaw, the Harlequin Duck, the White-winged Scoter, the Surf Scoter and the Greater Scaup. You can also find the Little Blue Heron, the Least Tern, Sabine's Gull and the Great Black-backed Gull. The Hudsonian Godwit has been seen in these parts, along with the Sanderling, Black-necked Stilt and the American Avocet.

Upper Mississippi River National Wildlife & Fish Refuge

The Visitor's Center for the Refuge at 7071 Riverview Road, north of Thomson, Illinois.

America's greatest bird flyway is along the Mississippi River. This route is blessed with an enormous variety of bird species. The Upper Mississippi River National Wildlife and Fish Refuge is a national preserve that extends 260 miles from the Quad Cities to Wabasha, Minnesota. It is administered by the U.S. Fish & Wildlife Service.

This national refuge contains 269 bird species, with another 36 species that have been accidental visitors that have showed up at the refuge.

Unusual species include the Black Scoter and White-Winged Scoter, the Greater White-fronted goose, the Red-necked Grebe, the Golden Eagle, the Long-tailed Duck, the American Avocet, the Upland Sandpiper and the Red-necked Phalarope.

Other unusual birds include the snowy owl, the Glaucous Gull, the Marbled Godwit and the Hudsonian Godwit, as well as the Loggerhead Shrike. The refuge also is home on occasion to the Carolina Wren, the Horned Lark, the American Pipit, the Northern Mockingbird, and the Kentucky, Connecticut, Hooded and Yellow-throated Warblers.

The Lapland Longspur calls this region home! And also the Red Crossbill, the White-winged Crossbill, the Hoary Redpoll and the Evening Grosbeak. You can also find Henslow's Sparrow and Le Conte's Sparrow. A complete checklist of birds found at the refuge is available at the refuge Visitor's Center.

Starved Rock region along the Illinois River

Starved Rock is an important birding resource. It is known for bald eagles. They winter in the area, finding fish along the Illinois River dam. The park region has habitat for waterfowl and shorebirds, and for woodland and field bird species.

Unusual species here include Snowy Egrets, White Pelicans, Little Blue Herons, Alder Flycatchers and Pileated Woodpeckers. And sometimes you find a Western Tanager in the area. Consult the latest *Starved Rock Almanac* for a full checklist. The best places at Starved Rock are Lookout Point at the park's eastern border and at Illinois Canyon.

Birders know that the best time for birding is in the morning and evening. The best places to look for birds are at the edges of fields and woods.

Everyone is a birdwatcher to some extent. And traveling along the GIT gives you an opportunity to become a beginner. It is a thrill to catch a glimpse of a bluebird, and a thrill to see the irridescent shimmer of a mallard's head. And anytime you see a bald eagle as it soars, you feel a deep and elemental charge.

The colors are fabulous: the red of a woodpecker, the heathery brown-red of a female cardinal, the black-white peppering of a chickadee, and the blues of a giant heron. Birdwatching gives you a bit of the thrill of a hunt combined with the joys of discovery and learning that come when you first identify a bird species.

Bird Watching

Tips for Bird Watching ————————————

Buy an inexpensive guide with color photographs.

Look at the bird, not at the book. Try to pick out its main features, and then look it up in the book.

When identifying, start at the top of the head and work down.

Try to figure out the three main features of the bird.

Don't worry if you don't make a positive identification. You'll get better at it as you go along.

Learn from your mistakes. Avoid noise and sudden movement.

Don't be afraid to ask another bird watcher for help or suggestions.

Use the checklist to determine your most likely times and places to see birds.

Use good quality optics, a 7 x 35 binocular is fine. Ask a bird watcher for suggestions about binoculars.

Respect the habitat; don't trample it.

Enjoy yourself: you're watching birds AND you're relaxing in the natural environment.

It's good to take along pen and paper, tissues, a bandanna and a field guide.

Bird watchers often keep lists, and these can be all kinds of list: a list of all birds send during their lives, all birds in one county, in one state, in the U.S., birds seen only in the day, and all the birds seen in one year's time.

Other Recreation

CANOEING / HORSEBACK RIDING / SNOWMOBILING

EAST SECTION

Fox River Valley

Much of the Fox River can be canoed and kayaked. There are dams in Carpentersville, South Elgin, Batavia and St. Charles.

Fox River launch points include Buffalo Rock Forest Preserve, Voyageurs Landing Forest Preserve and the Carpentersville dam. A new Duncan Avenue park in Elgin also accommodates canoe access.

SCHMIDT'S CANOEING SERVICE
1232 Ridgeway
Elgin, Illinois
(847) 697-1678
www.canoetrips.net

THE CANOE SHACK
42 W. 612 Steeple Chase Road
St. Charles, Illinois
(630) 584-8017
www.canoeshack.com

SOUTH SECTION

Vermilion and Fox Rivers/ Starved Rock Area

The Starved Rock area is next to two fine Illinois streams, the Fox River and the Vermilion River. The Little Vermilion River may also be paddled after some good rains, and this runs through La Salle, Illinois. The Vermilion River is one of the few places in Illinois where you can find real-life whitewater currents.

Fox River Canoe Rentals

AYERS LANDING CANOE RENTAL
Wedron (on the Fox River)
(815) 434-2233

C & M CANOE RENTAL
(Chet and Mary's)
3401 E. 2062nd Road
Wedron, Illinois
(815) 434-6690

FOX RIVER CANOE RENTALS
Ottawa, Illinois
(815) 433-4665

RIVER ADVENTURES
North of Ottawa at Dayton
(815) 434-2142

Vermilion River Rental

CANOE THE VERMILION
www.canoethevermilion.com
(815) 673-3218

VERMILION RIVER RAFTING
781 N. 2249 Road
Oglesby, Illinois 61348
(815) 667-5242

Hennepin Canal State Parkway

The Hennepin Canal is a wonderful canal for canoeing and kayaking. It features completely still water (this freezes over into an excellent wintertime skating surface). The best places for canoeing on the Hennepin Canal are stretches from Lock 22 to Lock 23 (9.1 miles), Lock 23 to Lock 24 (10.1 miles) and between Lock 25 and Lock 26. The whole feeder canal, a distance of 29 miles, can be done without portaging. But the entire route is good for canoeing and kayaking.

County road "improvements" in 2000 took out most of the substantial old steel-truss bridges, replacing them with low culverts at road intersections, so canoeing will include portaging across farmroads on occasion. Canoe rentals are available in Geneseo at the Geneseo Campground (309) 944-6465 and in Princeton through Willo-B Sports (815) 875-6088.

The Hennepin Canal Visitor's Center also has canoe access, and the center is northeast of Sheffield, Illinois at Exit 45 on Interstate 80.

Illinois & Michigan Canal

Dreamers (and some planners) hope some day to see the canal rightfully re-watered. In the meantime, the sections suitable for canoeing include: the Channahon State Park area to Morris, Illinois (about 15 miles) and from Utica, Illinois west to La Salle (about four miles). The Utica-La Salle route includes portaging around the Pecumsagen Creek area.

There is canoe access at Channahon State Park and Gebhard Woods State Park.

NORTH SECTION

There are canoe accesses at Rock Cut State Park and Lake Le-Aqua-Na State Park. Rock Cut features a 40-acre lake; Lake Le-Aqua-Na has a 40-acre lake.

Pecatonica River

The Pecatonica River offers good canoeing possibilities, and there are access points near the Pecatonica Wetlands Forest Preserve and off of Mill Road. Tutty's Crossing also offers access on the north side of Freeport.

PECATONICA RIVER
COUNTRY CANOE
824 N. Jackson Street
Pecatonica, Illinois 61063

Stephenson County

Stephenson County has been exploring the use of other streams for canoeing. Proposed blueways include:

Winslow/ Pecatonica Trail

This follows the Pecatonica River north to the Wisconsin state line, beginning at Orangeville Road on the west side of McConnell, Illinois.

Crane Grove Creek Trail

This runs from south of Freeport to Baileyville and further south toward Dixon, Illinois. One potential access point is at Lamm Road outside of Freeport. Access Lamm Road by taking Business U.S. 20 to Bailyville Road; Baileyville Road runs into Lamm; turn west on Lamm to reach Crane Grove Creek.

Rock Run Creek Trail

This runs at the eastern edge of Stephenson County, from outside of Lake Summerset to the Pecatonica Prairie Path.

Yellow Creek Trail

Yellow Creek wiggles across much of Stephenson County. Access this off of Mill Grove Road or Bolton Road, southwest of Freeport. There is a good access point immediately south of Freeport.

HORSEBACK RIDING

SOUTH SECTION

Hennepin Canal State Parkway

Current IDNR regulations allow horseback riding along the canal towpath from Lock 24 to Lock 3. Horseback riding is time-zoned on the Hennepin Canal parkway, with riding allowed from April 15 to October 31.

In many respects, riders have a wonderful untapped resource here. The terrain is mostly level, and the canal trail is multiuse. The IDNR has made an exceptional effort to provide equestrian access to the Hennepin Canal. The Wyanet, Illinois Lock 21 Park has 30 units for horse camping, but no water.

Equestrians need to be alert to the portions of canal trail open to them. From Lock 24 east, horses are allowed on the south side of the canal. At Aqueduct 6/Bridge 33 there is a switch back to the north side, and a return to the south side of the canal bank at Bridge 32. From there to Aqueduct 5/Bridge 24, horses should be on the north side, and at Bridge 23 there is a switch back to the south side. At Aqueduct 4 there is a switch to the north side, then a switch back south all the way to Lock 12. At that point there is a switch back to the north side up to Lock 3.

Horses are also allowed on the Hennepin Canal Feeder Canal, from the summit pool all the way to Rock Falls. They should stay on the east side up to Bridge 61, then switch to the west side

---

up to Bridge 60, and then resume the route on the east side of the feeder canal.

This may sound confusing, but it's important to minimize trail conflicts and to keep horses on pathways strong enough to support them. Aqueducts only allow passage on one side of the canal, so this kind of routing is essential.

For more horseback riding information, call the Sheffield Visitor's Center at (309) 454-2328 during regular working hours.

Matthiessen State Park

Eleven miles of trail through Matthiessen, with Class C horse camping for 25 units, with water. The terrain is gently rolling, occasionally timbered, with fields and ag land.

NORTH SECTION

Jo Daviess County

The Grand Illinois Trail route includes two local road sections suitable for equestrian use. In Schapville, Illinois a route runs from Schapville, Illinois on E. Stadel Road and W. Menzemer Road for about 3.5 miles.

Another equestrian option in Jo Daviess County is N. Broadway Road, a six mile stretch ending at Apple River Canyon State Park.

Lake Le-Aqua-Na State Park

Here there are seven miles of trails and 10 units for horse camping with water. There is a range of terrain here, including timbered areas, fields and grasslands.

Rock Cut State Park

At Rock Cut there are 14 miles of trail open to horseback riding, and the park also offers Class C horse camping, with 75 units with water. Trails are used for winter snowmobiling, and the terrain is slightly rolling, some open fields and some woodlands.

SNOWMOBILING

The outstanding feature of the Grand Illinois Trail for snowmobiling is the two canal trails making up "canal country" in the South section. The new and improved Hennepin Canal (phone (815) 454-2328) offers 104 miles of snowmobile trails. The I & M

Canal (phone (815) 942-0796) has over 60 miles of usable trail from La Salle to Rockdale in Joliet.

Another GIT snowmobiling option includes Rock Cut State Park (phone (815) 885-3311) with 14 miles of trails.

The Hennepin Canal is a new and improved resource for snowmobilers, hikers, bikers, fishermen, kayakers and canoeists.

State Park Camping

Some of the best camping possibilities on the Grand Illinois Trail are at Illinois state parks. Along the GIT route is Apple River Canyon State Park, Channahon State Park, the Hennepin Canal State Parkway, Illini State Park, Illinois & Michigan Canal, Lake Le-Aqua-Na State Park, Mississippi Palisades State Park, Rock Cut State Park and Starved Rock State Park.

There are several types of campgrounds at Illinois state parks, depending on what kind of camping you do.

Class A   showers, electricity and vehicular access.
                 Fee of $11 per day.

Class B/E   electricity and vehicular access.
                 Fee of $10 per day.

Class B/S   showers and vehicular access.
                 Fee of $8 per day.

Class C   vehicular access or walk-in with shower access nearby.
                 Fee of $7 per day.

Class D   tent camping or primitive sites (walk-in or backpack) with no vehicular access.
                 Fee of $6 per day.

Class Y   youth groups only, with minimum fee of $1 per person, minimum fee of $10 per group each day.

Class O   adult group camp, with minimum fee of $2 per person, minimum fee of $20 per group each day.

Fees are lower for senior citizens and the disabled. Also, the IDNR has an interesting "Rent-A-Camp" program. When you rent a camp, IDNR staff will set out a wall tent, on a wood platform, for you. You show up, and there's your campsite. No need to lug a tent with you. The Rent-A-Camp program is active in two GIT locations: Rock Cut State Park and Illini State Park.

KEY TIP: Make reservations early!

259

Camping fees are subject to change. Check with IDNR regional offices for additional camping information. For sites on the west side of the Grand Illinois Trail, contact (815) 625-2968 and for camp sites on the east side of the GIT, contact the IDNR at (815) 675-2385.

Apple River Canyon State Park
At Apple River Canyon, there is Class C and Class Y camping. The park totals 298 acres.

Channahon State Park
This 25-acre park has campsites for Class D and Class Y camping.

Hennepin Canal State Parkway
Hennepin Canal Parkway State Park Visitors Center
16006 875 E. Street, Illinois Highway 40
(815) 454-2328

The Hennepin Canal offers Class C and Class Y camping. There are 5,773 acres of state park here, reaching halfway across the state. Camping is permitted at these locations: Lock 11, Lock 17, Lock 21 (drinking water available), Bridge 14, Lock 23 and Lock 26. In many respects the Hennepin Canal trail is about the best possible camping trip you can take: the route is scenic, safe and the towpath is easy to travel.

Illini State Park
There is Class A, Class B/S and Class Y camping at Illini State Park. Illini also offers the Rent-A-Camp program. Illini State Park has 510 acres, sited along the Illinois River at Marseilles.

Illinois & Michigan Canal
There are Class D and Class Y campsites. The canal parkway is a total of 2,802 acres mainly spread through the Illinois River valley. An attractive feature of camping here is that you have many campsite locations to choose from.

Lake Le-Aqua-Na-State Park
At Lake Le-Aqua-Na, there is camping for Class A, Class B/S, Class C and Class Y. The park is 715 acres.

Mississippi Palisades State Park
This premier park has campgrounds for Class A, Class B/S, Class C and Class Y camping. Mississippi Palisades State Park is a 2,500-acre park above the Mississippi River.

Rock Cut State Park
There are campsites for Class A, Class B/S, Class C and Class Y camping, along with sites for Rent-A-Camp and disabled camping. There is also a horse campground at this 3,092-acre park.

Starved Rock State Park
Starved Rock State Park has a campground with sites for Class A, Class Y and disabled camping. An added feature is a horse campground. The 2,630-acre park is regionally noted for its hiking trails above and through marvelous stone canyons.

Crisp fall view of Gebhard Woods in Morris.

Trail Resources

Grand Illinois Trail Partners and Trail Organizations

ILLINOIS PRAIRIE PATH
P.O. Box 1086
Wheaton, Illinois 60189
(630) 752-0120
www.ipp.org

FOX RIVER TRAIL
KANE COUNTY FOREST PRESERVE DISTRICT
719 Batavia Avenue
Geneva, Illinois 60134
(630) 232-5980
www.co.kane.il.us/forest/frtrail.htm

PRAIRIE TRAIL
MCHENRY COUNTY CONSERVATION DISTRICT
18410 U.S. Highway 14
Woodstock, Illinois 60098
(815) 338-6223

LONG PRAIRIE TRAIL
BOONE COUNTY CONSERVATION DISTRICT
603 Appleton Road
Belvidere, Illinois 61008
(815) 548-7935
www.boonecountyconservationdistrict.org/
longprairie.htm

ROCK RIVER RECREATION PATH SYSTEM
ROCKFORD PARK DISTRICT
1401 N. Second Street
Rockford, Illinois 61107
(815) 987-8800
www.rockfordparks.org/recpaths.htm

GREAT RIVER TRAIL
BI-STATE REGIONAL PLANNING COMMISSION
1504 Third Avenue, P.O. Box 3368
Rock Island, Illinois 61204-3368
(309) 793-6300
www.bistateonline.org

ILLINOIS-MICHIGAN CANAL STATE TRAIL
ILLINOIS DEPARTMENT OF NATURAL RESOURCES
Gebhard Woods State Park
401 Ottawa Street
Morris, Illinois 60450
(815) 942-9501
http://dnr.state.il.us/

HENNEPIN CANAL STATE PARKWAY
16006 875 E. Street
Sheffield, Illinois 61361
(815) 454-2328
http://dnr.state.il.us/

OLD PLANK ROAD TRAIL ASSOCIATION
FOREST PRESERVE DISTRICT OF WILL COUNTY
22606 S. Cherry Hill Road
Joliet, Illinois 60434
(815) 727-8700
www.oprt.org

JANE ADDAMS TRAIL
CITY OF FREEPORT
230 W. Stephenson Street
Freeport, Illinois 61032
(815) 235-8207

PECATONICA PATH
P.O. Box 534
Pecatonica, Illinois 61062

FRIENDS OF THE I & M CANAL
P.O. Box 501
Willow Springs, Illinois 60480

FRIENDS OF THE HENNEPIN CANAL
410 W. Railroad Street
Sheffield, Illinois 61361
(309) 786-6681

BURNHAM GREENWAY
CALUMET MEMORIAL PARK DISTRICT
P.O. Box 1158
626 Wentworth Avenue
Calumet City, Illinois 60409
(708) 868-2530

CHICAGO LAKEFRONT PATH
CHICAGO PARK DISTRICT
425 McFetridge
Chicago, Illinois 60505
(312) 747-2200

OPEN LANDS PROJECT
25 E. Washington Street, Ste. 1650
Chicago, Illinois 60602
(312) 427-4256

FOREST PRESERVE DISTRICT OF DUPAGE COUNTY
P.O. Box 5000
Wheaton, Illinois 60189
(630) 933-7200
www.dupageforest.com

CANOEING & EQUESTRIAN GROUPS

ILLINOIS TRAILRIDERS
3588 Somerset Road
Harrisburg, Illinois 62946
www.illinoistrailriders.com

CENTRAL ILLINOIS WHITEWATER CLUB
Streator, Illinois
(815) 672-0408

ILLINOIS PADDLING COUNCIL
4905 N. Hamlin
Chicago, Illinois 60625
(773) 267-0146
www.illinoispaddling.org

HIKING & WALKING GROUPS

MISSISSIPPI RIVER RAMBLERS
1216 – 29th Street
Moline, Illinois 61265-3307
(319) 324-2525

WINDY CITY WALKERS
9725 S. Karlov Avenue, #610
Oak Lawn, Illinois 60453-3341
(708) 425-0211

BICYCLE CLUBS

ELMHURST BICYCLE CLUB
P.O. Box 902
Elmhurst, Illinois 60126
(708) 415-BIKE
www.elmhurstbicycling.org

CHICAGO CYCLING CLUB
P.O. Box 1178
Chicago, Illinois 60690-1178

WHEELING WHEELMEN
P.O. Box 7304
Buffalo Grove, Illinois 60089-7304
www.wheelmen.com

STARVED ROCK CYCLING ASSOCIATION
P.O. Box 2304
Ottawa, Illinois 61350
(815) 433-3237
www.geocities.com/colosseum/2947

STARVED ROCK RUNNERS
P.O. Box 1092
La Salle, Illinois 61301
www.starvedrockrunners.org

FOX RIVER TRAIL RUNNERS
P.O. Box 371
Geneva, Illinois 60134
www.frtr.org

FOX VALLEY BICYCLE & SKI CLUB
P.O. Box 1073
St. Charles, Illinois 60174
(630) 584-7353
www.fvbsc.org

OAK PARK CYCLE CLUB
P.O. Box 2331
Oak Park, Illinois 60303

JOLIET BICYCLE CLUB
1213 E. Cass Street
Joliet, Illinois 60432
www.jolietbicycleclub.org
Bicycle club that hosts events in suburban and downstate areas.

MCHENRY COUNTY BIKE CLUB
P.O. Box 917
Crystal Lake, Illinois 60039
(815) 477-6858
www.mchenrybicycleclub.org

FOLKS ON SPOKES
P.O. Box 824
Homewood, Illinois 60430

BLACKHAWK BICYCLE AND SKI CLUB
P.O. Box 6443
Rockford, Illinois 61125
http://members.aeroinc.net/bbsc/

QUAD CITIES BICYCLE CLUB
P.O. Box 3575
Davenport, Iowa
www.qcbc.org
Especially active bicycle club, with year-round
event calendar.

STATE AND NATIONAL ASSOCIATIONS

ILLINOIS HIKING SOCIETY
1142 Winkleman Road
Harrisburg, Illinois 62946
(618) 252-6789
www.illinoishiking.org

ILLINOIS VOLKSSPORT ASSOCIATION
3109 Valerie Drive
Champaign, Illinois 61822-1830
www.ava.org/walk/il.htm
*Organization that hosts noncompetitive hiking
and walking events.*

ILLINOIS ASSOCIATION OF SNOWMOBILE CLUBS, INC.
P.O. Box 265
2904 E. 24th Road
Marseilles, Illinois 61341-0265
www.ilsnowmobile.com
*Complete snowmobiling reference website. The
organization has long worked for trails in
Illinois.*

LEAGUE OF ILLINOIS BICYCLISTS
2550 Cheshire Drive
Aurora, Illinois 60504
(630) 978-0583
www.bikelib.org
*Bicyclist organization with practical
trailbuilding experience. Especially active in
Chicago suburbs.*

ILLINOIS TRAILS CONSERVANCY
P.O. Box 10
144 W. Main Street
Capron, Illinois 61012
(815) 569-2472
www.comnet1.net/ILLTrails
Illinois' chief trailbuilding advocacy group.

RIVER ACTION
822 East River Drive
Davenport, Iowa 52803
(319) 322-2969
www.riveraction.org
Promotes Quad Cities area trail network.

CHICAGOLAND BICYCLE FEDERATION
650 S. Clark Street, Ste. 300
Chicago, Illinois 60605-1719
(312) 427-3325
www.biketraffic.org
Advocate of Chicago bicycling enhancements.

STATE NATURE ORGANIZATIONS

ILLINOIS AUDUBON SOCIETY
P.O. Box 2418
Danville, Illinois 61834
www.illinoisaudubon.org

STARVED ROCK AUDUBON SOCIETY
605 Ninth Avenue
Ottawa, Illinois 61350

CHICAGO AUDUBON SOCIETY
5801-C N. Pulaski Road
Chicago, Illinois 60646-6057
(773) 539-6793

DUPAGE BIRDING CLUB
www.dupagebirding.org

SINNISSIPPI AUDUBON SOCIETY
P.O. Box 7544
Rockford, Illinois 61126
(815) 398-2974

THORN CREEK AUDUBON SOCIETY
P.O. Box 895
Park Forest, Illinois 60466

WILL COUNTY AUDUBON SOCIETY
P.O. Box 3261
Joliet, Illinois 60434

MCHENRY COUNTY AUDUBON SOCIETY
P.O. Box 67
Woodstock, Illinois 60098

SIERRA CLUB OF ILLINOIS
200 N. Michigan Avenue, Ste. 505
Chicago, Illinois 60601-5908
(312) 251-1680
http://illinois.sierraclub.org/

NATURE CONSERVANCY OF ILLINOIS
8 S. Michigan Avenue, Ste. 900
Chicago, Illinois 60603
(312) 580-2100
www.tnc.org

ADDITIONAL RESOURCES

AMERICAN DISCOVERY TRAIL SOCIETY
P.O. Box 20155
Washington, D.C. 20041-2155
(800) 6 33-2387
www.discoverytrail.org

MISSISSIPPI RIVER TRAIL
2001 Sargent Avenue
St. Paul, Minnesota 55105
(651) 698-2727
www.mississippirivertrail.org

LEAGUE OF AMERICAN BICYCLISTS
190 W. Olmstend St., Ste. 120
Baltimore, Maryland 21230
(410) 539-3399
www.bikeleague.org

NATIONAL SURFACE TRANSPORTATION PROJECT
www.transact.org
*This consortium tracks progress on federal
funding for transportation enhancements
including trail-building.*

ILLINOIS DEPARTMENT OF NATURAL RESOURCES
One Natural Resources Way
Springfield, Illinois 62702-1271
Camping information: (217) 782-6752
GIT information: (815) 625-2968
http://dnr.state.il.us/

ILLINOIS DEPARTMENT OF TRANSPORTATION
2701 S. Dirksen Parkway
Springfield, Illinois 62764
(217) 782-7820
www.dot.state.il.us/

AMERICAN BIKING TRAILS
Antioch, Illinois
(800) 246-4627
www.abtrails.com
*Reference resource for trail books and maps,
with particular strengths in midwestern trails.*

City Organizations

CITY OF CHICAGO
DEPARTMENT OF TRANSPORTATION
(312) 742-2453

CHICAGO PARK DISTRICT
(312) 742-PLAY
www.chicagoparkdistrict.com

CHICAGOLAND BICYCLE FEDERATION
650 S. Clark Street, Ste. 300
Chicago, Illinois 60605
(312) 427-3325
www.chibikefed.org

CRITICAL MASS
www.criticalmass.org

MAYOR DALEY'S LAKEFRONT BIKE RIDE
THE MAYOR'S OFFICE OF SPECIAL EVENTS
City Hall, Rm. 703
121 N. La Salle Street
Chicago, Illinois 60602
(312) 744-3370
www.cityofchicago.org/specialevents

Fairs and Festivals Along the Trail

NORTH SECTION

Galena

ANNUAL OLD MARKET DAYS
Held every Father's Day weekend, Old Market Days is an open-air market filled with crafts, produce and food, done in living history fashion by women in period costume. There are heritage skills and demonstrations presented at this event.

CIVIL WAR DAYS
Historic portrayals and battle reenactments of the Civil War, with Victory Ball, historic demonstrations and children's games. Held every second weekend in August.

FALL TOURS OF HOMES
Galena offers guided tours of historically important houses, and the tour is held on the fourth weekend of September in conjunction with an antiques and collectibles show and sale.

Freeport

OLD TIME THRESHING & ANTIQUE SHOW
A fascinating look at yesterday's great steam threshers and agricultural equipment. Includes an antique steam train. Held the last full weekend in July.

STEPHENSON COUNTY FAIR
Each year in mid-August, the Stephenson County Fair features displays and livestock and agricultural competitions. Includes carnival rides, food, activities and a major country-western act.

QUARRY DAY
This is a unique chance for families to explore a local quarry. Very hands-on: ride the massive quarry equipment and clamber on rocks. Held late September.

Pecatonica

THE WINNEBAGO COUNTY FAIR
This is a weeklong classic county fair that takes place at the Winnebago County Fairgrounds in Pecatonica every second week of August.

Rockford

ON THE WATERFRONT
This is a huge festival held downtown along both sides of the Rock River during Labor Day weekend each year. On the Waterfront includes foods, rides, big name entertainment and more. This is the third largest festival in the Midwest.

MIDSUMMER FEST
Rockford hosts the Midsummer Fest celebration each year in mid-June, showing a bit of its Scandinavian heritage.

CIVIL WAR DAYS
Civil War Days is held at Midway Village every year. This is a major reenactment of Civil War social life, camp life and combat, the largest such demonstration in Illinois.

Richmond

RICHMOND ROUND UP DAYS
Held the weekend before Labor Day, Richmond Round Up Days is a large town-wide festival with live music, a parade, kids games, talent show and a classic car cruise night.

EAST SECTION

Elgin

FOX TROT RUN
A celebration of racing with 5K and 10K races, a stroller brigade and two-mile walk held every Memorial Day weekend.

FOUR BRIDGES INTERNATIONAL BICYCLE CHALLENGE
The Challenge is a race and bicycle festival held in Elgin every year over the Fourth of July weekend. Includes an 8K race and family activities.

FINE ARTS FESTIVAL
Held late August, the Fine Arts Festival is a showcase for local arts with a full schedule of events interesting to the whole family.

Elmhurst

ELMFEST
Elmfest is a town-wide celebration with music, food and fun for the whole family. Elmfest is held on the second weekend of June.

Wheaton

THE DUPAGE COUNTY FAIR

The DuPage County Fair presents a weeklong schedule of county fair activities, including agricultural displays and exhibits, rides, shows and games. The fair is held at the end of July.

Lombard

LILAC TIME

Lilac Time, held in mid-May, celebrates the village's roots and love affair with lilacs. Includes the Lilac Parade.

TASTE OF LOMBARD

The Taste is an opportunity to explore and enjoy the fare of local restaurateurs. It takes place each year on the Fourth of July weekend.

Oak Park

SHAKESPEARE IN THE PARK

Shakespeare in the Park, an engaging presentation of Shakespearean themes and works, takes place at the end of July.

WRIGHT PLUS

An extensive tour of architecturally unique houses, including several by Frank Lloyd Wright. This is a fundraising event held on the third Saturday of May.

CHICAGO

TASTE OF CHICAGO

The Taste of Chicago is a major culinary celebration featuring food for every palate, held each year at the end of June.

CHICAGO AIR AND WATER SHOW

Held along the shores and skies of Lake Michigan, the show features exciting aeronautics each August.

GOSPEL AND BLUES FESTIVALS

Major music acts and artists perform in Grant Park each year during the first two weekends of June.

VENETIAN NIGHT

A floating parade of light and sound and blasting fireworks makes Venetian Night an amazing lakefront event. Generally held at the end of July each year.

CHRISTMAS TREELIGHTING

Some 10,000 attend the annual lighting of the city Christmas Tree downtown, igniting the Christmas holiday season on the first Friday after Thanksgiving.

SOUTH SECTION

Joliet

ANNUAL CITY CENTER CAR SHOW

This event is held at Billie Limacher Bicentennial Park, every Father's Day weekend. The show includes demonstrations and contests, displays, food and entertainment.

ANNUAL WATERWAY DAYS

A festival held at Billie Limacher Bicentennial Park downtown. Waterway Days celebrates the I & M Canal with concerts, displays, fireworks and lighted boat parades. Third weekend in July.

NASCAR NIGHT AT VAN BUREN PLAZA

This is a cruise night that features NASCAR drivers, cars and other events. First weekend after July 4th.

Channahon

THREE RIVERS FESTIVAL

The Three Rivers Festival features carnival rides, games, family stage entertainment, food, a softball tournament and more. Held every second Tuesday of August at Central Park.

Morris

ANNUAL SWEET CORN FESTIVAL

Held the second weekend in August, the Morris Sweet Corn Festival is a fun event with a carnival, flea market, beer garden and live entertainment.

DULCIMER FESTIVAL

Gebhard Woods State Park, Morris, held every second weekend in July. There are concerts and workshops featuring the hammered dulcimer and other folk instruments.

Princeton

HOMESTEAD FESTIVAL / CIVIL WAR RE-ENACTMENT

Held in September. A fun-filled family 3 day festival with parade, pork cookout, flea market, etc. Historic Owen Lovejoy tours. Civil War Re-enactment in October with period clashes and examples of living during the Civil War era.

Ottawa
RIVERFEST CELEBRATION
A ten-day festival with music, food and fun that runs from the fourth Wednesday of July to the first weekend of August. Check out the Polka Fest and try a Welcomeburger.

Utica
FLOCK TO THE ROCK
January through March, the Flock to the Rock offers views of bald eagles and natural lore. Illinois Waterway Visitor's Center at Starved Rock Lock and Dam, and at Starved Rock Lodge.

BURGOO FESTIVAL
Every year thousands come to Utica to eat Burgoo, a pioneer stew, and enjoy the Starved Rock area. Held each year on the Sunday before Columbus Day weekend.

Annawan
The Fun Day Celebration is a town wide festival held every first weekend in June. Annawan also hosts the World Rolle Bolle Tournament on the last Sunday of July.

Atkinson
Atkinson hosts an annual Antique Engine and Tractor Show on the second full weekend of September.

Geneseo
ANNUAL ARTS AND CRAFTS SHOW
Father's Day weekend in June. A wide variety of craft and food vendors in a picturesque, classic town park with musical performances/authentic gazebo.

VICTORIAN CHRISTMAS AND HISTORIC HOUSE TOUR
Geneseo opens her doors every second Sunday in December for the Victorian Christmas and Historic House Tour. This event includes touring some of the town's most beautiful houses and special downtown shopping opportunities.

Colona
Colona is host to a Memorial Day festival on the Hennepin Canal parkway featuring kids events, a parade, a carnival and a dance.

WEST SECTION

Quad Cities
GREEK CULTURAL FESTIVAL
This is an annual celebration of Greek culture featuring arts, live music, dance performances, food and more. Held in downtown Moline at John Deere Commons.

QUAD CITIES MARATHON
A USATF certified course, the 26.2-mile marathon is held every September. Includes pasta party and other activities.

ROCK ISLAND COUNTY FAIR
This is a traditional something-for-everyone county fair and agricultural show. Includes midway and carnival rides and daily grandstand entertainment, along with craft, hobby and produce displays.

FESTIVAL OF TREES
Held on Thanksgiving weekend, this is a ten-day extravaganza for the local arts. The Festival of Trees is one of the nation's biggest displays of Christmas trees, hearth and home displays, designer doors and room vignettes. Even Santa comes for a visit!

BACKWATER GAMBLERS WATER SKI SHOWS
These are professional water ski shows held on Wednesdays and Sundays during the summer, between Memorial Day and Labor Day.

MISSISSIPPI VALLEY FAIR
Held the last week of July, the Mississippi Valley Fair is a great celebration of the Quad Cities area.

Savanna
ANNUAL CHRISTMAS COOKIE WALK
A wonderful event featuring antique street lights, luminaries, horse-drawn wagon rides and homemade cookies. Contact the Savanna Chamber for more information.

Thomson
WATERMELON DAYS
Every September the town of Thomson, Illinois celebrates its famous melons. Sample some of the Midwest's finest watermelons.

Bibliography

Geology Underfoot in Illinois. Raymond Wiggers, Mountain Press Publishing Company, Missoula, Montana, 1997.

Guide to the Vascular Flora of Illinois, Robert Mohlenbrock, Southern Illinois University Press, Carbondale, Illinois, 1975.

Illinois: A Descriptive and Historical Guide (ed. Harry Hansen). New Revised Edition, Hastings House, NY. "Originally compiled by the Federal Writers Project of the Workers Progress Administration of the State of Illinois."

Hiking and Biking in DuPage County, Illinois. Jim Hochgesang. Roots & Wings, Lake Forest, Illinois, 1995.

Hiking and Biking in the Illinois and Michigan Canal Corridor. Jim Hochgesang. Roots & Wings, Lake Forest, Illinois, 1998.

The Structuring of a State: The History of Illinois, 1899-1928. Donald F. Tingley, University of Illinois Press, Urbana, Illinois, 1980.

Prairie Passage: The Illinois and Michigan Canal Corridor Photographs by Edward Ranney. Prologue by Tony Hiss, Essays by Emily Harris. Epilogue by William Least Heat Moon. Canal Corridor Association and the University of Illinois Press, Urbana, Illinois, 1998.

Illinois: Land and Life in the Prairie State, ed. Ronald E. Nelson. Illinois Geographical Society. Kendall/Hunt Publishing Company, Dubuque, Iowa, 1978.

A Guide to the History of Illinois, ed. John Hoffman. Greenwood Press, 1991.

Rockford. Works Project Administration in the State of Illinois. Graphic Arts Corporation, Rockford, 1941.

Made in Illinois: A Story of Illinois Manufacturing, Rolf Achilles, Illinois Manufacturers Association, Chicago, 1993.

Illinois Historical Tour Guide, D. Ray Wilson, Crossroads Communication, Carpentersville, Illinois, 1991.

Illinois State Parks, Bill Bailey, Glovebox Guidebooks of America, Saginaw, Michigan, 1998.

A Directory of Illinois Nature Preserves, vols. 1 & 2, Don McFall and Jean Karnes, eds., Illinois Department of Natural Resources, 1995.

Illinois Guide & Gazeteer. Illinois Sesquicentennial Commission. Rand McNally & Company, Chicago, Illinois, 1969.

Illinois Wildlife and Nature Viewing Guide, Mary Kay Judd Murphy, Ph.D., and John W. Mellen, Ph.D., Illinois Department of Natural Resources, 1997.

Illinois: Land of Lincoln. Illinois Sesquicentennial Commission. Children's Press, Chicago, Illinois, 1968.

Illinois, A History, Richard J. Jensen, University of Illinois Press, Urbana, 1978.

Illinois: A History of the Prairie State, Robert P. Howard, Eerdmans Publishing Company, Grand Rapids, MI, 1972.

Cahokia: Mirror of the Cosmos, Sally Kitt Chappell, University of Chicago Press, Chicago, 2002.

Rockford: An Illustrated History, Jon W. Lundin. Windsor Publications, Chatsworth, California, 1989.

The Chicago River: A Natural and Unnatural History, Libby Hill, Lake Claremont Press, Chicago, 2000.

The Quad Cities: An American Mosaic, Roald Tweet. East Hall Press, Augustana College, Rock Island, Illinois, 1996.

Illinois Architecture From Territorial Times to the Present, Frederick Koeper, University of Chicago Press, Chicago, Illinois, 1968.

Forever Open, Free and Clear, Lois Wille, University of Chicago Press, Chicago, Illinois, 1991.

The Time of the French in the Heart of North America 1673-1818, Charles J. Balesi, Alliance Francaise, Chicago, Illinois, 1991.

Illinois Wilds, Michael Jeffords, Kenneth Robertson and Susan Post, Phoenix Publishing, Urbana, Illinois, 1995.

DuPage Roots. Richard A. Thompson, et al. DuPage County Historical Society, 1985.

Galena. AAS reprint 1976. Originally published 1937 by the City of Galena, Workers Progress Administration.

Birds of Illinois Field Guide. Stan Tekiela. Adventure Publications, Cambridge, Minnesota, 1999.

Indian Villages of the Illinois Country: Historic Tribes. Illinois State Museum scientific Papers, vol. 2, part 2. Wayne C. Temple, Springfield, Illinois, 1958.

The Transportation Revolution 1815-1860, George Rogers Taylor, Harper & Row, 1951.

Hiking the Illinois & Michigan Canal and Exploring its Environs, vol. 1, La Salle to the Fox River. Phillip E. Vierling, La Salle County Historical Society, 1986.

The Living Legacy of the Chicago, Aurora and Elgin: An Illustrated History of the Chicago, Aurora and Elgin and Its Transition to the Illinois Prairie Path. Peter Weller and Fred Stark, Forum Press, 1999.

A Guide to Oak Park's Frank Lloyd Wright and Prairie School Historic District, Village of Oak Park, 1999.

Starved Rock Almanac 2003, FirstServePress, Peoria, Illinois, 2003.

Starved Rock State Park: the Work of the CCC Along the I & M Canal, Dennis H. Cremin and Charlene Giardina, Arcadia Publishing, 2002.

Historic Illinois from the Air, David Buisseret, University of Chicago Press, Chicago, 1990.

Trail Blazer Program

The State of Illinois officially recognizes those people who have completed the entire Grand Illinois Trail, awarding them the title of Trail Blazer.

To be a Trail Blazer, you need to complete the whole Grand Illinois Trail. It need not be done in one whole gulp. It just takes full completion of the Grand Illinois Trail within one calendar year.

And you must turn in a record of your journey. In this record, you should note your interesting experiences, comments on the routing, and remarks on any unusual sights you had along the trail. Your record also should include the date you stopped by each of the 17 official Trail Blazer checkpoints. The master map at the back of this book is designed to be used as a Trail Blazer record and application. Send in a copy of the master map in the back of this book or your own journal to the Illinois Department of Natural Resources, attention Greenways and Trails Program, One Natural Resources Way, Springfield, Illinois 62702.

Trail Blazers receive a handsome polo shirt, a certificate and a citation in the *Green Scene*, a newsletter of the Illinois Department of Natural Resources. New Trail Blazers are announced each year on National Trails Day.

Trail Blazer Check Points

Date	Check Point	Grand Illinois Trail Section
_____	Navy Pier	Chicago Lakefront Trail
_____	William Powers State Natural Area	Burnham Greenway
_____	Village of Matteson Depot	Old Plank Road Trail
_____	Billie Limacher Bicentennial Park	Joliet City System
_____	Gebhard Woods Visitor Center	I & M Canal State Trail
_____	Lock 14 Day Use Area	I & M Canal State Trail
_____	Hennepin Canal Visitor Center	Hennepin Canal State Trail
_____	Empire Park in East Moline	Great River Trail
_____	City of Fulton Windmill	Great River Trail
_____	Mississippi Palisades State Park	GIT local road route
_____	Old Market Square in Galena	GIT local road route
_____	Lake Le-Aqua-Na State Park	GIT local road route
_____	Village of Pecatonica	Pecatonica Prairie Path
_____	Rock Cut State Park	Willow Creek Trail
_____	Village of Richmond	Prairie Trail
_____	City of Elgin, Grand Victoria Casino	Fox River Trail
_____	City of Wheaton, Volunteer Park	Illinois Prairie Path

Trail Record South Section

TRAIL ROUTE	CHECKPOINT	DATE COMPLETED
☐ Joliet City System	Billie Limacher Bicentennial Park	_____
☐ Illinois & Michigan Canal	Gebhard Woods Visitor Center	_____
	Lock 14 Day Use Area in La Salle	_____
☐ Kaskaskia Alliance Trail		_____
☐ Hennepin Canal	Hennepin Canal Visitor Center	_____

Special sights along the way:

Comments on the ride and route:

Trail Record West Section

	TRAIL ROUTE	CHECKPOINT	DATE COMPLETED
☐	Great River Trail	Empire Park in East Moline	_____
☐	Great River Trail	Fulton Windmill, "the Immigrant"	_____
☐	West Section Road Route	Mississippi Palisades State Park	_____

Special sights along the way:

Comments on the ride and route:

Trail Record North Section

TRAIL ROUTE	CHECKPOINT	DATE COMPLETED
☐ North Section road routes	Old Market Square in downtown Galena	_____
☐ North Section road routes	Lake Le-Aqua-Na State Park in Lena	_____
☐ Pecatonica Path	Village of Pecatonica	_____
☐ Willow Creek Trail	Rock Cut State Park	_____

Special sights along the way:

Comments on the ride and route:

Trail Record East Section

	TRAIL ROUTE	CHECKPOINT	DATE COMPLETED
☐	Chicago Lakefront Path	Navy Pier	_____
☐	Burnham Greenway	William Powers State Natural Area	_____
☐	Old Plank Road Trail	Village of Matteson Depot	_____
☐	Prairie Trail	Village of Richmond	_____
☐	Fox River Trail	Grand Victoria Casino in Elgin	_____
☐	Illinois Prairie Path	Vounteer Park in Wheaton	_____

Special sights along the way:

Comments on the ride and route:

Trail Notes

Trail Notes

Trail Notes